Corporate Video Production

Corporate Video Production
Beyond the Board Room
(And Out of the Bored Room)

Stuart Sweetow

AMSTERDAM • BOSTON • HEIDELBERG • LONDON • NEW YORK • OXFORD
PARIS • SAN DIEGO • SAN FRANCISCO • SINGAPORE • SYDNEY • TOKYO
Focal Press is an imprint of Elsevier

Focal Press is an imprint of Elsevier
30 Corporate Drive, Suite 400, Burlington, MA 01803, USA
The Boulevard, Langford Lane, Kidlington, Oxford, OX5 1GB, UK

Notices
Knowledge and best practice in this field are constantly changing. As new research and experience broaden our understanding, changes in research methods, professional practices, or medical treatment may become necessary.

Practitioners and researchers must always rely on their own experience and knowledge in evaluating and using any information, methods, compounds, or experiments described herein. In using such information or methods they should be mindful of their own safety and the safety of others, including parties for whom they have a professional responsibility.
To the fullest extent of the law, neither the Publisher nor the authors, contributors, or editors, assume any liability for any injury and/or damage to persons or property as a matter of products liability, negligence or otherwise, or from any use or operation of any methods, products, instructions, or ideas contained in the material herein.

Library of Congress Cataloging-in-Publication Data
Sweetow, Stuart.
Corporate video production : beyond the board room (and out of the bored room) / Stuart Sweetow.
  p. cm.
ISBN 978-0-240-81341-7
1. Video recording. 2. Video recordings—Production and direction. 3. Business presentations. I. Title.
TR850.S94 2011
778.59—dc22   2011001527

British Library Cataloguing-in-Publication Data
A catalogue record for this book is available from the British Library.

For information on all Focal Press publications
visit our website at www.elsevierdirect.com

11 12 13 14   5 4 3 2 1

Printed in the United States of America

Dedication

This book is dedicated to my beautiful bride Sandy, who gave me her encouragement and patience, and who found us a home with an office for me to write.

CONTENTS

ABOUT THE AUTHOR

Photo courtesy of Cleo Brown.

Stuart Sweetow owns Audio Visual Consultants, a video production and consulting company in Oakland, California. He taught video production at the University of California Berkeley Extension and has written scores of articles for video magazines. On his company's website, www.avconsultants.com, are production-planning guides and tips on using video with social media.

Acknowledgments

I'd like to thank my supportive acquisition editors at Focal Press, Chris Simpson and Anais Wheeler, technical editor David McKnight and project manager Anne McGee. My attorney, Richard J. Lee, helped me with my contract and with the legal considerations chapter. Gini Graham Scott and Troy DuFrene helped me propose the book. Others who helped with writing the book include Erik Stinson, Jeffrey Marino, Greg Snyder, Steve Gilford, Debbie Brubaker, Larry Kless, Ron Dawson, Erik Westby, Dave Bolick and Jara Queeto.

INTRODUCTION

Corporate video production has come of age. At one time, cinematographers referred to corporate videos as "industrials," a genre to which they retreated between "real" films. Talking-head videos or unimaginative safety films dominated the field, and too often one might hear the word "boring" precede the term "corporate video." However, as professional video tools came down in price, corporations invested in cameras and editing gear. A generation of enthusiastic filmmakers who sought access to those tools took jobs in the corporate world. While broadcast television was reducing staff, corporate media centers grabbed up the best and the brightest.

The television producer who craves the excitement of a live broadcast will get that adrenaline rush by transmitting a shareholders' meeting live to viewers at home. The ambitious video professional who wants to meet a top corporate CEO has an opportunity to film him or her giving a talk and beaming it via satellite to employees worldwide.

In addition to TV producers entering the corporate arena, Hollywood cinematographers discovered that corporate execs were not as stuffy as they once thought. Over the years, innovative companies developed communication departments with creative staffs. They sought imaginative filmmakers to apply their cinematic artistry to produce engaging marketing and training videos. As corporations developed social responsibility programs and discovered YouTube as an avenue to reach the public, documentary filmmakers found they could support causes in line with their own humanitarian values.

Many companies have equipped their video departments with cutting-edge postproduction applications and network storage infrastructures. Some organizations send video messages via their satellite networks, and growing numbers use IP distribution. When researching this book, I found a trend where corporate video producers favored location filming over studio production. Smaller HD cameras enable speed and flexibility, and many video producers edit videos on their laptops during the flight home from a shoot.

Throughout this book I included examples of video applications that corporations use, such as customer communications, product announcements, employee training, and public relations. Social media has enabled corporations to relate to the public in an interactive way. Nearly every major corporation has a YouTube page, and many companies film their customers giving testimonials or offering praise for their products. Sometimes ordinary people say surprising things on camera, such as the Chicago woman who said she and her neighbors were praying that Wal-Mart would open a store in their community. You'll read about that and other unexpected uses of YouTube in the social media introduction.

Production values of some corporate videos now rival Hollywood. AT&T created a series showing 20-something singles texting and exchanging files on smart phones with AT&T data plans. An educational film from Honda about their humanoid robot, ASIMO, combines elements of a science fiction film with artistic cinematography. IBM produced a series of videos for their "Smarter Planet" YouTube page that incorporate multilayered imagery together with smartly edited interviews.

Savvy video producers have reinvented presentations by using innovative production techniques to create videos that remove the boredom factor. There is no reason why employees or customers should be sentenced to "Death by PowerPoint" now that video producers can create lively, dynamic presentations with creatively composed video clips, dynamic 3D graphics, and carefully crafted scripts.

A well-designed short video has the capability to reach viewers on an emotional level. Poetic writing, rhythmic camera work, and a compelling soundtrack create synergy to grab the viewers' hearts and convert visitors to customers. The market researchers understand the incredible impact that video could have to their companies' bottom lines. Corporations are investing in video services to utilize the medium to the max, and video has become an integrated communications tool in the enterprise.

In addition to learning about corporate video production techniques and applying some of the examples shown here, it is wise for you, as the video producer, to learn about the values of the company you work for, how they use their brands, and who their customers are. Then you can apply those principles to producing videos that align with the mission of the enterprise. The literal image of the company is in your hands.

CASE STUDIES

Introduction

Digital media and broadband connectivity have influenced the evolution of video production in corporations. Rather than distribute programs on DVDs, many companies use CDNs (content distribution networks) or satellite transmission. Employees watch videos via live streaming or VOD (video on demand), and videoconferencing has become an alternative to videotaping meetings.

While in past years organizations built their own TV studios, many video managers now prefer to film on location with portable production gear. Some organizations decentralize video services and train individual departments to use their own camcorders and editing software. Nearly all of the Fortune 100 companies have their own YouTube channels, creating further needs for in-house video production. Social media (including Facebook, Twitter, and YouTube) offer an opportunity to distribute videos to the general public, and this gives corporate video managers a major responsibility: to form the corporation's literal image.

Companies vary in how they structure their in-house video services. Corporate video units are sometimes called media departments or are part of a larger communications department or division. In some cases they charge their client departments for their services and operate as if they were an outside production studio. At other organizations, the video manager needs to propose each year's budget to the company-wide budget committee. Some video units get their funding from several different departments, and those video managers may have to juggle their priorities.

Let's take a look at some of the larger corporate video units headquartered in the United States to learn how they operate. You'll see that there is a wide range of video services that in-house departments offer, and the opportunities for employment or contracting are as varied as the companies themselves.

Corporate Social Responsibility— Google Heroes

Video producers with high ideals who want to have an impact on the world sometimes shun corporations as they turn to documentary production. At some companies, however, the corporate video team takes the task of documenting their firms' demonstrations of social responsibility. Such is the case at Google, the Mountain View, California company that spearheads the Google Earth Heroes project. According to Google, this is "a way to celebrate the individuals and organizations that have used Google Earth in their efforts to effect change."

One of Google's video productions documents how Google Earth helps track the movements of elephants in Kenya. The Google crew filmed an interview with the founder of the group Save the Elephants, and in the YouTube video, he explains how Google Earth links to the organization's remote tracking system. With B-roll of the elephants trekking across the Serengetti and animated graphics keyed over images from Google Earth, the short video serves as both a documentary discussing the problem and a corporate public relations piece to publicize the Google product. To protect the elephants from poaching or droughts, if an elephant stops moving during its migration, Save the Elephants sends a Google Earth file that shows where the elephant has stopped. Then the Kenyan wildlife patrol can dispatch a patrol to investigate.

Another video that the Google video team produced shows how the U.S. Forest Service uses Google Earth to track fires and plot the path through which a fire could spread. The video, also distributed on YouTube, includes animations of Google Earth displays. The Google video team shot on-location interviews with Forest Service personnel, who explained that climate change is contributing to fires starting earlier in the year, that the fires are larger than they once were, and that they burn more intensely. Google Earth helps the Forest Service's Aviation Coordinator track planes in the air from different agencies and coordinates the firefighting effort. B-roll of aircraft and fires add to the visual variety of the video.

A series of short, snappy YouTube videos, titled *Life at Google* (http://www.youtube.com/user/lifeatgoogle), helps new employees and recruits get an inside view of the half-million-square-foot Googleplex. Using rapid video montages of employees on the job, accompanied by their voices, and with quick shots of staff on-camera in the studio, the viewer learns about the corporate culture at Google. You can view more Google YouTube videos at Google's official YouTube channel http://www.youtube.com/user/Google.

The video team is part of the Marketing and Communications department at Google. The Studio G Team, according to Google, "consists of video production and operations professionals who harness their creativity to produce a variety of engaging, on-message 'Googley' video communications. We produce these videos for the YouTube audience, and examples include product launches, product demos, branding videos, and executive speeches. Our talented and creative staff shares the ideals of Google's mission, which is to organize the world's information and make it universally accessible and useful."

Hamburger University and Sustainability at McDonald's

Log onto McDonald's website and you can view *The Road to Sustainability*, a four-minute video the company produced that shows their work "toward sustainable agriculture production by addressing ethical, environmental, and economic challenges." A video montage set to music uses text rather than a voice-over narrator to explain such ecofriendly practices as recycling cooking oil and using recycled fiber in their packaging. The video producer interested in helping the environment will be pleased to see that this megacorporation partnered with Greenpeace to support a moratorium on illegal deforestation.

This video is also on the McDonald's YouTube channel (http://www.youtube.com/user/mcdonaldscorp), as are about 25 other videos, as of this writing, on other topics reflecting the company's efforts at corporate social responsibility. McDonald's joins many other major corporations that use YouTube to distribute public relations videos to the general public. Other videos are directed at potential franchisees, with a testimonial from a woman who started as a part-time employee at age 15 who now owns her own $2 million business. In another YouTube video, new employees and recruits hear crew and managers tell "the truth about working at McDonald's."

Employee training at McDonald's is done at the company's Hamburger University in Oakbrook, Illinois. With a student population of 5,000, the 80-acre campus includes a 300-seat auditorium and 12 interactive education rooms, and it employs 19 resident instructors. The company recently opened a new campus in Shanghai, China.

Still, the in-house video team produces 30 to 40 live webcasts per week; they also shoot and edit for the company's YouTube video channels, as well as their own social media distribution network. They produce product videos and tutorials in the studio and on location worldwide, and they frequently hire scriptwriters for customer service video productions. Location filming includes customer testimonials and documentary-style productions.

The company has an in-house video channel that accepts footage produced by many departments within the firm. Sometimes a department has purchased their own consumer-grade high-definition video cameras, and they send their footage to the in-house video team for editing. Then, the producer shoots a wraparound opening and closing with a host to create a news-style program that is streamed to internal sales and marketing teams worldwide.

The video group is not technically called a "department." It is a group that is part of the customer communications department that is within the company's enterprise business group. Different teams of video producers, editors, and crew work for dozens of different teams within the company. Asked what it takes to get a job or be selected as a freelancer for this company, we were told that staffers are selected to be on a team based on their depth of experience as well as their technical achievements. These may be demonstrated in their portfolios, which usually are part of the applicants' web pages. In addition to creativity, they need to have demonstrated that they have produced videos on time and on budget.

What challenges does a video producer at a large corporation face? Managers want television quality, but they don't understand the costs involved. Planning, research, scripting, hiring talent, producer and director time, other crew and staff time, postproduction, and distribution all contribute to large production budgets. The task of many video managers is to educate their clients and the department executives about the resources needed to produce top-quality video that is both effective and compelling. And, most of the time, the video manager needs to find creative ways to produce a video with a limited budget.

Another challenge is getting the client to commit to sticking to a production timeline and reviewing elements as they become available. The video producer needs to be clear with his client about the phases during production where their input is needed. If they are not ready to review materials, the production may risk not being completed on time.

Consulting Firm Booz Allen Hamilton

Consulting firms are different from manufacturing or distributing companies. They don't have a product to show, other than the ideas and solutions they provide for their clients. The company's video productions become tangible products that represent the intellectual capital they supply to the customers. Videos not only represent the corporation's image, but they turn out to be concrete examples of the company's output.

Senior associate Jeffrey Marino of Booz Allen Hamilton is in charge of a 17-person media unit that produces multimedia for the company's website and for its YouTube and Facebook pages. "Stay Connected" is the category on the company's home page that points to such social media as YouTube, and the media are mostly short video clips distributed on these user-generated content sites. As of this writing, the international consulting firm had posted 64 YouTube videos such as the CEO's minute-plus analogy of hockey strategy and business success, a three-minute clip from the company-sponsored FIRST Robotics fair, and a three-camera 1:20-minute conversation about environmental management.

Marino said the 22,000-employee company has 100 offices around the world, and some of the offices produce their own videos. At the Virginia home office, Marino manages a department that includes two production studios, four postproduction suites, and enough gear to shoot on location. They frequently use their green screen to incorporate live action with motion graphics and 3D animation to help explain concepts and ideas.

The company distributes its videos almost exclusively using digital media, rather than DVDs or tapes. Videos usually are embedded in a site together with other rich media such as Flash animation. Their postproduction facility includes two Avid Nitris and two Final Cut Pro suites. They use file-based workflows with a storage area network (SAN) and network attached storage (NAS) to share media.

Marino says that their file-based workflows enable editors to collaborate on projects and manage assets efficiently. However, he says the challenge is what to do with the assets after a project has been completed and delivered to the client. Footage on P2 cards and XDCAM discs needs to be removed and stored on hard drives. So they developed an asset management system using a Microsoft Access database.

The department also provides video support such as IMAG for large presentations and conferences. While they document these events with in-house crew and equipment, they subcontract with a staging company for lighting and PA. They use a chargeback process to recover labor and expenses, such as actors and narrators, from their client departments.

Productions are divided 50/50 between internal and external clients. External clients include the public sector agencies and organizations. Internal productions are developed for staff learning and development, marketing, and general communications. When they produced an orientation video for new hires, according to Marino, "We tried to put a human face to data and websites rather than use a PowerPoint presentation."

Marino said they recruit personnel for his department from production agencies and even from TV news stations. Sometimes they recruit staff who have as few as two years' experience out of college, especially if they are strong artists and know such graphics programs as Adobe After Effects. "That way, we can help them develop and grow with us."

Scripted Videos with Professional Talent at World Savings

World Savings' corporate video unit is a lesson in building a department from the ground up. When the organization decided to produce its training videos in-house rather than always contracting with outside production companies, they hired a corporate video specialist, Greg Snyder. The company wisely avoided the trappings of Hollywood filmmakers or broadcast television producers with big-name credits. Many of these ambitious producers merely leverage that cachet because they are looking for work and are willing to "settle" for corporate video. Snyder owned his own company that specialized in corporate video, Business Video Productions, and his experience and interest in employee training video helped propel World Savings to become a world-class financial institution that was eventually acquired by Wells Fargo.

When Snyder started, he was the only staffer in the department. During that first year he produced 12 videos. Fast-forward 15 years, and Snyder had built the video department to a staff of 13 employees in two facilities that produced 220 videos annually.

During Snyder's tenure, he hired staff based on what he calls a "generalist model." Producers would need to have skills in writing, directing, and editing as well as producing. And a senior producer would even fill in as a second or third camera operator or any other production support position when needed.

Together with his staff, Snyder's department scripted and produced training videos using professional actors as well as employees with strong presentation skills. Overhead costs were kept to a minimum, and all the videos were shot on location. The closest the company came to a shooting studio was the classroom next door to the diminutive room the video department squeezed into.

The department produced mainly sales training films for the loan department and customer service films for tellers and branch managers. Professional talent would reenact situations that frequently come up in the course of a day. A sales film might demonstrate how a model salesperson overcomes objections, or a film might introduce a new product or service. A customer service film would show ways to deal with difficult customers.

During the scripting process, Snyder would gather together groups of employees who represented his target audiences. Functioning similar to focus groups, he and his team would lead them in brainstorming sessions that he would record. To kick off the session, Snyder would describe a scene he had in mind, and the group would discuss it based on their own experiences. After the sessions, he would play back the recordings and modify his scripts based on the feedback from his focus groups.

Snyder's challenge was to take the somewhat dry subjects of banking and lending and make them engaging. He and his team had fun with their productions, especially when the audience was composed of younger employees. That's where they could get a little playful. While the scripts demonstrated real-life situations, occasionally Snyder would throw in a touch of humor or drama—just a tidbit to get the attention of his viewers and entertain them.

Finding and Directing Talent

Since World Savings was a nonunion shop, the video department would occasionally contract with talent agencies that could supply them with nonunion talent. However, they frequently used their own resources to attract actors for their videos. They would advertise on local job websites and casting-call portals to collect headshots. Three times a year, the department would conduct its own casting calls. These were two or three days of open auditions for those whose headshots best matched the looks and skills they sought for actors playing the roles of employees or customers.

At the auditions, sometimes a cadre of 16 candidates a day were given different scenes to act. The scenes were dramatic, humorous, and improvisational. The senior producers filmed the auditions and would work in tag teams to keep their energy up throughout the busy days of casting. Most of the time, the senior producers would select the talent from this pool, but in some cases the client would have the final say.

During shooting, Snyder's directors would frequently have the actors play a scene three different ways: one with strong emotions, one with light emotions, and one somewhere in between. Snyder calls this "emotional bracketing," and this would allow them to make edits later based on feedback from internal focus groups.

Snyder employed real employees to be news reporters for a company-wide news program that was part of a 24-hour satellite network at Wachovia Bank, which acquired World Savings before it became part of Wells Fargo. The video department would gather the news stories and then upload them via the Internet to the main office. When there was a need for live coverage, they would hire a satellite truck.

Evaluation Mechanisms

One of the distinctions of producing corporate video as opposed to entertainment films is that video managers need to demonstrate the effectiveness of the videos they produce. Either the training manager or communications manager needs to develop mechanisms to measure the outcomes and to demonstrate the value of video. Some media centers send surveys to their client departments.

However, Snyder maintains that questionnaires just don't cut it. "We would get maybe a 3 percent reply from questionnaires we send out, so we got our production team together to call the viewers and ask for their candid responses. We got a greater than 50 percent response, which was much better than before." Snyder also would visit classrooms where his videos were shown. He would act like a fly on the wall and observe the responses of the viewers to various scenes. This gave him first-hand knowledge of how his videos are received.

Rather than charge clients for the entire video production service, World Savings implemented a program to charge only for the outside services. These included talent, travel, duplication, and other peripheral expenses. The fees for a production, depending on the overall budget and scope, would range from

$2,000 to $15,000. The bulk of the budget came from the company, and Snyder, each year, would make his pitch to senior management and sometimes to the company-wide budget committee.

New Employee Orientation Video

Prior to Snyder's tenure, my company produced a new employee orientation video for World Savings. The savings and loan was expanding, with new branches opening in several cities in the West and Midwest. When they contracted with us, their vision was limited to showing the history of this mom and pop company. The organization grew because of the couple's tenacity with their business plan to service only their niche market: home loans.

As a producer who wanted my client to get the best bang for their video buck, I did some research about the company and asked lots of questions. I learned that most new employees were in the 18 to 24 age bracket and that the owners prided themselves on architecturally pleasing buildings and interior décor that reflected what I eventually referred to in the script as "understated elegance."

As a part of my research, I usually request photos and news headlines to illustrate the history and achievements of a company. I was allowed to rummage through old files, and I came across several newspaper and magazine headlines applauding World Savings for remaining profitable during a climate where several of their competitors were asking for federal bailouts. This was exciting material to create a robust visual montage.

Then I uncovered what became my Holy Grail: a videotape of the company president speaking before the Senate Banking Committee. He was an expert witness who was helping to explain how many savings and loan institutions had gotten into a financial crisis by extending their portfolios to risky commercial loans. He proudly exclaimed that World Savings remained profitable because it stuck to home loans only. That was my hook!

The script I wrote starts with news headlines accompanied by a voice-over narrator sounding like a news reporter talking about how well World Savings was doing despite the savings and loan crisis. Then came the video clip of the company president testifying before the Senate Banking Committee. The video was old, and it was even recorded on a home VCR in the extended play (EP) speed. Despite the low-resolution look, it was a powerful scene that helped grab the attention of the new hires.

The rest of the new employee orientation video proceeded to explain the job security of working at World Savings, and it showed the in-house technology, the advancement opportunities, and even a birthday cake at a party for an employee. We created scenes with customers speaking to tellers and other personnel. We showed training classes that used interactivity and employee support. We showed awards being bestowed on hardworking employees. And we included a photo montage of the history of the company and husband and wife team who built it from the ground up.

The video was a hit with the employee development department, and the VP of the division who oversaw that department wanted his own version with some edits and other scenes that were directed at personnel at the division level. Fifty copies of the video were produced and distributed to the branches. The corporation quickly recognized the value of video and set out to establish its own video department that would eventually produce over 200 videos annually.

A Consumer Products Manufacturer

A large consumer products manufacturer produces videos to assist its salespeople in the field. The videos show new advertising programs and support and the direction in which the company wants its brand to go. "A while back, it used to be PowerPoint, but video is replacing that; it really is the coin of the realm now," says their corporate video manager.

The company also uses video for market research ethnographies. They send researchers into customers' homes and videotape them discussing how they use a particular product. Why video? The video lets the researchers see the culture the product is used within. "What you are looking for in market research is not only what is spoken about, but behaviors, all leading to what are some of the unmet needs that aren't spoken about. Video or keen observation is a wonderful tool for this."

Setting Up an In-House Video Service

Previously, video equipment was very expensive and specialized. Now the tools are more accessible. The manager explains:

It has made the building of a department as easy as getting off-the-shelf equipment. The investment is not that expensive: decent-quality computers, a decent amount of storage, decent

*consumer video cameras. And with that we can do everything
from blue screening to matting to fancy graphics (as well as)
basic video capture and editing. The cameras that are being used
in the reality TV shows in many cases you can go out and buy for
a thousand dollars or less. I think the public is very used to
looking at images that are made on semiprofessional consumer
camera equipment. And any computer you get these days has
editing features on it that before you'd have to go to a
professional facility to get.*

In setting up its in-house operation, the company recognized
how desktop publishing and desktop video could eliminate
going to outside vendors. The company produced an in-house
three-camera shoot of an interview with the CEO. They edited
together video from the three cameras: "In the past that would
have been a pretty monster deal."

Using Outside Services

The company still uses outside services for particular projects. They look to particular contractors for the larger projects
for which they have neither the experience nor the equipment to
produce. As the manager explains, "Sometimes it's the tools and
the equipment that dictate a vendor; sometimes it's the wran-
gling of the ideas and the direction that the project has to take."

For example, they contract with a vendor to stream their
quarterly town hall meetings. The vendor brings in a satellite
truck and streams the meetings live to the entire company. In
another case, the company had a small production that they
might have been able to perform in-house. It required a blue
screen and After Effects—tools the company owned—but they
were looking for a level of elegance that they knew they could get
with a particular outside director they brought in for the project.

Scriptwriting

Some scriptwriting is done in-house, and some is contracted
out. The company states that it is moving away from producing
just short-form commercials to developing longer pieces. Its
writers used to either write for commercials or documentaries
or be technical writers. Now that the company is producing for
the Internet, it is producing longer videos, and it needs writers
who can write not only commercials and sales scripts but also
drama, comedy, and even sitcoms. "There is a need for writers

with different skills. This is a growth industry for writers," the manager explains. This mixed bag of written work integrates writing for video with other creative writing.

Chargeback

Most in-house departments have instituted a chargeback system for the users of their services. Generally, work is charged by the hour, and the rate may be lower than prevailing fees for outside vendors. The thinking here is that you need only cover your costs for labor and maintenance of the equipment. However, if you get busy and exceed your in-house capacity, there could be a problem. The manager explains it this way:

> *If you are envisioning a lot of production, and you institute a rate within the company that is cheaper than an outside rate, it is good until you exceed your capacity and have to go outside. Then it causes problems, because people get billed more. It is a continuing discussion for us: at what point should we make our rates competitive with outside rates, or do we ever?*

Social Media and User-Generated Video

Many corporations are moving from static websites to sites with a dynamic, ongoing presence that link to social media. User-generated videos that customers produce about a product, while seemingly a boon to boosting a brand, are being scrutinized by corporations and their legal departments. According to the video manager:

> *Just because you have a testimonial about a product's benefits, you can't use the claim without proper substantiation. The mere fact that somebody says something about your product doesn't give you the right to use it any differently than if you had paid an actor to use it. It doesn't make it legal to use it on your site without proof of the claim. User-generated videos can be a wonderful connection with the consumer, but now everybody is feeling their way around them.*

Shared Content at Safeway

Safeway is a leading grocery chain with stores in the western and midwestern United States. Its corporate headquarters produces 1,500 live broadcasts and over 100 scripted video productions. Productions range from videos for shoppers that are displayed on monitors in the stores to training and safety films. The company's corporate communications department delivers live and recorded video on two full-time broadcast channels and two streaming channels. This enables the firm to provide real-time connections with store managers and company managers at the corporate headquarters.

The company has several postproduction suites utilizing Avid and Final Cut Pro, plus an Omneon MediaGrid active storage system that handles content cut on the different editing systems. The MediaGrid is a cross-platform storage system that also supports the company's transcoding and streaming applications. According to Dan Pryor, Vice President of Corporate Communications at Safeway, the MediaGrid enables the company to "implement a true end-to-end workflow with content conveniently remaining on the Omneon system from ingest through postproduction to distribution."

Pryor says that the editors have access to a shared pool of content that is stored on the MediaGrid. The company uses hardware encoders that output different media streams to the appropriate formats. They distribute video programs in MPEG-4, and they have a separate system for webcasting. According to Pryor, the video network has proven itself by increasing sales and reducing costs.

Movie Production and IMAG Display at Berkshire Hathaway

Berkshire Hathaway is a conglomerate of companies owned by billionaire Warren Buffett. In 2010, the corporation's annual meeting drew 37,000 shareholders to the Qwest Stadium in Omaha, Nebraska (Figure 1.1). Buffett calls these stockholders' meetings "the Woodstock of capitalism." The event is transmitted to adjoining overflow conference rooms via microwave transmission, and several areas are set up for shareholders to ask questions of Buffett and his partner, Charlie Munger.

The meetings open with a series of short films projected onto large screens in the Qwest center and at the remote locations. A Berkshire Hathaway spokesperson stated that they do not produce the film in-house but would not provide the name of the film producer they contracted with. Shot with Hollywood production values, one of the films featured Arnold Schwarzenegger playing "The Warrenator," whose mission was to prevent the merger of Wal-Mart, Starbucks, and Microsoft. Sitting in the

Figure 1.1 Warren Buffett's Berkshire Hathaway annual meeting draws 35,000 shareholders to Omaha. The meeting begins with a short film with the likes of Arnold Schwarzenegger, Bill Gates, and the Desperate Housewives.

room during the film presentation was Berkshire Hathaway board member and friend of Buffett, Bill Gates. A later scene showed Buffett and Schwarzenegger arguing over California's Proposition 13, which limits taxes on residences.

At another of the shareholder meetings, the movie showed clips with Jamie Lee Curtis flirting with Berkshire's 80-year-old vice chair, Charlie Munger. Later, Munger played poker with the Desperate Housewives. In another clip, Bill Gates is on the phone, saying, "I'm sorry. I wanted to get you a good present for your birthday, but that is just too much." Melinda Gates enters the room and asks Bill what the conversation was all about. Bill replies, "That was Warren. I asked him what he wanted for his birthday, and he said he wants $30 billion so he could be the richest man in the world."

The films are a draw for investors who then have an opportunity to ask Buffett and Munger questions about the company and about economics in general. This six-hour shareholders' meeting may be one of the largest corporate events that an AV crew supports. The film and the live transmission of the meeting are not distributed; they are the private domain of Berkshire Hathaway Company.

Since Omaha has no single venue that can seat 37,000 people, the stockholders' meeting is transmitted to the adjacent Hilton hotel and to overflow rooms at the conference center. The video team not only oversees the film production and presentation, but they are responsible for sending it to all the locations that accommodate the members. They project the live video onto several screens in the Qwest arena, as well as onto large screens in the overflow rooms.

If you enjoy the excitement of live production, a company with a large contingent of shareholders can be the place for you. If you like hiring and directing actors, you are sure to find a corporation that produces in-house employee training videos where you can hone your craft. Want to work directly with the movers and shakers of corporate America? Then find a position with one of the Fortune 100 companies and offer to film the CEO; that should provide satisfaction and excitement. If you like to produce documentaries about the environment and want to help improve our world, then a position with a firm that has a commitment to corporate social responsibility can be fulfilling to you.

You don't need to limit your career choices to Hollywood and New York City. Omaha, Nebraska; Bentonville, Arkansas; and Irving, Texas are homes to some of the nation's largest corporations that offer opportunities for creative expression and career development. Corporate video production has matured, and there is a wide variety of opportunities for video producers to apply their particular skills and have an impact on the world.

Shooting the CEO

When filming a video with the corporate CEO, the video producer needs to be confident and efficient. The CEO looks to you as the expert in your field, and he or she expects the shoot to take as little time as possible. You need to have everything set up and ready to roll when the subject arrives on the set. There is no time for small talk; you don't need to charm the CEO.

While you need to remain polite with the CEO, you can also be firm with your ideas on how the shoot should go. As uncomfortable as it may seem, it is your responsibility to correct the CEO's delivery if necessary. For example, you may have to say, "Excuse me, but please focus your attention on the lens."

He or she needs to know that you are the point person directing the shoot, and other crew members should not chime in with their suggestions. They need to run any of their ideas past you in advance. Similarly, with the CEO's team, you need to demonstrate that you are in control of the shoot. Some assistants to executives are high-strung perfectionists, and they think they know what is best for filming. This can be a challenge, but you need to run the shoot. If you anticipate that there may be a control issue, prepare your response to the nervous associate in advance.

A corporate video producer we know who has worked with several CEOs at some of the largest companies enlightened us on this point. Currently employed in a 30-person video department for a Fortune 100 technology company, he said that even with a sizable staff, many departments within the company still choose to use outside contractors. They have longstanding relationships with outside video service providers for such services as live telecasts, sales support videos, and other video productions.

Job Listings at Corporations

To get an idea of jobs available, visit companies' websites. The listings on the following pages serve to show the job descriptions. The particular jobs were listed at time of writing. Visit the websites to learn of current jobs.

Job Listings at Google

Job Listing 1
Studio G Director of Photography—Mountain View

This position is based in Mountain View, CA.

The Area: Global Communications and Public Affairs

The Studio G team consists of video production and operations professionals who harness their creativity to produce a variety of engaging, on-message, "Googley" video communications. These videos are mainly created for the YouTube audience, and examples include product launches, product demos, branding videos, and executive speeches. Our talented and creative staff share the ideals of Google's mission, which is to organize the world's information and make it universally accessible and useful.

The Role: Studio G Director of Photography

The director of photography will oversee shooting of corporate videos produced by its internal video production department (Studio G). This is a key position requiring an individual who has a proven track record of shooting highly effective videos for communication of key concepts for internal and external communications in the corporate environment. You will head up the camera crew and will be responsible for gaffing, gripping, and sound engineering. You will work with the director and may direct some projects yourself.

Responsibilities:
- Lead all aspects of shooting during a production.
- Recommend shot composition, lighting, which camera(s) to use, what f-stop to use, what lens to use, sound, how to deal with problems of focus, and so on.
- Ensure that deployment of the cinematographic equipment for each shot will render exactly what the director desires.
- Mentor and guide team members in specific tasks as well as general team initiatives.

Requirements:
- BA/BS degree preferred with strong academic performance.
- At least 10 years in director of photography role, with at least 2 years of experience shooting in HD, and at least 10 years working in production environment (please include link to reel in application).
- Proven track record of shooting highly effective corporate communications videos.
- High level of familiarity with production equipment, including knowledge of P2 card workflow; experience with live broadcast desirable.
- Ability to solve problems in a cooperative and productive manner under pressure.

Job Listing 2
Studio G Video Production Editor—Mountain View

This position is based in Mountain View, CA.

The Area: Global Communications and Public Affairs, Studio G

The Studio G team consists of video production and operations professionals who harness their creativity to produce a variety of engaging, on-message, "Googley" video communications. These videos are mainly created for the YouTube audience, and examples include product launches, product demos, branding videos, and executive speeches. Our talented and creative staff share the ideals of Google's mission, which is to organize the world's information and make it universally accessible and useful.

The Role: Studio G Video Production Editor

This is a senior-level editor role supporting all editing activity taking place in Studio G. You possess excellent storytelling skills in the cutting room. You also possess experience in the use of high-definition editing, Final Cut Pro, Compressor, Photoshop, and Illustrator. You will work closely with clients and creative directors to execute creative concepts.

Responsibilities:

- Deliver superior service and reliability for Google's video needs.
- Create videos that speak to Google's message and brand.
- Collaborate with team members and internal clients to provide a consistent end product.

Requirements:

- BA/BS degree preferred, with strong academic performance.
- Experience in a video production environment and sample reel required (please include link to reel in application).
- At least 8 years of editing experience, with proven track record of using Final Cut Pro, Compressor, codecs, and other relevant production equipment (as relevant for position).
- Experience in a corporate setting is a plus.
- Excellent communication and organizational skills.

Job Listing at Schwab

These are job listings at Charles Schwab that were posted on the company's website.

Job Title: **Manager, Schwab Video Production Studio**

Job Description:

Charles Schwab's purpose is to help everyone become financially fit. Through advocacy and innovation, Schwab has worked to make investing more affordable, more accessible, and more understandable for all. For more than three decades, the Charles Schwab Corporation has been an advocate for individual investors and the independent advisors who serve them.

At Schwab, we respect the unique differences of our employees, our clients, and the communities we serve, striving to create a consistent and rewarding employee experience. If you share our enthusiasm for helping others and building trusted relationships, possess high ethical standards, and have a desire to learn and grow, there's a place for you at Schwab!

Organization Objective/Purpose:

The Events and Production Services team designs and executes events, webcasts, and media that recognize Schwab's valuable client base and support client relationships. Through strong partnerships within Schwab, with our clients, and with the industry, the Events and Production Services team creates and executes industry-leading events that build and strengthen awareness, confidence, and trust in Schwab's brand and strategic objectives.

Brief Description of Role:

(Continued)

Job Listing at Schwab (Continued)

This role is responsible for assisting Schwab Studio's Senior Manager with all aspects of video and media production and supporting day-to-day operations and reporting, including:

- Managing and producing audio, video, and webcast productions.
- Editing audio/video/webcast projects.
- Scheduling and maintaining the studio calendar.
- Updating monthly activity reports for internal webcasting and studio production activities.
- Maintaining studio process documentation.
- Maintaining and organizing studio filing systems (files, media, contacts).
- Responsible for media encoding and duplication projects.
- Ordering and maintaining inventory of studio supplies and consumables (office supplies, tape stock, etc.).
- Maintaining and organizing studio facilities (edit rooms, equipment room, studio, etc.).
  Technical/Functional Qualifications:
- Minimum 5 years of experience in the video production industry.
- Technical hands-on knowledge of video, audio production, and editing systems (Final Cut Studio).
- Technical knowledge and experience with digital video/audio encoding, duplication, webcasting, and web development.
- Proficient with Adobe Photoshop, After Effects, and Microsoft Office (Word, PowerPoint, Excel).
- Excellent organizational skills and strong attention to detail.
- Excellent time-management skills, with the ability to prioritize and multitask.
- Strong written and oral communication skills.
- Bachelor degree in communications, film, or related industry.
- Experience with WebTrends web traffic software and Lenos a plus.

Job Listings at Booz Allen Hamilton

This is from the Booz Allen Hamilton website that lists job openings.

Job Listing 1

Job Description:

Media Facilities Manager—01086229

Key Role:

Manage all aspects of Booz Allen's media services facilities, including the media lab, studio, and audio suite. Maintain the showcase appearance of the facilities, including general organization, cleaning, and developing; implementing; and maintaining showcase looks for each space, ensuring that the spaces are properly started up each morning and shut down each night. Keep all facilities in working order, including overseeing the repair of equipment and systems, troubleshooting computer problems, maintaining and installing software, ensuring tape archiving, assisting with data archiving, managing backend systems and video core, and troubleshooting issues. Maintain responsibility for the evolution of the spaces, including identifying, recommending, purchasing, and implementing new equipment, systems, software, and furniture. Work in conjunction with management and team members on these tasks and include them when appropriate. Participate in all stages of the media development process from initial meetings with clients through delivery, and collaborate with teams, project managers, and clients to produce final products as a secondary role. Lead tasks and apply skills in facilities management and functional media capabilities. This position is located in McLean, VA.

Basic Qualifications:

- 2 years of experience with media facilities management.
- 1 year of experience with media hardware and software research and installation.
- 1 year of experience with Avid, Final Cut Pro, or Adobe Premiere.
- Ability to obtain a security clearance.
- BA or BS degree in communication, visual arts, EE, or IT systems.

Additional Qualifications (Preferred):

- Experience with Editshare and Render Farms.
- Experience with maintaining Avid, ProTools, Final Cut, and Premiere systems.
- Experience with facilities design.
- Experience with IT and computer management skills.
- Experience with 3dsmax or Maya 3D modeling programs.
- Experience with shooting video using professional cameras.
- Experience with leading and developing video projects end to end.
- Experience with studio and location video production.
- Experience with developing DVDs, streaming media, and multimedia CD-ROMs.
- Experience with recording and editing audio.
- Experience with Adobe Photoshop, Encore, Audition, Illustrator, Flash, Captivate, Apple DVD Studio Pro, Autodesk Maya, and Autodesk Combustion a plus.

Clearance:

Applicants selected will be subject to a security investigation and may need to meet eligibility requirements for access to classified information.

Integrating the full range of consulting capabilities, Booz Allen is the one firm that helps clients solve their toughest problems, working by their side to help them achieve their missions. Booz Allen is committed to delivering results that endure. We are proud of our diverse environment, EOE, M/F/D/V.

Job:

Web Design

Primary Location:

United States-Virginia-McLean

Travel:

Yes, 10% of the time.

Job Listing 2

Job Description:

3D Motion Graphics Designer—01086167

Key Role:

(*Continued*)

Job Listings at Booz Allen Hamilton (Continued)

Develop media productions, primarily focused on designing and creating motion graphics. Participate in all stages of the media development process, from initial meetings with clients through delivery, including collaboration with teams, project managers, and clients to produce final products. Use creativity to design and produce visually interesting and compelling media. Lead tasks and project members and maintain responsibility for the overall program. Learn a wide variety of media skills and contribute to programs, including editing video, shooting video with professional cameras, recording and editing audio, and designing sound for video. This position is located in McLean, VA.

Basic Qualifications:

- 2 years of experience with 3D Studio Max.
- 2 years of experience with Adobe After Effects.
- 1 year of experience with Avid, Final Cut Pro, or Adobe Premiere.
- Ability to obtain a security clearance.
- BA or BS degree in communication or visual arts.

Additional Qualifications:

- Experience with leading and developing video projects end to end preferred.
- Experience with shooting video using professional cameras preferred.
- Experience with Render Farms a plus.
- Experience with Adobe Photoshop, Adobe Encore, Adobe Audition, Adobe Illustrator, Adobe Flash, Adobe Captivate, Apple DVD Studio Pro, Autodesk Maya, Autodesk Combustion, or Avid ProTools a plus.
- Experience with studio and location video production preferred.
- Experience with developing DVDs, streaming media, and multimedia CD-ROMs preferred.
- Experience in recording and editing audio with Avid ProTools preferred.
- Ability to learn a wide range of video and multimedia preferred.
- Ability to develop creative approaches to client requirements preferred.
- Ability to work independently and in team environment, depending on the project preferred.
- Ability to write scripts and develop estimates a plus.

Clearance:

Applicants selected will be subject to a security investigation and may need to meet eligibility requirements for access to classified information. Integrating the full range of consulting capabilities, Booz Allen is the one firm that helps clients solve their toughest problems, working by their side to help them achieve their missions. Booz Allen is committed to delivering results that endure. We are proud of our diverse environment, EOE, M/F/D/V.

Graphic Design

Primary Location:

United States-Virginia-McLean

Travel:

No

Salary Ranges for Video Production Employees

As of July 2010, salary ranges for video/media producers in the United States ranged from $38,265 to $68,004, with the average at $52,000, according to Simply Hired (www.simplyhired.com). The company states that "average video producer salaries can vary greatly due to company, location, industry, experience, and benefits." The range for a video editor is $32,047 to $56,680, and the range for a department head, film/TV postproduction is $42,155 to $79,087.

MARKETING YOURSELF AS A PRODUCER

"Big shots are only little shots who keep shooting."

—Christopher Morley

Introduction

So you want to be a small-business person. Well, start by removing the "small" from your consciousness. You can accomplish nearly anything you set your heart and mind to do, so dream big and work hard. Aim high when you set your goals. Talk with those in the field who have achieved them. Is your desire to be an independent video producer so great and your confidence in success so high that they will get you through those days of looming disillusionment? How will you feel when you see your employed colleagues get to take vacations, when you are faced with staggering premiums for all the different kinds of insurance you will have to purchase, or when your biggest customer has gone belly-up?

Perhaps you are an employee who sees little room for advancement in your organization, and want to go off on your own. Few corporations are large enough to offer several management positions in video, and sometimes the top managers in the video unit are no longer producing videos. They are supervising those who do, and their jobs have become those of business managers rather than executive producers. Or maybe you just think you can make more money on the outside.

If you have contracted with independent video producers, you know that their daily rates are much higher than the salaries of staff video producers. However, they pocket only a small percentage of the rates they charge. Overhead, taxes, start-up costs, insurance, and myriad other expenses can easily amount to two-thirds or three-quarters of the gross income—and sometimes more.

A Personal Message from an Independent Video Producer

I speak to you as an independent video producer. I worked in corporations for 12 years before starting out on my own. During a recession, my company laid off 10 percent of the workforce. I was shocked that they didn't need me, since I thought I was indispensible to the company. After the day my supervisor gave me the bad news, I was crying as I told my wife I had been let go. What would I do? How would we survive?

That was 26 years ago, and I wish now that I could tell that supervisor what a favor he did for me! I had been doing a little freelance work on weekends, and that client gave me more work. My now former employer called me in a couple of times to produce videos. I commiserated with a couple of colleagues who had also lost their jobs, and we formed a couple of small joint ventures. It took time, and it has been a roller coaster—the kind that malfunctions and leaves you hanging until help arrives.

I read books about starting a small business, and I took short courses in business management. I attended conferences. I taught classes in video production. I wrote for some of the video magazines. I worked as a production assistant. I even took on brief telemarketing jobs when things got really rough.

One of my colleagues asked if I would share a small office with him. The rent on the space was $300. I asked if I could take only a third, and he kindly agreed. Eventually he moved out, and I took on another officemate. Later, that man also left, and I took on all the rent myself. When business increased, I hired a part-time assistant, who later became full-time. Then I hired a part-timer to help out. Soon we needed more space, and the office next door was available. These were not the fast-paced success stories you see in the movies; they took place over the course of ten years.

Slow, gradual growth was what I had learned from reading and the courses I took. As much as I wanted to buy new cameras or editing gear, I usually rented equipment or hired colleagues. Only when I knew for sure that I would achieve a return on investment (ROI) did I purchase equipment. I also wrote business plans on several occasions. The business plans were required to obtain loans, but they also helped me determine my goals for the business and became the metric that I used to know if the business was on the right path.

Getting Started and Getting Business

While you may not be successful calling up Bank of America or AT&T to offer your video production services, there are other opportunities to earn money as a freelance videographer or contract video producer. Online video ads are a good way for any local store or service company to draw more business to its website. With a small investment in a camcorder and editing software, you can produce a video that you can post on their site and on the growing number of user-generated content (UGC) websites.

Find a specialty that you are good at, such as lighting or motion graphics, and offer your specialty to the active video producers in your area. Take in the excess video editing backlog of the wedding videographers and legal videographers in your town. Offer to be a production assistant to the video producers, or a production coordinator to help them get organized. Consider helping an established facility find clients to rent their equipment or studio. You probably have some skills that can be applied, and you might pick up a mentor in the meantime.

If your calls to those video producers and production facilities don't result in immediate work, ask if you can take the owner to lunch. Find a company that's been successful for ten or more years. Explain that you are getting started in the business and would like to learn his or her success story. Sure, several may think you are a formidable competitor, but plenty will be delighted to talk about themselves, and some may be generous enough to offer to be your mentor. If a local, successful producer won't take your lunch meeting, offer to do the same with one in a neighboring city. You won't be perceived as much of a local "threat."

Volunteer for Nonprofits

Look for community organizations that are having fund-raising dinners and offer to videotape them for free as a volunteer. Ask that your contact information be included in their printed program and that your website gets a link from theirs. Call the banquet hall in advance to tell them you are the official videographer and that you need a riser placed in the center of the room. Print your company name or website URL on your carrying cases and place them at the visible ends of the riser, next to a business card holder. Bring signs printed with "Video production donated by . . ." and place them on the stage, on your riser, and wherever else you can. Dress up and bring a friend or spouse as your production assistant. You want to look like a professional company.

Ask if the organizers plan to have a screen for a slide show or video presentation. Then offer to provide iMag (image magnification) by sending the video output from your camera to their projector. You'll need a fluid-head tripod and a handle-mounted zoom control to pull this off, and make sure no one shakes your riser during the projection. Large audiences will benefit from seeing the presenters on a ten-foot screen, and it makes your presence there more noticeable.

These dinners attract business owners and individuals who are active in your community. This is your chance to meet some of them. Arrive as early as possible and get your gear set up. Then take the time to socialize with the attendees. While you are setting up the equipment or during filming, your assistant can help make contacts by being on the lookout for anyone looking your way. He or she can initiate a conversation at the equipment riser or after the filming. While both of you can hand out cards, ask for business cards from those you speak to.

Perhaps the organization will let you interview guests at the close of the program. Then you can develop a rapport with those individuals and have an opportunity to call them at a later date. If you are generous enough to perform editing of the video, you could phone them and ask them how they want their names to appear on the screen. Do they have a particular title or company name they want to include? Would they like to receive a disc copy or website link to the video? This enables you to further your relationship with someone who at some time could refer you to an individual or company who needs video services.

You can take it a step further by offering to produce a public service announcement (PSA) for the organization. If the local TV station airs the PSA, you could send out press releases about your company's video production being broadcast locally. The PSA can be further distributed on the organization's website, on a UGC site, and on your own website and blogs.

As you develop a small database of charitable donors, you could offer to create family history video documentaries or biographies of individuals for a reasonable fee. Scanning old photos and putting them to music takes little time and, when produced with dynamic effects and appropriate music, they can be heartwarming family heirlooms

Your Business Plan

You'll need a formal business plan to get a bank loan—one that shows your expected income and expenses. Those kinds of plans require lots of research to learn how others in the industry are doing. It is tricky because corporate video production is not really an organized industry with a trade group that gathers data from its members. You'll probably want to enlist a bookkeeper or accountant to help you develop the data for your formal business plan.

However, even before you create a formal business plan, make an informal plan for yourself. Think through what you want for your business. Set goals for the near term and where you want to be five and ten years from now. You may already have a client or two, and you may have carved out a niche market for yourself, such as live streaming of meetings. As an independent video producer you are going to spend a lot of time at your business. Frequently, your business and your home life may have fuzzy boundaries. You may be entertaining clients at dinner, encoding at midnight, and blogging at breakfast.

Ask other independent corporate video producers how they run their businesses. Take them to lunch and ask them the following questions:

1. What are your overhead expenses?
2. How do you get new customers?
3. What should I *not* do?

In my early years, I was grateful to a producer who cautioned me against purchasing a broadcast camera. I rented them or hired shooters for many years until I knew I had enough regular customers to justify that expense. That tip probably saved me a ton of debt and even more grief.

According to Steve Yankee of Doc's Marketing Mojo (www. docsmarketingmojo.com), a business plan should include the following:
- Research on competitors' rates
- Research on my cost of operation
- Minimize start-up costs
- Operating with a minimum number of employees (just me)
- Offering modest salaries

Yankee also recommends that you set first, second, and third business goals. He suggests you explain to yourself why you are going into this business and state your personal objectives for starting or continuing your business. Keep these goals and objectives in mind as you market your business, seek new clients, and write proposals.

Writing the Video Production Proposal

So you have an opportunity to write a proposal for a prospective client. As a good listener, you have noted a problem or two that the prospect wishes to solve. You have gone through your bag of tricks and have come up with some video concepts that could solve that problem, and even help the company to grow. Now is the time to develop that proposal and turn that prospect into a client.

If you have not already set up a meeting, this is the time to do it. This is the time to gather more details about the client's problem and generally establish some rapport. It is best if one person at the corporation is assigned as the content specialist or project manager, but expect one of the executives to be in on an initial meeting. You want to clearly understand the problem and their objectives—both cognitive and behavioral. What resources are available at the company, such as filming locations, on-camera "talent," photos, and existing video clips? This is the time to gather any written materials such as procedure manuals, website text, and printed brochures. Ask about keywords and phrases that the company likes to use, and establish the demographic of the video's audience.

This may take more than one meeting, but since you are not yet being paid for your time, you will need to be careful not to become an unpaid consultant. The meetings and writing your proposal are your investments in producing a video that will solve their problem, enhance the corporation, and hopefully become an award winner for your portfolio.

In your written proposal state the problem and objectives as close to the way the prospect explained them to you. Once they see that you are a good listener, that you understand their needs and can clearly state them, you are at first base and heading for second. Then add some of your ideas on how video could solve the problem. Include one or two specific concepts, but don't give away the store. Explain that you would like to write a script and that the scriptwriting process starts with you writing a treatment for their approval. If they decide they want to see your script, explain what your scriptwriting fee is. You can decide for yourself if you want to just write the treatment for their approval and what that fee would be.

If they ask what the budget for the video will be, explain that once they approve a script or at least a detailed treatment, you can give them a production budget. (Later chapters discuss scriptwriting and budgeting.) In this early stage of the client-producer relationship, it is important to demonstrate how well you understand their problem and how great your video production will look. Try to use "we" in your correspondence with them. Refer to it as "our" video, and emphasize that they will retain control of the video while you apply your craft and artistry to make it effective and easy on the eyes.

Requests for Proposals and Requests for Qualifications

Some larger corporations, associations, and government organizations issue requests for proposals or RFPs. This is a way to notify contractors of upcoming projects, and it is a way for the organization to maintain transparency by creating a level playing field for all contractors. Rather than merely accepting the lowest bid, they look for companies that have the experience and any required facilities. Requests for qualifications (RFQs) are similar, but RFQs usually means that the organization wants to create a pool of qualified contractors for anticipated projects. RFPs generally have budgets already approved, and you'll be writing a concise proposal. RFQs are usually simpler; they ask for your resume and those of other principals on your production crew, as well as references from past clients. Usually the projects come with generous budgets, but expect to see plenty of competitors bidding against you.

To receive RFPs and RFQs, contact the department or section of the organization that may be called Purchasing, Procurement, Vendor Relations, or something similar. To find corporations and organizations, use such search terms as "Fortune 500," "Fortune 1000," "associations," and "corporations." To find governmental agencies, start with your city, county, and state purchasing or contracting divisions. For the federal government, the GSA (General Services Administration) and the SBA (Small Business Administration) are your best bets. Later in this chapter we provide information about those two agencies.

When the organization issues an RFP, sometimes the actual budget amount is stated, and the bidders, in their proposals, divide those funds into line items or tasks. The bidder explains how much time each item will take to complete and the costs of any materials. For example, one task on the RFP might be "write script for employee training video." Another item could be "film interview with manager at the power plant." Yet another task could be "create and film dramatic vignette demonstrating incorrect and correct way to drive a forklift." The bidder, in his or her proposal, shows the budget for each of these tasks.

While these contracts can be lucrative, there could be situations where you win the bid but never get to produce the video. If the contract includes a clause that the project may be cancelled due to withdrawal of funding, then your champagne victory party was not necessary. Governments during difficult economic times may not get the tax revenues they had counted on to produce the video.

The proposal process can get tedious because there usually is a large amount of paperwork to complete. Plan on including the resumes of the subcontractors you wish to hire, such as camera operator, sound recordist, and editor. You may need to obtain letters of referral from some clients. You probably will need to provide a copy of your city and state business licenses and a certificate of insurance. Some even ask for your last three years' tax returns! The proposal may require you to include a timeline for completion, and you may have to provide details of each of the processes you plan to undertake.

Some video companies have had experience working with government entities and have developed a boilerplate proposal that they can use to help streamline the bidding process. Other video producers don't want to be bothered with all this bureaucracy lest their creativity be hampered. You will have to decide if the process is worth the time commitment required to complete a proposal.

Business Accounting, Licenses, and Taxes

Retain a tax accountant, preferably one who has experience in the video business. Ask a colleague for a referral. If you prefer to perform your own bookkeeping, get a program such as QuickBooks from Intuit, and enter income and expenses every week. Use it to balance your checkbook and print out monthly profit and loss (P&L) statements.

If you don't regularly balance your personal checkbook, or if you don't like to record income and expenses on a regular basis, you should also get a bookkeeper. In my own business, things were very slow at first. Then I got very busy, and I was so consumed with productions that I was forgetting to invoice my clients. That is one of the many tasks a bookkeeper will perform on a routine basis. That person needs not know the video business, but a bookkeeper with clients in the service sector is probably better than one who works with a store or a company that sells products.

Register your business with your city; a city business license is cheap, and your city may offer services to new businesses. For example, some have arrangements with the Small Business Administration (SBA) to provide free business consulting with SCORE (Service Corps of Retired Executives). Some cities have a chamber of commerce and other business organizations.

Most states do not license video producers, although many will require a producer to register with the state's sales tax division, which frequently is called the State Board of Equalization. Most states charge sales tax, and sometimes the labor that goes into producing a DVD is also taxed. In most states, if the producer uploads the files and the client receives no disc or tape, no sales tax is levied. However, in some states, even if you are a consultant or a producer who sells only services, you still need to register with your sales tax office.

The state of California has what they call Regulation 1529 (http://www.boe.ca.gov/pdf/reg1529.pdf) that allows for "authorized motion pictures" to avoid sales tax, even when the producer sends a disc or tape to the client. Some other states have adopted a similar regulation.

Corporate videos are usually classified as an authorized motion picture. The rule is that the video has to have some commercial value—that it could possibly be sold and sales tax charged on its sale. A marketing or training video is usually considered an authorized motion picture. A video made for legal documentation or for a family, such as a wedding video, does need to be taxed, however. The regulation is not all that clear, and if you are operating in a state that has a similar regulation, ask your accountant about it. (That is another reason to choose an accountant who is familiar with film and video.)

Business Insurance

In the early days of my business, a client wanted me to perform a shoot out of town. So I called the local rental facility to schedule equipment. They asked that I send them an insurance certificate. I had no insurance, and the clerk there kindly gave me a brief explanation of business insurance. It is not the same as homeowner's or automobile insurance. He explained that I needed insurance to cover loss to their equipment, as well as any liability should someone trip over one of my cables. He explained that the liability insurance should be even more of my concern than the equipment getting ripped off. Business liability insurance can also cover your vehicle if it is used for business purposes.

If you produce videos on health or safety, or training about any procedure that if performed incorrectly could result in a loss to another person, errors and omissions insurance (E&O) is another policy you should look into. Even with a disclaimer at the opening of the video, if a viewer causes an accident or is injured, his or her insurance company could come after the video producer. This is a rare occurrence, but ask your attorney or accountant if you should consider this coverage.

As an independent contractor, you are responsible for your own health insurance and your own disability insurance. Some states offer a small policy for sole proprietors who want disability coverage. However, consider purchasing an additional policy on your own, and include coverage that will pay your overhead expenses during the time you are disabled. If you rent an office or lease equipment, you don't want to lose them because you are laid up. A disability could put you out of work for quite a while, and an independent video producer might overlook this kind of coverage.

If you are hiring employees rather than freelance contractors to help you, you probably need to get workers' compensation insurance. It covers employees in case of an accident. If you hire people as independent contractors, you don't need that insurance.

Hiring Help

When you have a chat with your bookkeeper or accountant, learn what you need to know about classifying helpers as independent contractors rather than employees. Generally a contractor works independently, and you don't control how he or she performs the work. Contractors need to have other clients, and they need to be able to demonstrate that they are available to take on other clients. Even if you have a written contract with a freelancer, if he or she has an accident and his or her insurance company decides he or she was working for you as an employee rather than a contractor, you could be in trouble.

Classifying helpers as employees is not a difficult task. You need to adhere to the employment regulations of your individual state, and your bookkeeper or accountant can help you with that. You will probably need to obtain workers' compensation insurance to cover the employee in case of an accident. You may even want to offer benefits such as health insurance. Some insurance companies offer group discounts to employers with as few as two employees: your assistant and yourself.

Consider contracting with a payroll service to write the paychecks and keep track of deductions. A payroll service will provide you with quarterly statements of taxes you need to pay and benefits deductions. Some payroll services even send the tax payments directly to the state and federal government for you; that relieves you of hefty fines should you be in the midst of a production when a tax payment is due.

Your helper, when classified as an employee, can feel more a part of your company than if he or she was hired as a contractor. The employee may help you get more customers, while a contractor could be competing against you. And even if you start with only a part-time employee, both that employee and you share a common goal of advancing up the ladder of You, Inc.

Business Formations

Sole proprietorship is a natural start. Even if you use your own name, have separate banking, checking, and credit card accounts. Register a fictitious name statement with your county or DBA (doing business as) even if it is in your own name. Counties differ on how this is handled, but it will prevent someone else from doing business as a filmmaker named John Smith. At tax time, you complete a standard tax return, but add a Schedule C for your business profit and loss. Check with your state if they assess income tax.

A partnership is another form of business, and it requires a different tax form with the IRS. You can have a virtual partnership with another video producer or with someone in a similar industry. If you are simply doing business together and splitting the revenue and expenses on individual productions, it may better be considered a "joint venture" rather than a partnership. For example, you may be a producer who routinely brings a particular client to a studio. The studio and you may form a joint venture where instead of you paying the studio for each day you use it, the studio gets a percentage of the income from the client. In a joint venture, each party files his or her own taxes.

In a partnership, you split every income and expense. It's like a marriage without a prenuptial agreement. If you and your partner part ways, you will need to divide the business assets. That can be almost as difficult as a divorce, as each partner may have been performing specific, different functions. For example, one may handle the marketing, while the other goes out on shoots. A partnership can be composed of more than two individuals, and the percentages of ownership need not be equal.

Some states allow for a limited liability partnership or limited liability company. An LLC is not a corporation but a form of partnership. General partners make the decisions and run the business, while "silent" partners, or those with limited liability, are mostly investors. States regulate these arrangements in different manners, but the partners in an LLC usually are shielded from personal liability.

A corporation provides that shield or what is known as the "corporate veil." Corporations exist in part to separate the owners from debts and personal liability of the corporation. Most states require that the corporation be managed by more than one individual. They require a board of directors as well as officers, such as a CEO and a CFO (central financial officer). Some allow one person to be the CEO and a spouse or domestic partner to be the CFO, and they allow them to be on the board of directors. Other states have different regulations. Your accountant is your best source of information on forming and managing a corporation in your state.

In addition to the veil, the corporation may offer tax benefits. You as the CEO are an employee. Rather than paying 15.3 percent self-employment tax, corporations pay FICA taxes at 7.65 percent. These rates are current with the writing of this book, and they may change. There are different types of corporations. A C-Corp pays income tax at the corporate rate, while an S-Corp handles income taxes in a similar way as if you were a sole proprietorship. There are a large number of documents to file if you operate a corporation, and you even have to conduct an annual meeting and keep minutes. It is best to consult your accountant to see if a corporation is best for you.

Doing Business with the Government

For federal contracting, go to the U.S. Government General Services Administration (www.gsa.gov), and look up Contracting Opportunities. There you will learn about the different programs to obtain a government contract and find assistance for small businesses. The GSA's Office of Small Business Utilization's (OSBU) outreach activities make it possible for the small business community to meet key contracting experts and be counseled on the procurement process. The GSA Forecast of Contracting Opportunities informs small businesses of anticipated contracts offered by the GSA for the current fiscal year, as well as known opportunities for subsequent fiscal years. The GSA fiscal year runs from November 1 to October 31.

Each state has its own procurement office or an office that helps small businesses to learn of contracting opportunities in their state. Note that some states, such as California, offer preference to Small Business Enterprises (SBE) and Disadvantaged Business Enterprises (DBE). Anyone with a business earning less than $5 million can qualify for the SBE, although they have to renew their status annually. The DBE looks at a combination of factors of the owner of the company, including ethnicity, assets, and tax returns. Some states give preference if you or one of your subcontractors is a disabled veteran. You will need to provide specific documentation to qualify for these preferences.

The Small Business Administration offers loan guarantee programs and business start-up advice. Are you ready to start a business? Take their test at http://web.sba.gov/sbtn/sbat/index.cfm?Tool=4.

- Do you think you are ready to start a business?
- Have you ever worked in a business similar to what you are planning to start?
- Would people who know you say you are well suited to be self-employed?
- Do you have support for your business from family and friends?
- Have you ever taken a course or seminar designed to teach you how to start and manage a small business?
- Have you discussed your business idea, business plan, or proposed business with a business coach or counselor, such as a faculty advisor, SCORE counselor, Small Business Development Center counselor, or other economic development advisor?
- Do you have a family member or relative who owns a business?

Personal Characteristics

- Do you consider yourself a leader and self-starter?
- Would other people consider you a leader?
- Are you willing to invest a significant portion of your savings or net worth to get your business started?
- Do you have enough confidence in yourself and your abilities to sustain yourself in business if or when things get tough?
- Do you like to make your own decisions?
- Are you prepared, if needed, to temporarily lower your standard of living until your business is firmly established?
- Do others turn to you for help in making decisions?
- Are you willing to commit long hours to make your business work?
- Would others consider you a team player?

(Continued)

Doing Business with the Government (Continued)

Skills, Experience, and Training

- Do you have a business plan for the business you are planning to start?
- Do you know and understand the components of a business plan?
- Do you know what form of legal ownership (sole proprietor, partnership, or corporation) is best for your business?
- Do you know why some consider business planning to be the most important factor determining business success?
- Do you know if your business will require a special license or permit and how to obtain it?
- Do you know where to find demographic data and information about your customers?
- Do you know how to compute the financial "breakeven point" for your business?
- Do you know how to compute the start-up costs for your business?
- Do you know about the various loan programs that are available from banks in your area and the SBA?
- Do you understand how a business loan can impact your credit?
- Do you know how to prepare and/or interpret a balance sheet, income statement, and cash flow statement?
- Do you know why small business loans are considered more risky than loans made to large businesses?
- Are you sure your planned business fills a specific market need?
- Do you know your target market?
- Do you understand the tax requirements associated with your business?
- Do you know how to prepare a marketing strategy for your business?
- Do you know how to learn about your business competitors?
- Do you understand marketing trends in your business industry?
- Do you feel comfortable using a computer or other technology to improve business operations?
- Do you have a payroll process planned for your business?
- Do you have a customer service strategy in mind or in place?
- Do you know how to obtain an EIN (employer identification number) for your business?
- Do you know if your business should have some form of intellectual property protection?
- Do you know where to obtain information about regulations and compliance requirements that impact your business?

VIDEO PROJECT PROPOSALS

Introduction

Whether you are a staff video producer or an independent freelancer, you probably will need to write proposals to get productions approved and funded. In this chapter we focus on project proposals and show you some examples of written proposals. Budgets are covered in detail in Chapter 4.

When a department wants to produce a video, they contact *you*. Your role is to flesh out the details of the video so you can estimate the amount of time needed to complete the process. They may not have thought through the details, and most likely they have not visualized the project scene by scene.

In my experience, many clients describe their idea for a video as if it were only a written document. They give little thought to the visuals and little regard to creating an engaging program that grabs the audience and maintains their interest. Their project description might include something like "John is going to talk about the history of the company. Then he is going to explain the features of the product. Finally, he will show a spreadsheet of sales projections." Talk about boring!

Businesspeople who have had little experience producing videos don't know how they can use the medium to enliven the content and motivate their audience. As part of your proposal, you can suggest frameworks to present the material in a dynamic and captivating way. Perhaps you can suggest that in one scene actors are hired to dramatize the hardships of not having the client's product. You could introduce the concept of filming a host in front of a green screen with a virtual background. Show an example of how motion graphics with data revealed in layers could substitute for a spreadsheet.

Corporate managers view video producers as creative types, and they expect innovation from us. Go beyond a mere budget proposal to include some of your ideas that utilize AV media. Your imaginative approach could help sell your proposal, and your novel ideas will make the video much more interesting and effective.

In addition to developing a budget estimate in the proposal, the producer needs to specify the functions for which he or she will be responsible, as well as what is needed from the client. For example, you could write, "The client will provide a content specialist to supply information for the scriptwriter. The producer will send the client links to audition clips of proposed on-camera spokespersons for the client's input on talent selection." The proposal may also include an estimated timeline that shows approximate dates by which each phase of the production will be completed.

The freelance video producer, especially when he or she may be working for the client the first time, will need to provide samples of some of his or her own marketing materials to help sell the project. These include descriptions of the producer and crew members, contact information from past clients, and sometimes even a cost-benefit analysis. Businesspeople love case studies, and you can include brief descriptions of similar video projects you have worked on. If your proposal is in an electronic form, such as a PDF, you can include links to video clips from your website. Let's examine some actual proposals that I wrote when my company was responding to RFPs (requests for proposals).

Sample Proposal: The Metropolitan Transportation Commission

Here is a proposal to produce a series of video clips and to be a consultant for live webcasting. The Metropolitan Transportation Commission coordinates public transportation and vehicle traffic in the San Francisco Bay area. The RFP stated that the cover letter—what they call the "transmittal letter"—and the other elements must be included in the proposal.

(Date)

(Individual's Name)

Project Manager

Metropolitan Transportation Commission
Joseph P. Bort MetroCenter
101 Eighth Street
Oakland, CA 94607-4700

Dear Ms. (Last Name):

This transmittal letter is part of Audio Visual Consultants' (AVC) proposal to be the video production services contractor for both Part I of the RFP for the video production of MTC's Excellence in Motion awards and for Part II of the RFP for on-call webcasting, video, and editing services. AVC will be able to provide the services as indicated in the RFP by August 13, 2008.

I, Stuart Sweetow, am the owner of AVC and will be the person signing the contract and managing the video production. I will be your contact person and will make sure we adhere to the production schedule. I will directly supervise AVC employees and subcontractors.

The AVC Advantage

- Audio Visual Consultants recently produced the awards video for the East Bay YMCA. This was very similar to your video in that we interviewed CEOs and other executives in their offices and homes. We also produced three years' of awards videos for Summit Hospital prior to their merger with Alta Bates. These included production and presentation.
- AVC has experience projecting completed DVDs at presentations and projecting live video of the talks as well. We use a special lens for live projection.
- The University of California, Haas School of Business uses AVC to produce tape-delay webcasts of the Business Plan Competition. We produce eight videos for Haas each year and have been their regular contractor for over 12 years. We also incorporate speakers' PowerPoint slides and digitally zoom into them during the video editing process.
- AVC is only five minutes away from MTC. This will allow for quick and frequent viewing of footage and supervision of the editing process.
- AVC specializes in corporate and public sector informational videos. We do not produce entertainment films or videos. We have experience working with company staffs on camera.

This proposal includes the following: a production treatment plan, AVC company information, experience of AVC and key personnel, description of equipment to be used, client references, signed price proposal form, and AVC sample DVDs.

Please let me know if there is any additional information you need. Should there be irregularities in this proposal or in the cost and price analysis form, I will be happy to make corrections.

Sincerely,

Stuart Sweetow

Producer Director

Encl.: Proposal to Produce "Excellence in Motion" Awards Videotape

(*Continued*)

Sample Proposal: The Metropolitan Transportation Commission (Continued)

I created a title page (not shown) that would serve as the cover for the bound proposals. The RFP called for a number of duplicate proposals. I added the single transmittal letter to the stack of bound proposals.

Introduction
Part I Excellence in Motion Awards

In October 2008, MTC will host the Excellence in Motion awards program. AVC shall produce approximately 13 presentation clips, each approximately three minutes in length, that highlight the people, programs, and organizations that will be honored. These clips will be composed of interviews with the honorees and with nominators or others close to the winners. AVC shall get shots of the work they performed when available, as well as shots of the location of their worksite or the location of the activity for which they are being honored.

AVC staff shall coordinate with interviewees and MTC to record the interviews on broadcast-quality videotape, edit them appropriately, and assist with their presentations at the awards program.

The individual award clips shall be combined in a finished compilation video, together with an introduction by MTC's executive director or his/her designee. The running time shall be approximately 30 minutes in length.

Part II As Needed/On-Call Video and Webcasting Services

In addition to producing the Excellence in Motion videos, AVC shall be an on-call contractor to provide such services as webcasting, videotaping, and editing of workshops and meetings, and producing video news releases.

Approach I, Stuart Sweetow, serving as the AVC producer, will meet with the MTC project manager and other appropriate staff members to assess their particular needs. I'll review previous awards videos and will ask the project manager what MTC likes and doesn't like in the videos.

AVC is client focused, and we do all we can to assess client needs and preferences. If appropriate, we will conduct a brainstorming session to develop ideas for the interview segments and for the voice-over narration.

Preproduction I will create a written treatment for MTC approval. The treatment will be a description of the video project and will serve as a blueprint for the script. The treatment for the interview segments will describe such details as interview questions, B-roll video clips to be shot, photos, and other graphic elements that MTC will provide.

The treatment for the compilation video will describe such elements as the opening shots, how the director's introduction will be incorporated, what the voice-over narrator will say, how transitions will be developed between interviews, and what will be in the conclusion.

The project manager and I will meet to discuss what elements need to be included in the video and what resources are available.

Upon approval of the treatment, I will then write the draft script. The script will include all the visual elements and will include the wording for the voice-over narrator. It will describe the interviews and the order in which they will be compiled, and it will provide details on the opening, the introduction, and the conclusion of the compilation video. Upon approval of the draft, I'll write the final script.

While the project manager is reading and approving the script, I will provide samples of male and female narrators with whom we work. The project manager will choose the narrator.

The project manager and I will collect photos, TV news clips, video clips, and other visual elements from interviewees and MTC to provide visual support to the interviews and narration sequences.

Upon approval of the script, the project manager and I will work together to coordinate scheduling the videotaping of interviews. We will try to combine interviews to minimize the shooting days. We send each interviewee a link to a guide on our company website that suggests appropriate clothing, makeup, and jewelry. We also send a location filming guide to the facilities where we will be filming. It covers the logistics of bringing equipment in and out, and it discusses such issues as having a quiet area and locating interesting backgrounds for the interviews.

The project manager and I will meet to discuss the best approach to filming MTC's executive director or his/her designee for the introduction. We will also discuss the room setup of the awards ceremony and options to

(Continued)

Sample Proposal: The Metropolitan Transportation Commission (Continued)

videotaping the ceremony. We will consider audio, lighting, and possibly projecting the live camera signal onto the screen.

Production   I will compile the shooting crew and will be responsible for working with outside video contractors. We will determine the appropriate equipment and will arrange to bring backup cameras, lights, and microphones. I will be briefing the filming crew on the project and our policy to have minimal adverse impact on workers at the videotaping locations.

I'll direct the crew to set up the lighting equipment to best flatter the interviewees and to create aesthetically pleasing compositions with the backgrounds. I'll supervise the crew to make certain they capture the best-quality audio and video. I'll be watching the clock to make sure the interview segments that we plan to use don't exceed the allotted time lengths. If necessary, I'll coach the interviewees to help them relax on camera.

Some interviews will take place at MTC, and others will be at the interviewees' office locations. When our production crew is shooting at those locations, we will shoot B-roll of the facilities and processes to provide visual support to the interviews.

We will make window-dub copies of each day's video. The project manager may review the copies to select the most appropriate portions of the interviews.

Once the project manager has selected the narrator, I will schedule a sound studio to record the narration. I'll direct the narrator to speak with proper inflection at appropriate segments of the narration. I'll also direct the studio technician to maintain proper audio levels and to provide audio editing as necessary.

Postproduction   I'll supervise Mitch Silver, AVC's in-house editor, to create a DVD with a menu for the awards presentation video clips.

The production manager may visit AVC at any time to supervise the editing process. We will provide music choices for the project manager's approval.

When all the audio and video elements are together, I'll supervise Mitch to piece together the scenes into a rough-draft video for client approval. Upon approval, the video will be finished and distributed on DVD or over MTC's website.

Videotaping and Presenting the DVD Videos at the Awards Ceremony   The AVC staff will provide professional video production services to videotape the speakers at the awards ceremony and other relevant activities. Whether the ceremony will be at MTC or a remote location, I will contact the facility representative to discuss the following:

- Room layout
- Placement of camera on a riser
- Lighting, both of the room and of the stage
- Coordinating light dimming during DVD presentations
- DVD playback equipment
- Video/data projection
- Possibility of feeding the live camera image to the projector

At the ceremony, AVC staff will provide the following services:

- Videotaping the ceremony
- Connecting to audio from the PA system and monitoring audiorecording
- Possibly showing live camera on projection screen
- Start and stop DVD segments
- Dimming lights if dimmer is accessible

Production Equipment AVC will use a broadcast digital camcorder for top-quality production. Professional lighting with softening filters will give the video a clean look and will not be harsh on the performers. A sound recordist with a boom microphone will be used to capture audio clearly, and wireless microphones may be used for additional audio as needed. The equipment can be set up and taken down quickly. AVC has many years of experience shooting in the workplace and will minimize the impact on the workers and on the facility by using the least amount of equipment and accessories required.

Postproduction and video editing will take place at our storefront studio, about five minutes away from MTC. Staff editor Mitch Silver knows how to get the most out of our hardware and software for digital video editing. We use sophisticated DVD production software and hardware, and perform video duplication in-house to exacting specifications.

Company Description

Audio Visual Consultants, now in its 25th year, specializes in producing corporate training videos on location. Clients include East Bay YMCA, EBMUD, the University of California, and the city of Oakland. AVC provides scriptwriting and production services and contracts with outside professionals in particular specialties, depending on the scope of the production. AVC is client-focused and designs the video programs to meet the needs of the client.

AVC maintains its own broadcast-quality camera, portable lighting equipment, and sound recording equipment. It has an in-house editing facility and a full-time editor with a variety of software applications and DVD authoring equipment. Clients may supervise the editing as it takes place, or they may come in to approve different stages of the process.

AVC also maintains an in-house DVD production and duplication facility, as well as DVD duplication. Discs are checked using a quality-control procedure, and AVC provides labeling and packing of discs.

Description of Personnel

Stuart Sweetow, producer director, manages the overall production and supervises in-house and outside personnel. He will direct the shooting and postproduction. Mr. Sweetow has nearly 30 years of experience as a video producer and director specializing in corporate training videos. He previously taught video production at the University of California, Berkeley Extension, and has written scores of articles for professional video journals. He has won several first-place awards and managed in-house instructional video facilities for 12 years prior to starting Audio Visual Consultants in 1983.

(Continued)

Sample Proposal: The Metropolitan Transportation Commission (Continued)

Michael Fleming, the camera operator, has 15 years of experience in video production. He previously was the manager of audio visual services for Mervyns and has extensive experience working with nonprofessional talent in corporate settings. He has served as camera operator on several video and multimedia productions.

Allen Lam, the sound recordist, has 17 years of experience recording audio on location for video productions. He recorded the audio for training videos for American Medical Response, DHL, St. Mary's College, and several musical and theatrical performances.

Mitch Silver is the AVC full-time staff editor who will perform video editing and other postproduction services. Mr. Silver previously worked at Cision as the lead editor and was responsible for producing promotional videos for public relations firms.

Jara Queeto, the production assistant, has 8 years of experience as a professional audio and video technician and camera operator for a variety of organizations, including Audio Visual Consultants, where he is employed. His technical expertise and easygoing manner help keep the on-camera personnel calm and the production running smoothly.

Audio Visual Consultants maintains general liability insurance and workers' compensation insurance and can obtain insurance certificates and riders to insure individual productions.

Previous Similar Video Productions

Client: Oakland East Bay YMCA

Project: Awards video produced and shown at banquet

AVC was the sole contractor to videotape interviews at various locations in Oakland and Richmond. These interviews were with CEOs, board members, religious leaders, and students. We worked with our client to develop a shooting schedule and contacted facility representatives to arrange logistics, such as bringing equipment in and out, using facility electricity, and getting into offices in advance to set up lights and audio. Locations included the Kaiser Permanente executive office, the Highland Hospital CEO office, the Richmond YMCA, and others.

AVC provided postproduction of the interviews to include subtitles and a DVD with a menu to enable clips to start and stop at will. The video clips ranged from 1 to 3 minutes in length and were shown at the awards banquet.

Client: Summit Hospital

Project: Employee Recognition awards, videotaping and presentation

Duration: Three years

Summit Hospital contracted with AVC to produce short video clips of long-tenured employees that were shown at employee recognition banquets for three years in a row. The project involved setting up a filming schedule for employees at all three shifts, filming them at their jobs, including photos of them when available, talking about their work history at the hospital, and adding additional footage. We used stock photos, newspaper headlines, and TV news clips of the decades during which they started working at the hospital.

Kaiser Permanente Emergency Preparedness Training Video Audio Visual Consultants produced the emergency preparedness video for Kaiser Permanente. It was used to train employees to perform triage and other procedures should a disaster, such as an earthquake, take place in the San Francisco Bay area. Stuart Sweetow served as the director and scriptwriter, and he worked with Kaiser physicians and other staff to utilize procedure manuals and other tools in developing the videotape.

Mr. Sweetow directed hospital staff as on-camera actors and supervised the videotaping of a scheduled disaster drill to get additional footage. AVC also has news footage of the 1989 earthquake that could be incorporated into MTC's video.

Mission Possible—Safety Training at Kaiser Richmond Using nursing and administrative staff, AVC produced a training video to reduce the number of work-related injuries. Incorporating a *Mission Impossible* theme, the hospital's safety committee assumed roles of investigators and impromptu training staff when encountering unsafe practices.

Stuart Sweetow was the director and scriptwriter. He met with the content expert and developed a treatment. Upon approval, he wrote the script and scheduled the filming. Vignettes demonstrated such hazardous conditions as workers using poor body mechanics, nurses throwing away used needles in regular trash bins, and employees verbally abusing one another.

Approval Stages

AVC's style is to work in a collaborative manner with clients. Several approval stages are built into the production process. These include:

- Treatment approval
- Script approval
- Talent approval
- Rough edited draft approval
- Approval of final edited master

Estimated Timeline

July 15—30: Review materials at the EOCs. Conduct meetings with client and content specialists.

August 1—15: Write draft treatment, client reads and comments on treatment, write final treatment.

August 16—31: Write script draft, client reads and comments on script, write final script.

Sept 1—15: Break down script into a shooting schedule. Contact locations to arrange filming times. Gather existing visual materials. Produce rough drafts of graphics.

Sept 15—30: Filming at the EOCs including interviews and B-roll. Record voice-over narrator at studio.

Oct. 1—15: First cut of edited versions of videos. Deliver to client for approvals.

Oct 15—31: Final audio mix, final cut of video, author DVDs, replicate DVDs, and deliver to client.

Note: This is an estimate based on information in the RFP. Once the process gets started, AVC will draft another timeline for approval of client.

(*Continued*)

Sample Proposal: The Metropolitan Transportation Commission (Continued)

Budget—AVC Spreadsheet

(Please see also Appendix B-1, Price Proposal Form.)

Quantity	Unit	Description	Rate	Amount
12	days	Producer director	700	$8,400
6	days	Camera operator	500	3,000
6	days	Audio recordist	500	3,000
6	days	Production assistant	400	2,400
60	hours	Postproduction	120	7,200
6	days	Camera equipment	500	3,000
6	days	Lighting equipment	300	1,800
6	days	Audio equipment	250	1,500
1	each	Scriptwriter	3,000	3,000
1	each	Voice-over narrator	1,400	1,400
2	hours	Audio studio w/technician	350	700
6	each	Digital videotape master	45	270
				$35,670
1	each	10% contingency		3,567
				$39,237

Following these pages, a page with reference names and contact information is provided. I did not include one with this sample, but here are some other data pages or appendix materials.

Sample Proposal: Accounting Training DVDs

In this proposal, we included a profit projection, since the client would be selling DVDs. We created two versions of the proposal with two different budgets. This is a technique that gives the freelance video producer two chances at winning the contract.

(Date)
(Individual's Name)
HMC, (Name) Management Group
100 First Street
San Francisco, CA 94105

Dear (Name):

Thanks for the opportunity to produce a DVD video for HMC and for taking the time to list the shots you want. This Word document explains the project and your profit potential. Two attached Excel spreadsheets show two different estimated budgets. Budget #1 represents a professional video that will incorporate Magic Bullet film look filtering and additional pre-production and post-production time. This would result in a more polished look than the more economical Budget 2.

The AVC Advantage

(As in the previous proposal, we list the advantages of using our company.)

Approach

The AVC producer will meet with HMC representatives to gather information and brainstorm ideas for the video. He will also review existing printed and graphic materials. The producer will conduct a brainstorming session to determine the most effective filming and postproduction techniques. In the alternate Budget #2, AVC will eliminate the brainstorming session.

Filming will take place in a client-provided conference room in Oakland. Client will provide PowerPoint slides that will be incorporated into the DVD during the postproduction process.

The video will consist of your lecture plus PowerPoint slides and other text graphics. Transitions and graphics will be accompanied by professional voice-over narration. Budget #1 includes motion graphics and layers that gradually reveal data. This is not only an eye-appealing process, but this technique helps the viewer understand and retain data. Client may choose the narrator from among candidates AVC will provide. Client may also choose optional background music from the royalty-free CDs that AVC owns.

Supervised by the producer, AVC's in-house editor will piece together the scenes into a rough-draft video for client approval. Upon approval, the video will be finished and distributed on DVD.

Assumptions

You will be the liaison with AVC. After the filming, you will review "window dubs," or copies of the videotapes that show time code (minutes and seconds). You will indicate the time code start and stop points. This will allow for an efficient editing and postproduction process.

HMC will provide printed materials for AVC to review. Appropriate photos, artwork, or video clips may be included in the video. The running time of the video will be approximately 90 minutes.

HMC will provide the location for the filming, and no professional studio, other than a sound studio for narration, will be rented. HMC will provide all on-camera subjects.

Production Equipment

AVC will use a Panasonic DVC 60 broadcast digital camcorder for top-quality production. The camcorder has a special "movie mode" that creates a film look. The first budget includes the option of using a postproduction digital filter called Magic Bullet. Professional lighting with softening filters will give the video a clean look and will not cast harsh lighting. AVC will provide a clip-on wireless microphone for you to wear. It will be for the filming only.

(Continued)

Sample Proposal: Accounting Training DVDs (Continued)

DVD Production and Duplication

As part of the postproduction process, AVC will create a DVD with a menu and chapters. You will be able to select the menu style from a variety of templates. Users of the DVD will be able to select the chapters they want from the menu, and they will be able to navigate from one chapter to another.

AVC will subcontract for DVD replication and packaging. You will be able to supervise this process and will select the graphic styles for the package printing.

Estimated Income

You mentioned that you train 200 students per month. If the DVD has a life of three years, that would be 7,200 students. With a conservative estimate of one-third of students purchasing the DVD at $20 each, the income would be $48,000 from student sales. Additional, the SBDCs would be selling the DVDs to nonstudents who want to develop bookkeeping skills. If they sell the DVD at $25 and you offer the DVDs to the SBDCs at $15 each, that means a $10 profit. If they sell 20 per month × 36 months, that's an additional $7,200 profit. Total income over three years would be $55,200.

See the attached Excel spreadsheets for two production budgets based on different levels of sophistication.

HMC Budget # 1

4 hours	Production planning	110	$440
1 day	Video production	900	900
10 each	Digital videotapes	10	100
10 each	Window dubs	25	250
50 hours	Postproduction	115	5,750
1 each	Narrator and studio	600	600
10 hours	Graphics production	115	1,150
15 hours	DVD authoring	115	1,725
5 hours	Magic Bullet digital filter	115	575
3,000 each	DVD copies	0.85	2,550
1 each	Packaging & printing	1,873	1,873

(Package design will be outsourced at an additional fee per client artwork)

Total			$15,913

HMC Budget # 2

2 hours	Production planning	110	220
1 day	Video production	900	900
10 each	Digital videotapes	10	100
10 each	Window dubs	25	250
25 hours	Postproduction	115	2,875

1 each	Narrator and studio	600	600
2 hours	Graphics production	115	330
10 hours	DVD authoring	115	1,150
3,000 each	DVD copies	0.85	2,550
1 each	Packaging & printing	1,873	1,873

(Package design will be outsourced at additional fee per client artwork.)

Total		$10,848

Notice that Budget #1 is the higher budget, and in the preceding narrative, I explained the benefits to the viewer.

These are just two examples of project proposals. Each production has its own individual objectives and considerations. You will be doing your viewers a favor by considering the audience demographics as part of your proposal. Emphasize your and your crew members' past experiences with similar video productions. Detail your individual competencies that relate to the specific project. Consider offering two or more alternate budgets so you can increase the odds of becoming the winning bidder.

Sometimes the bidding process includes a "bidders' conference" where the client meets with all the video producers who wish to submit proposals. The company representative answers questions from the bidders and sometimes will provide additional information not included in the RFP. While it may feel awkward to be in a room with your competitors, you can use this to your advantage by collecting their business cards or contact information. In the unlikely chance that one of them is chosen for the production instead of you, you can contact them to offer to be their associate producer, researcher, or scriptwriter.

With each successive proposal that you write, you learn more about answering RFPs, and you can use much of the material from previous proposals for new ones. As you compare your proposed budget with the actual production budget, you will refine your budget-estimating skills. Remember to offer your innovative suggestions about frameworks that you can apply to the client's video production. Businesspeople sometimes get so wrapped up with budgets and deadlines that they may overlook the importance of designing a video program that is engaging and motivating to the viewers. The proposal is an opportunity for you to demonstrate your creativity, your expertise and your professionalism.

BUDGETING THE CORPORATE VIDEO PRODUCTION

"You can do pretty dumb things when you've got a big checkbook."

—Warren Buffett.

Introduction

As your video production career advances beyond operating cameras and performing editing, you will find yourself in the company of corporate executives and business managers. You may be proposing creative concepts for videos and distribution via cutting-edge networks, but your manager/client will always ask the same question: "How much will this cost?"

As a producer, you are now a business manager yourself. Perhaps you can arrange to get the title of "executive producer" so you can feel more comfortable dealing with the financial aspects of video production. As you contract with camera operators and animators, you find yourself asking that familiar question: "How much will this cost?"

This chapter shows you budgeting techniques used by video producers, and they are not all that different from techniques used by business managers in other service industries. Construction contractors bill in what they call "time and materials," and consultants use the term "billable hours." Accountants and bookkeepers develop what they call "profit and loss statements" and "balance sheets."

In essence, you are doing what any business person does: estimating the cost of a project based on individual "line items" such as equipment rental, staff time, and travel. If you forget a particular line item, such as insurance or baggage fees, you may have to make up the difference by reducing the number of shooting days or editing hours. If you are an independent contractor, you may have to reduce your salary to make up for those forgotten items. You don't want to risk the quality of your production suffering (or your family suffering) because of an unforeseen administrative cost; it's better to have a list of as many line items as possible that can go into a video production.

There are software packages on the market such as BoilerPlate, Movie Magic, and Easy Budget. Many of these applications are designed for Hollywood movies with million-dollar-plus budgets, but you need only use the line items that apply to your own production. It is helpful to have everything laid out for you so you don't miss anything.

Most budgeting applications run under Microsoft Excel or a similar spreadsheet, and they include columns for estimated and actual budgets. After the video has been completed and all the bills are paid, you compare the estimate with the actual figure, and you come up with a variance for each line item. The variance is a percentage either above or below the estimate of the budget for that line item. If you estimated four days of shooting and it took five, the variance is +25 percent. The next time you prepare a budget, consider that variance when you make your estimate. The more videos you produce after taking into account the variances, the more likely the variances will diminish.

In addition to tracking variances, or before you create your first budget, you will need to develop the art of estimating time required for different tasks. This is done by analyzing the script or detailed treatment and determining the amount of time it will take to shoot each scene. Besides the estimate of the number of shooting days, other line items include the staff, talent and equipment requirements, post-production time needed, and other administrative expenses such as pre-production planning, auditioning talent, travel, meals and many more.

Successful budgeting comes with experience, but if you are relatively new to budgeting, ask some of the subcontractors to show you how they estimate times for specific production tasks. You can also contract with a production coordinator who may have more experience with budgeting, and there are companies, such as Entertainment Partners, that provide budget consultation services.

Determining the Costs

Depending on the scope of your video production, you may be able to wait until a treatment has been approved, or even until the entire script has been approved, before estimating your budget. It is best to aim for the latter. Then you know what you have to work with during the process of breaking down the script to organize shooting. With that structure in mind you can start figuring out the most efficient way to meet your needs for talent, locations, crew, equipment, postproduction, and all the ancillary and administrative costs.

Most corporate video departments have a chargeback system where the department requesting the video becomes the client and is billed by the video department or entity. If you are an in-house producer with the goal of going independent, this chargeback system can help you learn how it is to work with a client. You'll be operating as if you were an outside production facility, so you may need to "sell" the video production idea to the client. Also keep in mind that within companies that have chargeback systems, the requesting department is usually free to go to the outside to use one of your competitors.

In some cases you may have been given a fixed amount to produce a particular video and are asked, "How can we get the best bang for our buck?" You need to explain the type of production that may be purchased for the fixed amount, as well as the limitations. For example, you may not have the budget to hire actors to play out vignettes, so a lower-budget video could be structured as more of a documentary with interviews and voice-over narration.

When you get a fixed budget, reserve at least 10 percent of that as a contingency. Consider a contingency figure closer to 20 percent for lower-budget productions. It is easy to spend an additional $1,500 in postproduction just to create graphics or for revisions. If your entire budget is only $10,000, that is 15 percent right there. While justifying a 20 percent contingency fee may be difficult, it is easier than apologizing afterward for going over budget. There is nothing worse than having your bubble burst at your premiere when all that the big boss can say is it went over budget.

Even when you develop a budget based on a line-by-line estimate, that 10 to 20 percent contingency amount will no doubt come in handy to cover those unforeseen expenses that are deemed by Murphy's Law. When I produced a patient education video, on the final day of filming, our content specialist hit me with a surprise. The plastic model of the neck that we had been using during three days of filming had a hole in the side that their staff used for live demonstration purposes. However, the client didn't want that hole visible in the video. We had loads of footage of it with its hole, since that is how the content specialist had positioned it on-camera. In postproduction we had to perform the equivalent of an animated Photoshop "healing brush." That took several hours in added postproduction time and over a thousand dollars—out of my pocket!

Above and Below the Line

In budgeting, "above-the-line" refers to preproduction, scripting, producer and director fees, actors' pay, music rights, and administrative costs. These are costs that need to be paid, even if for some reason, the video never gets shot. "Below-the-line" budget items are the equipment and technical production costs. These include equipment rental, pay for camera operators and other technicians, transportation and meals, permits, props, and postproduction. With lower-budget productions, the distinctions between "above" and "below" the line may not be important. The line may also be blurred with in-studio productions.

Some producers ask for larger contingency percentages for below-the-line expenses, offset by a smaller contingency for above-the-line items. Based on the script, you can probably do a good job of estimating the costs for the producer, director, and actors. However, after the production is underway and you need to purchase unforeseen permits, rent the cameras for an extra day, and animate the company logo, these unplanned below-the-line expenses can build up quickly. It is not uncommon to see 5 percent contingency for the above-the-line budget and 20 percent contingency below-the-line.

Itemizing every expense is a process that corporate managers do nearly every day. They will appreciate seeing that you have a concise budget and that you have considered all the different expenses and contingencies that go into a production. With an itemized budget, the video is no longer this magical process populated by artists and starlets but a project just like any other, with a detailed budget and a timeline for completion.

The Executive Producer

It has been said that if the producer is the one with the pockets, the executive producer is the one with *deep* pockets. In corporate video production, the executive producer could be your boss or the manager of the department who orders the video. In the nonprofit world, it could be the fund-raiser who obtained a grant to produce the video. In most cases, the producer answers to the executive producer.

However, in some structures, the producer hires an executive producer. This person's job is to handle the budget and the other administrative aspects of the production. With higher status than an associate producer, the executive producer is the one who is responsible for the money. If the video is produced by a contractor rather than in-house, the executive producer may be the one who actually writes the checks to the subcontractors and bills the client. Someone with bookkeeping experience or a production manager would make a good executive producer in this situation.

What to Leave In, What to Leave Out

Probably the two most common errors that cause productions to go over budget are unrealistic estimates and forgetting to include something. Ask other producers how they estimate time and what line items you could mistakenly overlook. Consult with technical people for advice on rates and how long it really takes to shoot one page of a script. If possible, ask them to review your budget; perhaps you can hire them as consultants.

If you are not experienced with estimating time and don't have the resources to get a consultation, consider asking the director and actors if they are willing to work on a flat rate rather than by the hour or day. Overtime adds up quickly, and it could be a production-killer. Scriptwriters frequently bill as a flat rate, and directors interested in a particular project may flat-rate bill, too. Union actors need overtime and all the fringe benefits, but nonunion actors may be willing to work a reasonably long number of hours without charging overtime. Before considering nonunion talent, however, check with your company to determine if they are a union signatory.

If you are using union talent, consider using a payroll service that specializes in paying actors. They will include all the fringe benefits such as insurance, pension, taxes, and union fees. The payroll service can help you determine your budget, but if you choose not to use one, a talent agency can be another source to help you get the talent budget accurate.

If you will be rehearsing your actors, you need to add those hours to their billable time. Do you need to rent a space to conduct rehearsals and hire a videographer to videotape them? How about costume fittings and costumes? Some actors will provide their own wardrobes for an added fee. If you plan to hire children as actors, you'll need to pay a welfare worker and perhaps a teacher during school hours.

Transportation costs can be difficult to estimate. Airline ticket prices vary widely, depending on when you book them. Airlines each seem to have different fees for checked baggage and additional fees for cases weighing more than 50 pounds. Rental car companies tack on fees for insurance and surcharges for fuel when the production assistant forgets to stop at the gas station before he or she returns the vehicle.

"Craft services" include catering, snacks, and drinks, as well as tableware, tables, and all the extras such as coffee in the morning. If your budget is extremely low, you can consider letting the crew and cast get their own meals. However, if they take too long to return, you may be losing money by having to pay them overtime at the end of the day. That's why craft services are usually money well spent. Don't forget to include feeding the others who are on the set, including the executive producer, the department executives, the writer, the unpaid interns, the security guard, the parents of children, the producer's boyfriend or girlfriend, and so on.

How about location services? A location scout is an expense well worth considering. That person can make your day run smoothly by knowing where to park cars, where to load in equipment, where the bathrooms are, where the circuit breakers are, when the sun sets, when the garbage truck makes noise, and so much more.

Renting a studio, a conference room, or a private home includes not only the rental fees but an insurance certificate and perhaps someone to clean up when the crew leaves and maybe even to touch up scratched paint. Studios charge for setup time, and many charge extra for lights and other equipment. There may be a need for set design and props. Have you arranged to have equipment and materials shipped to the studio? Will there be a securely locked room you can leave equipment in overnight, or will you need to hire a security guard? If you are renting a conference room or a suite in a hotel, there may be added fees for an Internet connection, the parking garage, a room safe, and the minibar.

Postproduction fees can include such unexpected expenses as capture fees, download fees to get your logo and photos, and fees for scanning artwork. Depending on the facility, you may be faced with separate fees for color correction and digital filter processing. You will need to purchase rights to music and even sound effects. How about a voice-over booth or an insert stage? Audio mixing and sweetening may carry a separate fee, and they may have to be handled at a different facility.

Insurance will help you to sleep at night. Your company may already have liability and workers' compensation insurance, but you may need to purchase what is called "negative insurance" for any recording media that gets damaged and needs data recovery or the scenes to be reshot. Errors and omissions (E&O) insurance may or may not be covered by your company. This protects you and your company from lawsuits from viewers who may have followed the procedure in your training video but still managed to injure themselves. Speak with a production insurance specialist to discuss if you need cast insurance to cover an actor who gets sick on the day of the shoot. The insurance specialist can let you know if you need a completion bond, especially if you are working with a relatively high video production budget and there is a chance it could go over budget.

Your company may have a legal department, but if you are a contractor, you probably should add in an amount for legal fees so your attorney can review the contracts with actors and subcontractors. He or she can also help you to secure distribution rights and avoid any potential lawsuits.

Budget Management

The appendix contains sample budgets for different levels of video productions. The rates were current for the time the budgets were developed, so be sure to use the current fees of your cast and crew. Talent agencies, post union and nonunion scales, and many production facilities, have printed rate sheets or post their rates on their websites. Note that rates vary from region to region, and even from production company to production company within a city. If you work for a large corporation, you may have clout to get a discount from a production facility that wants your company's name in its list of clients.

You can download budgets for films and videos at http://shop.mwp.com/pages/film-making-resources. This is the website of Michael Weise Productions, which publishes *Film and Video Budgets* by Deke Simon and Michael Weise.

If you are not already familiar with spreadsheet applications such as Microsoft Excel it may be time to learn some of the basics. Once you set up a "boilerplate" template for your first budget, it is easy to plug in figures for future budgets and proposals.

Budget management is an ongoing process during the production. Don't just wait until the video is finished to tally your expenses. Keep invoices and receipts for all expenditures, and maintain a running balance for each line item. If certain categories are running over budget, you can reduce expenses in another category. While Hollywood seems to wink at films that go over budget, corporate managers take their budgets seriously. Video productions easily can go over budget when a large number of small expenses quickly pile up.

Distribution and Marketing Budget

You should learn early on if your production budget includes distribution—online and on DVDs or other media. You don't want to be surprised at the premiere screening to learn that your budget included distribution. Content distribution networks (CDNs) charge by the viewer and running time of the program. Some companies have their own distribution networks.

Frequently the budget for a video includes its distribution. A request for proposals might ask for the rates for video on demand for X number of viewers per month, or it may want DVD replication and packaging. In addition to the costs for duplicating or replicating DVDs, consider the budget for graphic design for the DVD label. Packaging is another item to consider, as are the labor and fees for mailing the DVDs.

If your company seeks to recover its costs by selling DVDs or uploads of the video, there may be marketing costs involved to promote or advertise the video. If this is the case, early on try to estimate the expected revenue from the distribution of the video. This can justify marketing and distribution fees, and perhaps could make the video profitable for the company. Once your video unit is a profit-making entity, you'll have many more opportunities to produce additional videos in the future.

The Bottom Line

The budgeting basics can be spelled out in three steps:
1. What do you need?
2. How long you will need it?
3. How much will each item cost?

You don't want money to get between you and your creativity. Having to worry about pinching pennies or constantly consulting the calculator can drain your energy. Developing a budget based on sound practices, consultation with others on the production team, and prior experience lets you do what you do best: produce exciting and motivating informational videos.

Justifying the budget for a video production can become the purview of the video manager and video contractor. The question to ask is, "How much is it going to cost if we don't produce a video?" You may find a less direct way of making your point by referring to the problem that the video is intended to solve or by reviewing the objectives and see if they can save the company, over the lifetime of the video, more than the video will cost. This cost-benefit analysis is covered in Chapter 15.

THE ROLE OF THE PRODUCER IN CORPORATE VIDEO

"If you can keep your head when all about you are losing theirs and blaming it on you..."

—From the opening lines from the poem, "If..." by Rudyard Kipling

Introduction

In this chapter we discuss the functions of the producer in the corporate video setting. The producer is responsible for the overall video production, and he or she is usually the one who develops the budget; hires the scriptwriter, director, crew, and talent; and supervises the production from start to finish. Often the producer is also the director and scriptwriter, and in small organizations, he or she may fulfill additional roles. Since the producer works closely with the company executives, the successful corporate video producer has developed skills in business management and is aware of the culture of the corporation he or she is working with.

The Producer-Director

In many corporations, the roles of producer and director are rolled into one job. This two-hat rule is frequently the case both for in-house video production units and for video producers working as freelancers or contractors. This dual role is not unique to corporate video; low-budget movie production and documentary videos frequently have a single person taking on both roles. Depending on the budget of the video and the skills of the producer, he or she may need to take on additional roles such as scriptwriter and production coordinator.

While there may be advantages to delegating some tasks to others, the producer who assumes the multiple roles avoids

Corporate Video Production.
© 2011 Stuart Sweetow. Published by Elsevier Inc. All rights reserved.

personality conflicts and has the opportunity to apply his or her own creativity to the project. If you like the hands-on approach to filmmaking, working as producer-director may be more satisfying than acting as the producer alone.

Above the Line

While the director works mainly during filming and postproduction—what is known as "below the line" in filmmaking jargon—the video producer's main functions take place prior to the filming—"above the line." These include meeting with the client, developing the budget, determining concepts for the video, hiring a scriptwriter, and assembling the crew. Either the director or the producer may select the talent or supervise the postproduction.

The producer is responsible for obtaining permits for location shoots, permissions from those appearing on camera, insurance, and music clearances. The producer may deal with the legal department to craft contracts and accounting to arrange payments for personnel. Depending on the particular production, the producer also hires such ancillary personnel as a location scout, a set designer, a makeup specialist, one or more production assistants, and in some cases security personnel. Some productions have budgets for a production manager or coordinator, which we will discuss later.

As part of the production planning process, the producer should inventory existing content and visual resources. Has PR written press releases, or are there annual reports that can help the scriptwriter? Are there photos on file that can be scanned, rather than sending a production crew to a remote site for B-roll? What about graphs and charts from slide shows? Is there existing videotape or DVDs in the archives that could be sources for clips?

The corporate video producer sometimes comes up with the idea for a video and then needs to sell the idea to the appropriate department manager or company executive. Since the executive is the one with the budget, it is appropriate to call this person the "executive producer." When that person sees his or her name in the credits, you can expect that you now have an ally in the company to help you fund the next video production.

While selling the video idea to an executive is required when the producer is a freelancer or contractor, this can also be a task for the in-house video producer. As an employee of the company, you probably see several areas where training or corporate communications could be improved with a well-produced video. The producer's enthusiasm for the company's mission, whether he or she is a member of the staff or a contractor, encourages upper management and others in the organization to come on board with a proposed video production.

The Producer As Team Motivator

If you want to enroll management in supporting your video aspirations, do what you can to support the mission of your corporation. While we all enjoy learning more about video, you may want to brush up on your business skills, too. Books or courses on basic business principles, corporate management, and marketing strategies will help you develop the understanding and the vocabulary to create a rapport with the corporate execs. The relationships you build from attending meetings, serving on committees, and general schmoozing will serve you well with future productions.

When you are in meetings discussing a proposed video, listen carefully for the reasons why management wants to produce the video. What are the problems they wish to solve? What would happen if no video were produced? Can you put a cost estimate on the effect of no video, such as reduced employee productivity, travel fees for a training specialist, or an embarrassing lawsuit? With this data, you are ready to show how the video will be cost-effective. Management rarely cares about key lights and green screen effects. A business plan with metrics is what turns on corporate execs, and it could be the key to a green light for your production—with a decent budget, too.

You will win the confidence of management once you demonstrate that you know how to manage the company's money. Completing productions on time and on budget gets you on the path to earning their confidence. The more they trust that your opinions and decisions about producing videos are correct, the better position you will be in should your ideas for the video ever be in conflict with those of the executive. You may have to fight for what you think works right on the screen—maybe even convince a powerful manager that he or she is wrong. The only way you can succeed at this daunting task is to have earned their respect through relationship building and consistent performance.

Once the production planning is underway and during the production process, you'll need to motivate your team to give the production a high priority. Your enthusiasm is contagious, so spread it around. Repeat how the finished video benefits the company and how proud everyone will be to show and distribute the video. Don't hesitate to repeat the positive impact the video will have on the company's bottom line as well as management's pride in a job well done.

The In-House Producer

If you are an in-house producer, your department's future and your own tenure with the organization rest as much on your ability to forge relationships with management as on the quality of each of your videos. Some executives look at the video department as an opportunity for them to flex their creative muscles. Others think that the video producer is a pretentious artiste. The time may come when you need to justify the cost of the firm maintaining an in-house video department. Some managers know nothing about video; they see only a large capital outlay for staff and equipment without the department generating any revenue. Your job will be to show them how video saves money in the long run.

In some organizations, the video producer has filmed the CEO or has produced a video for the stockholders' annual meeting. This puts the producer in an enviable position: membership in the "executive club." These are opportunities to forge relationships with the CEO and his or her administrative team. On more than one occasion, when the CEO learned that a merger or financial issue was going to result in the video department being eliminated, he or she stepped in and came to the rescue.

Another of the hats the in-house producer wears is that of a business manager. Plan on writing reports detailing budgets for your video productions and your unit's operating expenses. If you have a staff, you'll be plenty busy completing employment forms. You'll need to justify your expenses, and you'll be expected to estimate your budget needs for the next fiscal year, if not for three years out. When you estimate a budget for a particular production, keep track of the actual expenses as the production takes place. Then figure a variance between the estimate and the actual expenditures for each line item. This will help you to create better estimates for each successive production.

As the production requests increase, you may be in a position to hire outside producers to handle some of the video projects. Now you take on the role of management because *your* eyes will be on the budget and other business concerns. Develop a request for proposal (RFP) that states the parameters of the video and asks for proposals from the candidates.

The proposal should include information on the backgrounds of the producer and his or her staff. The prospective producers should give you an idea of the concept or treatment they propose for the video, and their proposals should include the timeline and budget

When shopping for a producer, look at a sample production and ask how much that would cost to produce in current dollars. Also, make sure you meet the actual producer or director you will be working with, not just a salesperson. If the camera operator who shot the demo is not available, can you see a sample of the current camera operator's work?

Once you hire the producer, be open to his or her ideas. The objectivity of the outsider can bring a different perspective to your project and may shine a light on some of your blind spots. Don't discourage creativity just because you may not agree with his or her ideas. You will want the contractor to get a good feel for the corporate culture, so spend time explaining some of the key players and the mission of the firm. Finally, have them sign a confidentiality agreement, and confirm that your company owns all the rights to work performed by the contractor.

Corporations like to evaluate their projects, so plan on developing an evaluation mechanism and use it for each video produced. It could be an online survey that pops up at the conclusion of the video, or it could be in paper form. When possible, include quantifiable metrics, such as the number of people who viewed the video, the number of viewers who performed a task taught in the video, and, most important, a dollar amount of travel or consulting fees not spent as a result of the video being in existence. This will help you justify the next production budget request.

Your manager may want to approve the video production at various stages. You could go as far as asking for initials or signatures to approve the treatment, the script, the selection of talent, and the final video. Build in multiple stages for the manager's approval. That way, you are not only sure that you are on the right track, but you are involving the manager more in using video in general. This buy-in helps ensure the longevity of the video unit and your own job.

As in-house producer, you may be asked to perform as an on-camera host at times. While you may feel more comfortable behind the camera, this could be an opportunity to become better known within the company. However, each producer must decide if this is right for him or her. Some may have already found talent who can play the role as on-camera host—someone who better looks the part.

Appendix A

Instructional Video Evaluation Instrument

Video Title: _____

Name of Evaluator: _____

Phone: _____ Date Viewed: _____

Please rate the video according to the following quality

indicators by CIRCLING one response for each item (1 equals Poor

and 5 equals Exceptional). Give comments where appropriate.

Poor-----Exceptional

Content

1. Accurate   1 2 3 4 5

    Was the content of the video accurate and up-to-date? If

not, then the video is not ideally suitable for learning. There

may be portions of the content that should NOT be used, as well

as sections that are usable. Please note unusable content in the

space provided or on a separate attachment.

Comments:_____

2. Useful   1 2 3 4 5

    Was the content of the video generally useful? The video

should stimulate, motivate, and inform the learner to act on the

information that was being presented. Will you incorporate the

ideas presented into your life?

Comments:_____

3. Bias-Free   1 2 3 4 5

    Was the video bias-free, including stereotyping with

regard to age, sex, ethnicity, race, physical impairment, values,

dress, language, or social class?

Comments:_____

Instructional Plan

Figure 5.1 A video evaluation sheet. Copyright © by Extension Journal, Inc.

4. Stated the Objectives   1 2 3 4 5

Did the video begin with a motivating introduction to stimulate interest? Were the objectives or key elements made clear in the introduction?

Comments:_____

5. Content Presentation   1 2 3 4 5

Was the content detail controlled to promote understanding? Did the video simplify complex tasks and avoid introducing extraneous information? Did it try to cover too much material or introduce too much detail?

Comments:_____

6. Learner Application   1 2 3 4 5

Did the video suggest methods for the learner to apply the newly acquired knowledge? Were suggestions for practice of what's being discussed considered? Practice can be designed into the overall program design as well as into the video itself.

Comments:_____

7. Learner Reflection   1 2 3 4 5

Did the video allow for learner reflection? Was reflection, silence, or time allowed for the learners to react to a scene or statement? It is also important for the facilitator to interact with the student to provide feedback on the learner's application of the material.

Comments:_____

8. Met the Objectives   1 2 3 4 5

Did the video meet the learning objectives and needs of the learner? Did what was being visually depicted fit the learning objectives? As in the introduction, people also remember the last things that are presented in a program; therefore, did the video have the key learning elements repeated in the summary or conclusion?

Comments:_____

Figure 5.1 continued

9. Learner Interaction   1 2 3 4 5

   Was the video conducive to learner interaction? Videos can
often be used to promote active learning.

Comments: _____

10. Integration into the Learning Environment   1 2 3 4 5

   Can the video be easily integrated into the learning
environment by adding emphasis to or supplementing more
traditional methods? Did the video bring remote experiences and
places to the learner?

Comments:_____

Technical Production

11. General Video Design Characteristics   1 2 3 4 5

   Was the video well planned, organized, and structured?
Was the technology transparent and non-threatening to the
learner? Did the video demonstrate its ability to transcend space
and time? The camera can go where the learner cannot and the
video is an excellent media for presenting information or
demonstrations that are timely; however, care must be taken to
prevent giving a false idea of reality.

Comments:_____

12. Focused on Intended Content   1 2 3 4 5

   Did the video avoid content not related to the subject
matter stated in the introduction? Digressions could lead to
confusion and may be a waste of video time.

Comments:_____

13. Visual Quality   1 2 3 4 5

   Is the camera looking at the scene from the learners'
point of view? This is especially important when psychomotor
skills are being taught. Did the scene changes appear to be
appropriate? Were special effects used to enhance learning by
drawing attention to specific attributes of what is being seen?
Were varying types of camera shots, close-ups to long shots, used
to provide variety in the video?

Comments:_____

Figure 5.1 continued

14. Audio Quality   1 2 3 4 5

    Was the vocabulary of the narration appropriate for the
intended audience? Was the speed of the narration slow enough to
be understood? Was the music fitting for the visual effects or
audio narration? Were background noises used that were conducive
to learning? Were sound effects used to add emphasis to the
visual tract of a video to enhance learning?

Comments:_____

15. Audio-Visual Relationship   1 2 3 4 5

    Was the audio-visual combined well? The audio and visual
components should not contradict one another but complement each
other. Was there a variety of differing types of sounds and
visuals to attract and hold attention?

Comments:_____

Included Supplemental Materials

16. Provided Introductory Information   1 2 3 4 5

    Did the included supplemental materials include the
purpose and objectives of the video? Did the video accomplish
what is stated in the supplemental materials?

Comments:_____

17. Clarifies and Summarizes Content   1 2 3 4 5

    Were job aids or diagrams provided to help in
understanding the material? Were terms defined? Were sources for
further investigation included? Are there suggested activities in
the materials to aid in understanding? Such as, discussion
questions, role plays, or simulation exercises. Is the summary
useful in understanding the nature of the video and does it match
what is on the tape?

Comments:_____

        Total (Sum the Scores, 85 Max.) _____

Additional Comments:---

Figure 5.1 continued

Navigating the uncharted and sometimes murky currents to understand the corporate culture is a skill any corporate team player must develop. Unfortunately, these are not topics covered during new employee orientation. Perhaps you should propose to produce a video on the topic? (Or maybe not. . . .)

The unstated dynamics that go on in a large company don't show up on the firm's organizational chart. You learn this over time with your keen observations of the subtle nuances. Some who are new to the organization will seek a mentor (even someone below them) to let them in on "trade secrets." Consider being willing to do an exec's pet project or incorporate his ideas (even though they stink). You don't have to be obsequious to get on the good side of an influential manager; just be cooperative.

The successful team player in big business needs to let go of democracy. While some companies do let lower-level managers and their employees make decisions, most companies operate as a caste system. The CEO and top-level execs get paid large sums of money (and bonuses), while the hourly paid workers get only industry-prevailing salaries. You aren't going to change the system because the system works for most organizations. The captains who steer the ship and take on the responsibility for the company's profits or losses get the lion's share of the benefits. Your role as video producer usually resides somewhere between the lower-level workers and the corporate execs. The more opportunities you make to work with and hang out with the suits, the better chance you will need to wear one, too.

The Contract/Freelance Producer

The independent video producer needs to work at finding opportunities to hang with the suits. In addition to being a video producer, he or she needs to be a salesperson. Read books on personal and professional development, including sales. Take a community college class on public speaking. Join professional online social networks and include a link to a video clip whenever you can. The link should be to your website so the readers get to see more of what you do. Use search engine optimization (SEO) techniques for your site and for the video links. Submit your videos to user generated content (UGS) sites such as YouTube and Vimeo. Use contact management software to keep track of prospects and the content of your calls and meetings with them.

Attend conferences and trade shows—not video conferences but the meetings your prospects attend. Visit displays at the trade shows, and offer to produce videos for the vendors to display in their booths. Belly up to the bar during happy hour. Arrive early to conferences and ask if they need volunteers. Offer to speak at a seminar or a local trade organization's meeting. An entertaining and short presentation with visuals may be just the diversion that the meeting planners are looking for to break up the monotony.

Do you like golf? Are you a member of your local chamber of commerce? How about a local business networking organization? Read the business section of your newspaper to learn of companies that are expanding or merging. Volunteer to videotape the speakers at nonprofit fund-raising dinners; this is where you'll find the corporate executives in your town.

Unless you are one of the lucky few with a client who fills your time with production work, you'll need to always be on the lookout for new clients and people who could refer you to prospects. Even if you have a big client with regular work, if they decide to drop you, you could be in the unemployment line. So develop your sales skills so you can market yourself and have plenty of clients with interesting video projects.

One consideration of which the independent producer should always be aware is the possibility that a corporate video could be repurposed for distribution nationally or internationally. A forklift safety video could be used by any company that owns forklifts. A training video on employee supervision could be generic enough that nearly any manager could learn supervision skills. Think early on of including the option of you widely distributing the video, perhaps with only a change to the opening and closing titles. Alternately, you can shoot some extra shots that would be substituted for the company-specific scenes, and those would be edited into the generic version. Check with your attorney so you can craft a contract that gives you the distribution rights. We cover more about contracts and media law in Chapter 9.

Script Development

The producer usually works with a content specialist at the company—the person who best knows the subject and may be the one initially requesting the video. The producer, in conjunction with this person (sometimes known as the "subject matter specialist"), forms the foundation of the team that will produce the video. The content specialist knows the material but may not know the best way to present it clearly and visually for the target audience. That's where the producer's skills come in.

The producer sets up meetings with the content specialist and frequently that person's manager or department head. This is the time to listen to their concerns and perhaps to play devil's advocate. Ask why they need the video. What are the benefits to the company, to the employees, and to the customers? Establish the objectives—both cognitive (what do they want the viewer to know after viewing the video?) and behavioral (what do they want the viewer to *do* after watching the video?). This is the time to conduct a brainstorming session.

During brainstorming, encourage everyone to come up with every idea he or she can, and don't discount any of them. It's good to assign one person to be the scribe who writes each idea on a flipchart or types it through a data projector. Then you are free to guide the brainstorming session and encourage even the most outrageous ideas. Some of these ideas will be completely off the wall, but you might be surprised at what comes out of some of these "no holds barred" brainstorming sessions. Once the completely outlandish ideas have been identified and removed, then ask them to decide which of the remaining ideas are feasible.

We will discuss script and concept development more in Chapter 8, but the most important role of the producer is selecting the best scriptwriter (yourself or another writer) and guiding the production planning process. Company managers may overlook the necessity to take enough time to come up with creative concepts that result in the most effective video for the target audience. Your role as producer is to demonstrate to them the importance of thorough planning and writing the best script.

If you will be selecting a scriptwriter, choose one who has experience working in the corporate arena. A Hollywood fiction writer may not be the best choice, nor would a technical writer. An experienced corporate scriptwriter can make or break the production. Choose one who can be a part of your team and can participate in planning sessions. A corporate scriptwriter knows how to take mundane information and enliven it with clever concepts and snappy wording. You want the writer who thinks in visuals; that way, the video will limit talking head scenes.

Production Management

Some corporate video producers are blessed with budgets sufficient enough to hire production coordinators, while others assume that role themselves. Choose a production coordinator who can work within the constraints of a corporate setting and budget. Many coordinators have feature film experience, and they are used to working with budgets that may not be appropriate for a corporate video. They may be frustrated by your small crew size or the small office where shooting takes place. A good coordinator knows to rent plants and flowers to spruce up the office. He or she can juggle the schedules of the execs and those of the actors and crew. The coordinator may also have a plan to silence the noisy construction project that was scheduled on the shoot day.

The production coordinator makes travel arrangements when needed, orders meals and other craft services, and arranges to have releases signed by those appearing on camera. The coordinator rents camera and other production equipment, and even a generator if needed. Such details as parking for staff and crew vehicles, maps and floor plans, dressing rooms, and even renting portable toilets are included in this job description. A good coordinator is nimble enough to handle any contingencies that may come up during the shooting days.

If you are not both producer and director, you may be hiring a director. Choose one who can work with your particular script and possibly lower-budget talent. If the director will be working with nonprofessional actors, such as employees at the company, he or she needs to know how to treat them. See Chapter 6 for details on this, as well as suggestions for directing the CEO.

Usually the producer is responsible for hiring the cast and crew. Determine early on if the company needs to hire union crew and talent. Talent is available through talent agencies, and you will need to contract with SAG or AFTRA, the two national talent unions. Union crew positions can be filled by working through the local stage hands' union. Nonunion crew may be found by asking other producers and directors, by placing a notice on a local online video production forum, or by placing a help wanted ad. Local theater groups and the college drama department are also sources for nonunion talent.

It is possible that a director may hire you as a producer. In that case be certain to clarify your role. Sometimes a producer working for a director is acting more like a line producer, handling the budget, hiring crew, and dealing with the day-to-day production tasks. Similar to a production coordinator, a line producer rarely has much input in the creative process.

Whatever your role as producer, from the top person in charge of the production or acting more like a production coordinator, you have an important responsibility to manage the production and coordinate the various talented individuals. These can include the CEO, the content specialists, the director,

1. Locate decision maker

2. Identify the need or problem to be solved

3. Write proposal, including budget

4. Secure finances

5. Set up planning meetings, focus group or brainstorming session

6. Develop and obtain approvals for concept, treatment and script

7. Hire cast and crew

8. Arrange shooting location and secure use of equipment

9. Obtain permits and permissions

10. Schedule and perform shoot

11. Log footage and create edit decision list (EDL)

12. Supervise postproduction

13. Obtain management approval of video

14. Finalize video, encode and distribute

15. Evaluate video

Figure 5.2 A producer checklist.

the crew, the actors, and the editors. You may work with the IT department to distribute video, or you may select a content distribution network. Your abilities as an organizer, a coach, a creative producer, and the calm ship's captain moving steadily on course in sometimes stormy waters will result in a video program that can help large numbers of employees to do their jobs better. Your video productions may outlive you, and they can be your contribution to the continued success of the organization.

DIRECTING CORPORATE VIDEOS

Introduction

In a corporate setting, the video producer will probably have times when he or she is asked to videotape a company executive. Other corporate clients may want to act out a skit or vignette they wrote, and there may be training programs where only a staffer trained in a particular procedure could show how it is done.

This chapter focuses on particular considerations when selecting and directing employees and actors to represent the company image. We will discuss the role of the on-camera narrator-host in corporate videos, as well as directing talent in dramatic vignettes. In the "Shooting the CEO" section, you'll learn some techniques for getting the best performance from the executive without becoming intimidated.

This chapter does not cover the basics of directing. Read some introductory books to learn about the different types of shots, camera positioning, and angles. Focal Press and other publishers' books cover composition, continuity, the use of cut-ins and cutaways, and how to avoid jump cuts. They will help you learn about blocking your shots as well as pacing and timing.

Here, we will discuss the issues of using employees as talent and ways to coach them to act naturally and be relaxed on camera. This chapter includes techniques on multicamera direction, both in the studio and on location, as well as considerations when directing the editing and postproduction aspects of your video.

Directing Professional Talent

If you have training or experience producing or directing actors in films or television, you will be an asset to the corporation that wants to produce videos with professional talent. Your contract may require that you hire union talent from an agency, or you may simply want to hire the best. Talent agencies usually can help you find the types of actors you need, and some even have website videos where you can see them in action. However, if you are on a tight budget and the video will be used in-house only, you may want to hire nonunion actors. Many of them are excellent actors with a wide repertoire, and they know how to take direction.

Whether you hire union or nonunion talent, audition your prospects, and record the auditions when possible. Ask them to read a portion of the script, and keep your eye on the actors, not on the script. It doesn't matter if they miss a word or two; your attention needs to be on them. How well do they communicate with you? Can they easily bring to life the mood you are looking for? How do they react when you stop them and give redirection? Even though you may have a video to view, how you and the actors relate to each other during the audition will predict how you will relate during shooting.

Once you choose your actors, let them know how much memorization will be required. Will they be able to read from a teleprompter during the shoot? Will there be a rehearsal? What are the other roles, and who are the other actors they will be working with?

Get them their copy of the script with their sections clearly marked. You don't need to give them the entire script if they will be on camera for only an individual segment. Explain the video's objectives and how the roles they play will help achieve that objective. Discuss your interpretation of the role, and elicit their ideas or suggestions on how they can apply their own methods of acting to add impact to the performance.

Rather than show the actors how to perform, let them interpret the characters and find their own styles to give life to the characters. Most actors prefer minimal direction so they can invoke their own feelings and energy. Try to be open to the actors' suggestions and ideas to improve the wording or adding an action. Encourage some spontaneous improvisations, even if you leave those takes on the cutting room floor. You want to get the best performance out of your actors, and sometimes that means directing with a lighter touch.

Some producers and directors in television and motion pictures consider two different approaches to styles of directing: "selective" and "creative." The director who employs a "selective" style lets the talent select their own interpretations of the script and create their own movements and other staging. Working together with talent as a team, they review the program objectives as well as the demographics of the target audience. The selective director even encourages talent to suggest changes to the script based on their own interpretations.

The "creative" director develops his own visualization of the script and directs talent to fulfill the director's interpretation of how scenes should be performed. The creative director will determine the blocking, the talents' movements, and other staging elements. A good creative director knows what concepts will work for the particular audience and can mold the video into an engaging and effective presentation.

Shooting the CEO

When the "talent" is the CEO or another powerful executive, the creative director may need to take the role of the selective director. The CEO knows the target audience best and will want to determine what his or her movements and staging will be. The director can be creative in producing a roll-in to the CEO's section, determining B-roll shots to illustrate the CEO's talk, and creating the set, backgrounds, and staging. In some cases the CEO may let the director make all the decisions, but in most cases the CEO or one of his or her assistants will want to call the shots.

Many corporate chief executives are charismatic speakers who can engage an audience. They may want to be filmed for a variety of reasons, and their personality may be an important asset to the organization. The video director's job is to make them look good and to maintain the interest of the viewers.

One of the challenges is to keep their on-camera message clear and focused. The corporate culture will dictate whether the CEO's presentation will be more formal, such as that of the president of the United States, or casual, as if he or she were buddies with every employee.

Younger CEOs, especially those in newer, entrepreneurial companies, will probably opt for the casual approach. Executives in more established companies may prefer the more buttoned-down look. In either case, the job of the video director is to help their true selves come out in as a relaxed and polished manner as possible.

One problem could be the older CEO who wants to change his image and be "one of the guys" or the young newcomer who wants a formal image despite his discomfort with that demeanor. Preproduction meetings with the executive's assistant or the company's public relations department can help you determine the best approach.

The CEO may want to simply rally the troops in a quarterly address, distributed live or playable as needed. He or she may want to introduce a new product or service at the shareholders' annual meeting. The video presentation could be directed documentary-style, as if it were an interview. The CEO may want a brief clip of herself welcoming viewers to the company website.

The director will need to be flexible with the format of the video, as well as provide direction to create the most effective presentation. Getting a feel for the corporate culture and advance planning sessions and determining the setting for filming are some of the steps the director can take in advance to ensure that the process will go smoothly.

While it is best to have the opportunity to meet with the CEO in advance and discuss some ideas for the filming session, the director may have to conduct these planning sessions with the administrative assistant or PR person. Ask to see a photo or video clip of the CEO, if available. This will help you determine if you will need to coach him or her, or need to have special lighting. If he is bald or wears eyeglasses, you will know to arrange appropriate makeup or lighting. For the CEO who wears glasses, one solution is to light from the side—not too much, just enough to avoid picking up glare in the eyeglasses.

This is the time to discuss the production and the script. Listen for their concerns both for the content of the presentation and logistical considerations. What if the CEO needs to back out at the last minute, or on the day of the shoot he or she has less time than previously allotted? Explain to the assistant that you and your crew will make the filming process run as smoothly as possible and that you will work together as a team with the CEO's staff.

This is probably a good time to discuss wardrobe and makeup. Ask that the CEO bring a change of clothing or at least a shirt, tie, and jacket. A finely striped shirt or tweed jacket can cause an undesirable moiré effect. If the CEO is male and reluctant to use makeup, explain the professionalism of the makeup artist. For the female CEO, provide instruction on appropriate makeup for television.

Even if you like filming at your studio, be prepared to shoot the exec at his or her location. If the CEO is going to your studio, make sure everything is in place before he or she arrives. The exec will probably arrive with an assistant or two, and you don't want anyone tripping on cables or becoming distracted by a messy studio.

Before their arrival, use stand-ins to set up the studio lights, and have them on when they arrive. That way, they won't be bothered by a harsh light suddenly being turned on. When the CEO and team arrive, focus attention on them and assure them of your keen interest of what they have to say. Then introduce the group to your assistant and explain that you have some last-minute things to attend to. Your assistant will offer them coffee, show them the dressing room if available, introduce them to the crew, and show them the set. If you have a makeup person available, your assistant can make sure there is privacy for its application. Your assistant needs to assume the role of the CEO's new best friend and be at the CEO's side throughout the process.

The CEO's assistants will probably have their own agendas and useless suggestions. Hopefully you have a location that can serve as a "green room" where they can relax with coffee and snacks and watch the filming on a monitor. If they want to be on the set during filming, your assistant needs to diplomatically explain how any slight rustling of clothing can be heard through the sensitive microphones.

During the filming, since the CEO probably has not had experience on a shooting set, consider raising the light levels behind the camera. That may help the CEO feel more in control rather than being in the spotlight and not being able to see anyone else.

If the exec fidgets with his or her hands, you'll need to go for a tighter shot. Sometimes the first take is the best, but make sure you shoot at least one more safety take. When you start getting into multiple takes or if he or she is making mistakes, pretend there are technical difficulties and take a break. Or if you aren't a good liar, simply say that you need to stretch or take a break yourself. If you have the opportunity, ask the CEO to walk with you to a private room where the two of you can practice some deep breathing, tell jokes, or do whatever you can to help him or her relax.

If the CEO is speaking to the camera and reading from a teleprompter rather than a simple talking head shot throughout, consider dividing the scene into two shots. At the close of the first shot, the CEO gets up and walks to another location. Cut to the different location and move in close for a close-up. This serves three purposes: it gives the CEO a break, it attracts the attention of the viewer, and it allows for a close-up with a strong impact.

Employees as Actors: Directing Nonprofessional Talent

One my first assignments as a freelancer occurred shortly after I was laid off from my staff job as video producer for a teaching hospital. The outpatient surgery department wanted to produce a waiting room video for patients. Rather than staff repeating the same information for each new patient, the video would show a typical patient checking in and following the postsurgery regimen.

The doctor in charge of the outpatient surgery department approved my script, and I had completed talent auditions for the roles of doctor, receptionist, patient, and patient's spouse. Then the doctor (the real one) told me that he would play himself in the video. Sensing danger, I politely explained that we needed him to be the executive producer and to make sure the content and procedures we filmed were accurate. He told me he was in theater in college and that he had performed in a commercial. He was insistent, and I didn't want to lose my first freelance job.

I offered to rent a teleprompter for the doctor to be able to read his lines as he looked into the lens, but the doctor said he would be able to remember his lines. I asked what would be a good time for us to rehearse, and he said he didn't have time to rehearse. On the set, as our crew was setting up equipment and I was blocking the talent and camera movements, the doctor started rushing the crew. I should have understood that he was nervous, but I focused more on calming the crew, who by now sensed trouble with our "executive-producer-turned-star" and were threatening to leave.

With the lighting artfully set and the camera perfectly balanced, we started filming one of the scenes with the doctor. My goal was to complete his scenes first and let him get back to work (and out of our way). The camera rolled, and I gave the doctor his cue to start. Once he started speaking, I knew the production was going to be a failure. He was as stiff as the bodies in the morgue! His delivery was in a slow monotone. Later, I learned that after the nursing staff saw the video, they always referred to him as Dr. Rogers, after Mr. Rogers, the soft-spoken children's show host of that time.

That video died a quick death, and my career would have, too, but I decided to learn all I could about directing nonprofessional talent. I bought Thomas Kennedy's book *Directing Video* and paid close attention to the chapter about nonprofessional talent. Kennedy stresses that the video producer must develop a working relationship with any employees who are to appear on camera, whether it is the company president or the cafeteria cashier. If you'll be filming the CEO, whenever possible planning should be with the executive who will appear rather than his or her assistant. Probe for concerns the exec or employee may have about the production, and explain the process in clear terms. Use this personal meeting to assess potential concerns such as wardrobe or speech patterns.

Kennedy also advises that the video producer explain how the shooting will progress, the need for lights, and where the microphones will be placed. He suggests that you be frank about the invading force of a camera crew who may be moving furniture and closing window blinds. Try to set up a quiet area where the on-camera staffer can sit between takes and make phone calls or check e-mail. Do your best to shoot all their on-camera scenes at one time so they don't have to wait while others are on camera.

When filming with nonprofessional talent, allow more time to shoot their scenes. Plan for them to require several takes, and try to limit the length of each of their shots. If you are accustomed to directing professional talent, you'll need to be much more patient with the nonpros. Explain to them that you need them to pause a second before you say "Action!" (In fact, it may be better to do a countdown to silence or find a softer way to ask for action.)

Explain that you need them to pause and stay in character at the end of a take so you have room for editing. You will probably have to coach them to look into the camera lens. I sometimes say that if they look deep into the lens, they can see their best friend listening intently to what they say. For scenes when they shouldn't be looking at the camera, especially when you are both director and camera operator, they need to be guided to listen to but not look at you.

On the set, don't make them wait while the crew sets up equipment. Try to give them an accurate time to arrive, and make sure the crew is going to be ready by then. Early on, give some positive reinforcement; find something they did right. When you need to correct them, limit it to *one* specific thing they need to correct so they don't take it as criticism of them personally. You could wait for another take to ask them to correct an additional mistake. Be quick to admit your or your crew members' mistakes. This relieves the pressure on someone who is being too hard on himself. If you are filming a large number of takes to shoot a single scene and the talent is getting hard on herself, consider taking a break to "see what is wrong with that light over there."

Limit the number of shots you plan to complete during the time you have with nonpro talent. If you appear to be in a hurry, the on-camera staffer will probably pick up on this. Thinking she is trying to please you, she may perform too quickly and cause even more time to be wasted. Slowing down the process can help ease her nerves as well as those of the crew.

Auditioning the Talent

Auditions are an important technique for determining the choice of talent. Many producers and directors record the auditions to help them select talent, and sometimes the client watches the videos when they want to participate in choosing which actors best match the company image.

Watch for the talent's particular mannerisms and gestures that are a reflection of his or her personality. They can be appealing and complementary to the corporate image, or they can be a distraction. Unless the script calls for drama, the prospective actor will need to keep his or her performance straightforward. In any case, watch for overacting; it can be a deal-breaker. Don't let the too-enthusiastic actor onto a corporate video set unless he or she can readily accept direction to tone it down.

When choosing an on-camera spokesperson, in addition to finding an actor to match the corporate image, look for the actor who appears genuinely enthusiastic and natural. Good eye contact with the camera is an important trait, as are appropriately timed smiles and other facial gestures. Appropriate head-nods and arm and body movements can add life to an otherwise mundane talking-head segment.

If shooting in a factory or another noisy setting, it can be difficult to capture a clean voice track. Consider using a chroma key or green screen technique to allow the on-camera narrator to speak in a studio with the location keyed into the background. You may need to create virtual moves in the background if the talent moves or you move the camera on a dolly.

Directing the Crew

While crew size varies by the budget, the type of company may also be a consideration when selecting your crew. You may already have crew members you like to work with, but some of them may not want to work on a surgery video. You may need a Steadicam operator in some instances, or you may need a gaffer with particular skills in low-light settings.

Some subjects may require that crew members be particularly sensitive to talent or nonprofessional on-camera personnel. For example, if you are making a training video on avoiding sexual harassment, make sure crew members don't make inappropriate comments.

Provide appropriate portions of the script for particular crew members, and let them know such relevant tasks as a certain type of lighting or a particular camera movement needed. Be open to suggestions from crew members. Just because someone is a production assistant does not mean he may not have a good idea for the director. The camera operator may have suggestions for a particular type of dolly or crane, and the gaffer may have an idea to illuminate the nearby plant.

Try to conduct a preproduction meeting. This is a good time to elicit suggestions from the crew. Discuss call and strike times, lunch and other break times, and any other logistical concerns the crew or client has. If you don't have a full rehearsal, plan some time to rehearse complicated moves of talent and equipment. Sometimes production assistants can be stand-ins for talent for lighting and blocking.

One way to pace your crew is to start the shooting day with some easier shots. Then later in the morning, perform some more critical scenes. After lunch, cast and crew may have lower energy; this is the time for some easier shots. An afternoon snack break can be followed by more energy-intensive shots. If possible, plan some fun moments near the end of the day. That helps bring your crew together and gives them an opportunity to review with you, in a relaxed atmosphere, what went well and what did not.

Directing Live Switching

With the accessibility of flash and hard drive recording, many productions can be easily switched in post while retaining all the footage from all the cameras. However, day-long conferences and videos requiring quick turnaround frequently are more cost-effective when you perform live switching.

While broadcasters are accustomed to long setup times and cables strung over doorways and down halls, businesspeople usually find this arrangement unconventional, if not uncomfortable. If you are shooting in a studio, then all you need to do is show the client the studio in advance and make sure he knows that there could be some delays in getting started or between takes.

When the shoot is in the company conference room or auditorium, let the client know far in advance what logistics are involved. Assure your client and the staff at the location that while it may appear the crew is turning their world topsy-turvy, you will return everything to its original place (and make sure you do!).

Assign each camera a number, and use that associated number on your monitor panel. Rehearse some moves and switches so you can get an idea how long it may take for a camera operator to reposition and refocus for the next shot. Be clear and consistent with your camera directions. Some newer camera ops may not know that "push" means "zoom in" or the difference between "truck" and "dolly."

Avoid getting another camera in a shot. Plan all shots and camera moves in advance. Think of backgrounds so they complement the shot rather than having a vertical pipe looking as if it were growing out of the talent's head. Watch for lighting issues, such as a camera lens casting a shadow. Block movements so actors and crew don't bump into one another or are in the way of camera movements. Plan in advance how much time is needed to move a camera from position A to position B.

When directing your crew through intercom headsets, talk quietly and ask all crew members to turn up their volume so they can hear you. Make sure that camera operators know to limit their talking through the intercom, and if they have to say something, they should talk as quietly as possible. You, as director, can also speak quietly and calmly through the intercom. In a corporate setting your "control room" may be in the same room as the cameras. Certainly you have your own style of directing, but if the company CEO happens to tour his client through your control room, you want to make sure they see a relaxed, confident director.

Script Markup and the Shot Sheet

Rather than read each word during a take, you want to be able to take a quick glance at the script and then back to the action. Highlight cues on the script, and develop your own shorthand. For example, "C1" is camera one, or a slash mark (/) on the script can indicate where to cut from camera 1 to camera 2. An "X" might mean a dissolve between cameras rather than a cut. Use the highlight tool to color-code for camera 1 and camera 2. You can have a different color of highlight to tell you when to cue a camera or graphic.

Camera operators, the floor director, the boom mike person—everyone should have a shot list that includes such details as position, angle, and size of shot. The director should be able to minimize explanations so he or she can concentrate on the production without getting distracting questions from the crew.

Multitasking is a skill required for directors. You need to watch *all* the monitors, not just the preview and line monitors. Glance at the line monitor only during a cut. Keep your eyes moving in a pattern to see all the monitors, and glance at the script only when absolutely necessary.

Try to be one or two shots ahead of the script. Be certain you know what comes next after a particular move or sequence. Rely on your technical director or assistant director to correct your mistakes. A good technical director will know when the director calls out the wrong command, and the director should set the tone so the TD feels comfortable correcting him.

Directing the Edit

In the corporate world, the video you shoot, including the out-takes, may be the property of the company. Your client or even the legal department may want to see the raw footage. Many video producers would rather give up their first-born child than let the client see unedited dailies. However, if you are required to relinquish this wart-infested footage, make sure the client knows why they are going to see lots of stuff they don't like.

Write "raw footage" or "unedited footage" on the tape, flash card, or disc label and on the box. Insert the words "raw footage" on a slate before the footage, or key in a disclaimer throughout it all. If the footage gets passed from department to department for approval or edit notes, someone may think it is a finished video and may want to put your head on the chopping block.

Some producers provide the client with window dubs where the time code is keyed into the lower third of the screen. Then they include a simple list of instructions asking the client to note the start and stop times of the shots they like (see Figure 6.1).

At some point you'll want to take the field logs and view the raw footage (sometimes called "rushes" or "dailies"). You might notice some bad takes that the PA in the field labeled as good and vice versa. Perhaps the camera was rolling when the talent

Shot or Scene #	Tape or Disc#	In Point	Out Point	Description
1	1	1.32	4.27	Mary introduces herself
2	2	8.51	12.02	Mary holds up book
3	1	16.42	21.03	John introduces himself

Figure 6.1 An edit decision list (EDL) shows the start and stop times of the takes you want to include in the final edit. The director or assistant prepares an EDL after logging footage and prior to the editing session.

did not know it, and he gave a cute expression that could be used as a cutaway or cut-in shot.

Since the scenes were shot out of sequence, this is the time to put them back in order. Enter the time code numbers of each good take to each corresponding scene. Now you have the start of an edit decision list (EDL), a document that will save loads of time and headaches when you are in the edit room.

Hopefully, you have an editor who can push the buttons while you direct the edit. Many editors lead a double life— directing their own projects on weekends—so include the editor in your decision making. Ask him or her for opinions and suggestions. Fill them in on the objectives and audience for the video, and let them know the style and mood you are looking for. Is this going to be a straightforward educational video, or is the intention to create emotion in the viewer? Do you want any sequences to be fast-paced with graphics and effects? How will music and other sounds be used?

The problem arises when the client wants to join in the editing session . . . and bring her friends! Some edit rooms include a producer's table with a phone, located behind the editor. I've heard editors say they put the phone there so the producer can busy himself with calls and leave the editor alone.

When the client brings his client and an art director and maybe even legal staff, then you know the session is going to run long. The company may very well need this group to approve scenes and statements. Certainly, the time for this was in the script stage, but nevertheless, there you are with a cadre of suits who have taken over your director's role.

One way to avoid this potential debacle is to schedule an edit session—with just the editor and you. Don't let anyone else know about it. Then send the edited video to that team as an online file or on DVDs. Let all involved know that it is a rough draft for them to preview and provide their comments. Give them a deadline for responding, and try to build in a way for them to approve or comment. That way you remain the director, but you still are working on the team with the client to address his or her ideas for the video.

In Summary

The corporate video director needs to be a strategic diplomat with the corporate suits, an enthusiastic motivator of cast and crew, and the energetic, creative force driving the video project. Sometimes the director of corporate videos is also the producer, production coordinator, and even the shooter and editor. Depending on the budget, the director will need to take on the role of gaffer or sound recordist. This role requires versatility and flexibility.

If you are the in-house producer/director, your job may be somewhat more defined than if you are a freelancer or contract video director. You'll need to learn about the company and its culture. Developing alliances with key management personnel can help you to learn about the people and the processes that drive the corporation. Your colleagues will look to you for creative direction only after you have gained their respect. You may be the manager of the video department, or you may be an employee if the department is large enough to have a staff position for a director or producer-director.

Whether you are a department manager or you report to the manager, you are part of a team that will help the company train employees and communicate to the public. The director is the center-point of many video productions. His or her creativity, combined with communication skills and the ability to lead a team, makes or breaks the video.

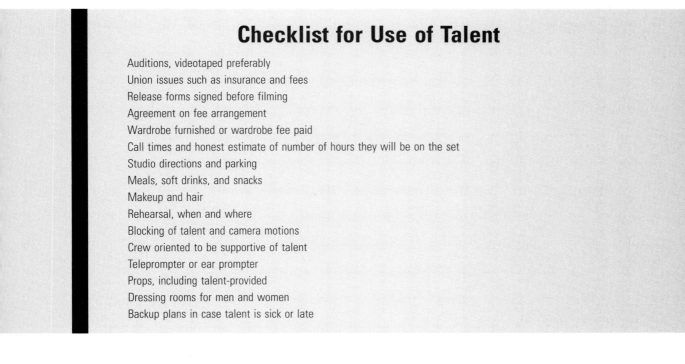

Checklist for Use of Talent

Auditions, videotaped preferably

Union issues such as insurance and fees

Release forms signed before filming

Agreement on fee arrangement

Wardrobe furnished or wardrobe fee paid

Call times and honest estimate of number of hours they will be on the set

Studio directions and parking

Meals, soft drinks, and snacks

Makeup and hair

Rehearsal, when and where

Blocking of talent and camera motions

Crew oriented to be supportive of talent

Teleprompter or ear prompter

Props, including talent-provided

Dressing rooms for men and women

Backup plans in case talent is sick or late

PRODUCTION COORDINATION

Introduction

While feature films and television broadcasting have clear job descriptions for such roles as unit production managers, production coordinators, line producers, assistant directors, and script coordinators, frequently in corporate production many of these jobs are rolled into one. In some cases, especially with low-budget productions, the video producer or his or her assistant is tasked with these duties. No matter what the production budget, video managers should consider the value of contracting with production coordinators, even if it is for only a short period of time. In most cases you can justify their fee in the savings they generate for the production budget.

At some corporations an in-house project manager with no film experience or an administrative assistant assumes the role of production coordinator. How helpful this person is to the producer depends on the background of the individual and how well the producer explains his or her needs. In the corporate world a professional production coordinator cannot only make the producer's and director's jobs easier, but they can have an influence on the outcome of the video production overall.

According to Wikipedia, "The duties of a POC (production office coordinator) are often undefined and extremely varied, ranging from office manager to human resources, to controller, to accountant. The position requires adept organizational skills, resourcefulness, and the ability to handle a multitude of tasks simultaneously under often high-pressure situations. The POC is often the first person in the office and the last to leave, since they hold the responsibility of tending to the needs of the crew."

The production coordinator is the one who makes sure the script is properly formatted and numbered. He or she acts as the location scout to find the best setting for scenes filmed away from the studio. The coordinator arranges for the use of any outside studios and makes sure they have the appropriate equipment, access, and accoutrements for the crew, the cast, and the company executives who inevitably will show up.

The coordinator handles the paperwork for insurance certificates, location permits, talent permissions, and security releases. He or she is the one who walks through a proposed location to make sure there is adequate electricity, that the doorway is wide enough to accommodate your dolly, that your soundtrack will not record the flushing sounds in the bathrooms adjacent to the filming rooms, and that the windows have drapes or blinds. If they don't, she or he will rent enough C-stands and sound blankets to cover them so the gaffer can artfully light the set.

While film and TV studios provide "green rooms" for actors and craft services for the cast and crew, corporate video productions frequently are shot in an office building or a factory. Production coordinators either arrange for everyone to eat in the company cafeteria, or schedule another conference room for food service, and perhaps arrange equipment storage and green room monitoring.

Production Management

Production coordinators on a corporate shoot take on the role of unit production managers (UPMs) by helping to select the cast and crew. They may schedule a casting call and arrange for it to be recorded. They could secure rentals of cameras, grips, and special production equipment and arrange for its pickup and return.

The production manager may also handle financial details of the production, or at least those during location shooting. These include payment for cast and crew, fees for permits, travel costs, and payment for craft services. Additionally, the production manager or production coordinator (in corporate video production, probably the same person) obtains insurance certificates and sends them to the equipment rental facility and the contact people at the filming locations.

If you are an in-house producer, check with your manager to make sure the company's liability insurance policy covers equipment rentals and liability for injury or damages when filming on location. Your company must have workers' compensation insurance and business liability insurance. However, you may need to provide your company with resources for production insurance. This insurance covers contracted crew and cast members and loss to the camera original recordings on flash cards, hard drives, or tapes. Additionally your company may need errors and omissions (E&O) insurance in case there are claims about the originality of the script or if the viewers of the video follow the instructions and perform a task that results in an injury.

Script Breakdown

Either the production manager or the assistant director is the one who breaks down the script to create a shooting schedule. In the corporate world that is usually the same person. The scenes are frequently shot out of order, and you will want to organize the sequence of shooting to minimize the crew's camera setups. You also want to use actors and settings most efficiently. Frequently all the scenes with a key actor are shot together, and all the scenes at a particular location or setting are filmed at the same time. The scenes that can be shot with a limited cast and a smaller crew may be scheduled at a later time.

The script breakdown starts with marking the script to divide it by the category of shot and by the actors scheduled to perform. Software applications are available for script breakdown, such as Final Draft Tagger or Movie Magic Screenwriter, that tag the different elements with color codes. Then you export the tagged elements by category into a schedule app such as Movie Magic EP Scheduler.

Some people use the old-school method of printing the script, assigning different-colored highlighters, and marking the script to a color code. Some save the script as a pdf file and use screen highlighting. Either way, Figure 7.1 shows the color-coding used in the industry. At this stage, once you have a full script breakdown, revisit the budget to make sure it is in line with the shot list, the script, and the estimated days of production

We asked San Francisco film producer and production manager Debbie Brubaker to give us an idea of the number of shooting days a video script might have. She said that corporate videos vary depending on the material. However, she said you could shoot four to eight pages a day, depending on the amount of action and the skill of the actors and the crew.

Jeffrey Marino at consulting firm Booz, Allen, and Hamilton said they average one to three days of shooting for their studio shoots and about five days to shoot on location. He said that if

Element	Shape or color	Description
Cast	Red	Any speaking actor.
Extra (Atmosphere)	Green	Any extra or group of extras needed for the background.
Extra (Silent bits)	Yellow	Any extra needed to perform specifically, but has no lines.
Stunts	Orange	Any stunt that may require a stunt double, or stunt coordinator.
Special Effects	Blue	Any special effect required.
Props	Purple	All objects important to the script, or used by an actor.
Vehicles/Animals	Pink	Any vehicles, and all animals, especially if it requires an animal trainer.
Sound Effects/Music	Brown	Sounds or music requiring specific use on set. Not sounds added in during post.
Wardrobe	Circle	Specific costumes needed for production, and also for continuity if a costume gets ripped up, or dirtied throughout the movie.
Make-up/Hair	Asterisk	Any make-up or hair attention needed. Common for scars and blood.
Special Equipment	Box	If a scene requires the use of more uncommon equipment, (e.g., crane, underwater camera, etc).
Production Notes	Underline	For all other questions about how a scene will go, or confusion about how something happens.

Figure 7.1 When breaking down scripts to a shooting schedule, they may be color-coded. This is the industry standard for showing which elements are needed with particular scenes.

the script calls for talent in front of a green screen and motion graphics, they spend most of their time in postproduction. Marino adds, "I don't have a formula for determining the length of time it will take to shoot something. We consider as many variables as possible when scheduling the production—how many actors, how many locations, geographic locations of the particular sets, travel, interior versus exterior, the weather, number of extras, size of the sets, number of cameras, type of camera we're using (HD, SD, DSLR, 35 mm DOF kit, etc.), and then a few of us review the production schedule to see if it makes sense from our experience."

Daily Call Sheets

Daily call sheets provide the cast and crew with their arrival times, descriptions of scenes scheduled to be shot, and logistics about the filming location. While a feature film may have the production coordinator, unit production manager, and assistant director dividing the task to produce a call sheet, in corporate video it is usually created by a single person. The daily call sheet specifies which scenes will be filmed that day and includes such details as wardrobe requirements and lighting.

Call sheets include the address and phone numbers of the location and a map. If they are sent electronically, such as by e-mail or a Twitter post, they can include a link to the location and other information such as parking, public transportation, and nearby stores. The sheets include the names of the cast and crew scheduled for that day and individual schedules, if appropriate. For example, a call sheet may state an earlier time for the gaffer and grips to set up lights. The cast and crew shouldn't have to wait for on-set preparations.

Daily Production Reports

The daily production report goes to the producer and perhaps the department manager. It states how many shots were completed, how many camera setups were conducted, and the number of screen minutes that were shot. It also points out any shots that were not completed and have to carry over to the next day, as well as any additional shots that were completed but not on that day's schedule. This serves as daily feedback on whether the production is coming in on budget, below budget, or possibly over budget.

Generally the production coordinator or director reviews the footage shot that day (dailies) prior to writing the report. The report includes relevant details such as any problems with lighting, camera moves, or sound. Were there any issues with the location or with security? Noting these early can allow the crew to correct any problems for the next day's shoot. The report could also suggest filming additional shots or B-roll that may not have been included in the script. Depending on the needs of the video manager, the report could detail finances of the day, such as overtime of cast and crew, costs for equipment rentals and meals, travel fees, and other relevant budgetary items.

The Assistant Director

The production manager, when developing shooting schedules and call sheets, ventures into the role of what may be considered that of an assistant director (AD). While Hollywood and broadcast television define individual roles, lower-budget corporate videos frequently combine several roles into one person. As an assistant director, this person may take production management a step further by tracking the daily progress of the shoot against the prepared shooting schedule.

In much the same way as a production manager compares the projected budget against actual expenses to track variances, the assistant director looks for variances between the planned schedule and the actual progress. If it looks like more time may be needed to complete a shoot, he or she reports it to the director or producer to discuss paying overtime to cast and crew and perhaps planning for an additional day of studio rental. While Hollywood studios seem to garner resources when a film goes over budget, in the corporate world budgets need to be adhered to.

The assistant director may schedule and direct rehearsals of cast and crew and block the action for the camera operators and the director. In some cases the AD may direct the crew while the director directs the talent. This position may include supervising a makeup artist (highly recommended for filming aging CEOs, by the way) and supervising production assistants.

The assistant director may be the one operating a slate or clapboard—calling out scene and take numbers—and may have the honor of saying "quiet on the set." In this role, the production coordinator may also act as a camera assistant and focus puller. Some of the functions that require less skill could be relegated to production assistants.

The Production Assistant

PAs are the assistants to the production coordinator. They perform many of the routine tasks that don't require much skill and can be thought of as the interns of the video/film world. Many are students who are looking for experience. Tasks include picking up crew and cast at airports, carrying equipment in and out, taping cables to floors, and picking up lunch—pretty much anything that is needed by the production.

One of the distinctions of corporate shoots that PAs need to consider is to tone down their appearance. On features and documentary shoots, tattoos and torn clothing represent the creative spirit of these newcomers to the industry. However, if the crew enters the corporate headquarters where staff are dressed in business attire, the artistic look could become a distraction that could interfere with an otherwise smooth-running production. Some corporations have a casual approach to attire and employee freedoms, but most companies adhere to some version of a buttoned-down look. Be sure to find out in advance what the appropriate dress for the crew should be.

One advantage for PAs working in corporate video rather than in Hollywood is that within a smaller crew they have a greater chance of working with equipment than if they were part of a larger team. The PA may be asked to hold a microphone boom (fishpole), or be asked to operate a second camera or be a sound mixer. The PA may be the one running extension cords from one room to another to divide up the electrical load. While a PA on a Hollywood film may be asked to bring over a light, during a corporate shoot he will be allowed to set it up, add gels, and adjust it.

Interview with a Production Manager and Producer

Debbie Brubaker is a San Francisco–based corporate video producer, line producer, and production manager. In addition to feature films and documentaries, her corporate credits include such Bay area companies as Apple Computer, Sun Microsystems, and Electronic Arts. I had the pleasure of hiring her as a production coordinator several years ago for a training video I produced for Kaiser Permanente.

Ms. Brubaker coordinated our efforts to obtain a permit with the city that allowed us to film in a city park. Although the park was a beautiful set, the area that we filmed in had a monochrome background—totally unnoticed by me—that would have been less than effective. Ms. Brubaker took it upon herself to rent a hundred artificial roses that she tied to the trees present in the shot. This gave the background a touch of warmth that helped convey emotion in our final scene—that of an older couple kissing. She even obtained a selection of ascots that were an important element for our main actor to wear.

Ms. Brubaker explains that most corporate video productions these days don't have budgets large enough to hire a coordinator, but her job is more accurately that of a line producer. She said many companies provide their own staff to handle much of the coordination. This is especially true when the company has an in-house communications, multimedia, or video department with its own equipment. While they may call in an outside producer and camera operator, they have had enough experience with video productions that they can handle the production coordination.

However, according to Ms. Brubaker, "When they take on those duties themselves, it's onerous for them because they have to wear a bunch of hats. If I'm producing or line producing, and if the money is there, I hire a production coordinator who can be my in-between. If I have a crew of ten people, generally I'm able to hire a PA/craft service person. I can give them money, they do it, and I don't have to think about it. Otherwise I get stuck doing it. For some corporate gigs I do it all. I'm taking the craft service in, I'll hire somebody to help me once I get there, but I'm there buying the fruits and vegetables and the bagels."

Ms. Brubaker explains that the production coordinator is almost like being a secretary. There is a litany of tasks to perform: making sure insurance certificates get sent out, reserving equipment and filming rooms, setting up appointments between key production personnel. You support whoever is next up the ladder, such as the line producer or producer. Every job is different, according to Ms. Brubaker. "It's a job in logistics, if you are bringing in people from out of town, you need to arrange for their hotel, their car reservation, and provide a welcome packet for them with suggestions of what to do in town and where to eat."

Crews for Corporate Shoots

What is the difference between coordinating corporate shoots and coordinating feature films or documentaries? Ms. Brubaker says she brings in crews "who can work stealthily, who can get the job done, who have a good attitude and not dress funky. When you do corporate, you have to dress a little differently. It is important for production managers to remind their crews of this, although many already know the drill. I have a different set of people I hire for corporate than I do for features. That's what they do regularly; they know what they will be doing."

With regard to filming in corporate offices and conference rooms, she says, "There is an art to taking a conference room and making it look like a studio. It is good to hire crew who know how to do that." She adds that you need to arrange where you are going to feed your cast and crew, since company offices and conference rooms are probably not appropriate locales for chowing down. You also need to arrange where your cast and crew are going to park. "I don't believe it is fair to hire people and tell them they have to worry about where they are going to park. If you are working at a place where parking is very tough, it is okay to tell people that you won't cover their parking, but you can identify a garage for them."

Talent and Union Crews

Some companies have existing contracts with unions and guilds and will always work with union crews. Others may hire actors from a guild and do not need to hire union crews, especially for smaller video productions that will be used in-house. AFTRA is the American Federation of Television and Radio Artists, and SAG is the Screen Actors Guild.

SAG allows organizations that already have a union contract to hire an actor who is not in SAG on a one-time-only basis. Known as the "Taft-Hartley" clause, you will still need to pay the nonunion actor at the SAG rate. Those actors are required to join SAG if they want to work a second time. Another union from which corporate video producers hire is SEG: the Screen Extras Guild. SEG actors have less experience and work at a lower rate, but SEG is not active in all cities.

Ms. Brubaker explains that while guilds have national offices, they vary from state to state. In "production cities" such as New York, Chicago, Philadelphia, Los Angeles, San Francisco, and Miami, the unions are very active. Other cities would be in what are called "right to work" states, where SAG does not require producers to hire cast and crew with union backgrounds.

If you plan to use a truck to deliver gear for a larger production at a hotel or conference center that has a union contract, expect to hire a driver from the International Brotherhood of Teamsters. Workers in that union also bring in your equipment, or at least the heavy items such as a stage and flats.

Some venues and corporations will require you to only use the stage hands union: the International Alliance of Theatrical and Stage Employees (IATSE, or sometimes referred to as the "IA"). This is an umbrella organization for a variety of location filmmaking specialties, such as camera operators, electricians, grips, set designers, and editors.

While the terms "union" and "guild" are sometimes interchanged, guilds generally protect workers who want to maintain their intellectual properties. In addition to SAG and SEG, guilds that the production coordinator should be familiar with are the WGA (Writers Guild of America) and the DGA (Directors Guild of America). The latter covers production managers. There is also a Producers Guild of America for producers and the American Federation of Musicians.

According to Ms. Brubaker, "Some people are afraid of unions, but they shouldn't be. Working with unions is quite easy; it takes time and it takes diplomacy. I think it's important for video producers to know that people join the union for a reason.

A lot of camera operators are already in the union. They don't wear it on their shirtsleeves, but they are in the union already."

She advises that if you have a short-running production, you can arrange a "one-off" contract with the union for a single event. In addition to the union wage, you would also pay such fringe benefits as health and welfare, and pension at a certain rate. The workers would be paying union dues, even if they work only one day. Similarly for talent, such as an on-camera narrator, AFTRA or SAG will pay them for as little as a single day of work, although you probably will want to hire them for at least a half-day of rehearsal. All this is usually handled by a payroll service.

Ms. Brubaker uses a San Francisco area payroll service called Talent Fund, but for productions elsewhere she uses such national companies as Media Services and Entertainment Partners. "I recommend pricing them out; different companies cost less. It also depends on how much attention you need; you pay more for some and get more attention. They're going to be more meticulous. Depending on how fast and furious you put something together, you may want somebody who has good attention to detail so that nothing slips through the cracks. That way you're not spending a day here and there two weeks after the project trying to clean up after a payroll company that didn't quite do the job they should have because you were too cheap to hire a better one. If you are doing a job that takes only a week, it behooves you to spend a little more money. If you are in it for the long haul, if there are glitches, you have time to iron them out."

Locations

Many corporate videos are filmed in company conference rooms or at industrial facilities. Scout the location and listen as well as look. Are there ventilators that turn on and off that could interfere with the soundtrack? Will construction suddenly be scheduled on your shooting day? Will there be a surprise birthday party with raucous revelers?

Frequently your client's department is not in the same location as that of the video. Some corporations have a campus of office buildings, and your client may not even know any staff at the filming location. In an effort to be helpful, they may think they know the routine at the remote building and that you can be fooled. This means that the production coordinator needs to be diplomatic to find out who the appropriate contact people are.

Ms. Brubaker suggests that you scout the location and get in touch with the building maintenance people. "You are going to be in a situation where you need those people or somebody you can call. If they won't shepherd you around, you will need to have their name and number and touch base with them. Let them know where you are going to be in the building. You may have power issues; lights consume lots of power. They may have to turn off some of the lights for you because it is a smart building and you don't know where the switches are. Or you may have no ventilation, or it's freezing. Scout it out, and if necessary, be prepared to explain to the client why this particular conference room doesn't work."

Another reason to establish contact with the building maintenance staff is to arrange parking for your truck. Arrange to use a loading zone where you can load in your gear, and maybe if you are on good terms with maintenance, perhaps you can leave it there. Ms. Brubaker adds, "Ask where you can park where it will be convenient for you so it doesn't have to get into the back-40 corner and you forget something and send a grip or PA who gets lost for 45 minutes."

Ms. Brubaker also suggests that you double-check the room reservations. She explains that office personnel don't look at the production the same way we do. They don't realize how important every detail is in order to make the shoot successful. Even if your contact people say they have reserved a room, check again and make sure there is enough time to get in early to set up and leave late to strike the gear.

When you are scouting a location and meeting with the site representative, you'll need to ask myriad questions about the facility and the logistics. This questioning may start to sound like an inquisition, so try to ease that person's mind, especially if he or she has never had a film shot at his or her location. Whether it is an office manager or a factory supervisor, that person may feel intruded upon just by your presence. Explain that you are there to ensure that things will go smoothly and to anticipate any possible problems in advance. Reassure this person that there will be no permanent alteration to the physical space and that you have production insurance should anything go wrong. Demonstrate your respect for the person as well as the property, and remove any mystery he or she may have about what the film crew will be doing there.

Early on you may need to address some issues that might cause some tension. Will employees need to leave their workstations during the filming? Will you need to paint walls or bring in flats and other set design? Will you need to access the ceiling to hang lights, or will you bring in some rigging gear that may need to be attached to a wall? Assure the property manager that if you do any painting or alterations, the crew will return the location to its original look after the filming is completed. And make sure you have obtained an adequate budget and skilled personnel to perform this redecorating.

Take photographs of the location and even video if you wish. It will be helpful for the director and camera operator to better visualize the scene and decide where to place and move cameras. Consider creating a panorama of a series of photos and stitching them together. Then the director can have a virtual tour of the location.

Producer Support

Another way the production of corporate videos differs from documentaries and educational films is that you have more people to answer to. In addition to sorting out who the decision makers are among your client's team, you need to create an environment where the clients may easily express their opinions. The producer needs to be ready to hear them and address their concerns, even if they ask for unreasonable changes in the midst of a previously planned shoot.

During the shoot and in postproduction, the producer needs to be super-attentive to the client—what Ms. Brubaker calls "handholding." The production coordinator or production manager needs to provide logistical support to the producer so he or she can attend to the client or the cadre of clients on the set.

During preproduction, the producer and production coordinator need to map out their roles with almost as much detail as the shooting script. The coordinator can double-check to make sure the client and any managers or associates that may suddenly appear have seen and approved the script, storyboards, and talent ahead of time. Make sure they all know the shooting schedule and understand that sequences frequently are filmed out of order. Do they like what is being planned? Does anyone have an opinion that's different from yours? That needs to be ferreted out well in advance of the shoot. You never want to find yourself in a position late in the project where someone new shows up with a different opinion or new set of requirements.

The producer and the production coordinator need to clarify their roles. They need to identify the different needs of the client and the client's team. The producer needs to hold the client's hand during the process, and the coordinator needs to provide support so the producer doesn't get bogged down with logistical details. The producer shouldn't have to wear two hats. He or she has the responsibility to make the client happy, while the coordinator needs to take responsibility for the nuts and bolts of the operation.

For example, the production coordinator needs to make sure the clients have their copies of the script and that their comments and approvals have been included. During filming the coordinator needs to position a monitor so the client can easily see it, and he or she should make sure they are watching it during the filming. Do they like what is being shot? They have to be allowed to weigh in and have an opinion of what is being done.

During postproduction the coordinator can limit the number of personnel who are looking over the back of the editor by offering to send roughs of scenes as soon as they are compiled. Then the coordinator collects the comments from the clients, discusses them with the producer, and relays them to the editor. That way the client feels they have control of the finishing process as well as the planning and filming.

Communicating with the client, supporting the producer and director, managing the cast and crew, handling myriad logistics, keeping the production on time and on budget—these are among the functions of a production coordinator. Sometimes in an effort to keep costs down, the budget leaves out this important person. Then the producer is tasked with details that could detract from producing the video with creativity and panache.

The corporate video coordinator plays the role of production manager, assistant director, line producer, and babysitter to the crew or the client. This is the job for someone with plenty of filmmaking experience, and it should not be relegated to an office assistant or a project manager. The production coordinator needs to know what is involved in producing videos and how to support the producer, talent, and crew. Not only should this person be highly organized, he or she needs to be resourceful enough to find a rental camera when the company's camera fails to operate, find vegan food for a particular cast member, and break down a script to a realistic shooting schedule—all the while remaining cheerful and supportive. It takes a special person to wear this many hats, but it an essential role in corporate video production.

Guilds and Unions

Screen Actors Guild (www.sag.org)

International Alliance of Theatrical Stage Employees (www.iatse-intl.org)

Directors Guild of America (www.dga.org)

Teamsters (www.teamster.org)

SAG Industrial and Educational Pay Rates as of April 30, 2011

According to the SAG website, this is the minimum compensation for training, sales, educational, and public relations programs. Rates for commercials are higher.

On-Camera Narrator/Spokesperson: $857–$1,015 per day

On-Camera Actor: $471–$586 per day

Voice-Over Narrator: $385.50–$429.00 for first hour; $112.50 each additional half-hour

General Background Actors: $122.50 per day

Pension and Health Contribution Rate: 15.3 percent

You can find the complete list of rates at http://www.sag.org/files/sag/documents/ 2009_Industrial_and_Educational_Rate_Sheet.pdf.

CORPORATE SCRIPTWRITING

Larry: "Slap a happy ending on it, and the script will write itself."

Griffin: "I was thinking what an interesting concept it is . . . to eliminate the writer from the artistic process. If we can get rid of the actors and directors, maybe we've got something."

—From Robert Altman's *The Player*

Introduction

In an effort to reduce video expenditures, sometimes the scriptwriting budget is eliminated, or this creative endeavor is relegated to an overworked copywriter. Corporate scriptwriters can charge thousands of dollars for a carefully researched and well-written script. At times the video manager or producer will write the script. This can work well if he or she doesn't have myriad other tasks on the proverbial plate. The video manager or the executive producer needs to allocate appropriate resources to scriptwriting, and sometimes this even means convincing upper management that the budget for a proposed video needs to be increased.

The script serves as the blueprint for the construction of the company video. It is the document that determines whether the video will be a sensational success or merely mediocre. Since the video literally reflects the image of the corporation, expect that the script will need to be approved by upper management, if not the CEO.

Determining Objectives

Generally, a department manager or project manager contacts the video producer to request the production. The producer either writes the script or hires a scriptwriter. Then the scriptwriter and the content specialist meet to start the planning process. The producer or video manager can operate more efficiently if only a single person acts as the content specialist; decision by committee usually slows down the process. As the scriptwriter submits treatments and script drafts, expect that the content specialist (or specialists) will need approvals from higher up. The producer will need to decide if it's best to have management attend early planning meetings.

At the initial meeting, the scriptwriter might want to play devil's advocate and ask why the company wants a video at all. What is the problem that the video might solve? How would that problem be solved without a video? For example, if management wants to produce a video to train supervisors to be sensitive to cultural differences among employees, it might have been due to an employee taking legal action against the company. Averting a million-dollar lawsuit can be the objective—one that can also help secure the video department's value during budgeting season.

In this case there was a clear behavioral objective: altering the behavior of supervisors so employees won't sue the company. Other examples of behavioral objectives could be employees properly using the computer network, customers purchasing a particular product, or stock brokers encouraging their clients to purchase shares in the company. If the objectives of the video are particular actions that you want your viewers to take, you are well on your way to clear sailing during the scriptwriting process. Likewise, providing a way to measure these actions—the results of the changed behaviors—increases your worth as a producer.

In addition to behavioral objectives, the video may be designed to fulfill cognitive objectives. These refer to concepts and ideas that you want the viewers to know after watching the video. Cognitive objectives include teaching employees about the history of the corporation or educating them on the products or services the company provides. With the objectives in mind—both behavioral and cognitive—you will be better able to write a script or simply plan the shots for your video.

Research and Concept Development

After meeting the content specialist, the scriptwriter gathers the available printed and visual material and sometimes must go outside the organization to obtain more visuals, such as news headlines or general information on the subject. Frequently, the writer interviews the content specialist and other key personnel to learn more about the subject. This is the time to get a good idea of the problem to be solved by the video. What happens if the video is not produced? What are the objectives of the video? Every scene the writer creates should have these objectives in mind.

Sometimes the producer and writer will schedule a brainstorming session, hopefully with some of the actual stakeholders and maybe sample audience members. This is the time to develop all sorts of ideas, both on the content and on the concept. What are the key facts and ideas that need to be presented? What resources are available? What is the best way to show this procedure?

During brainstorming, the writer/producer simply asks questions and elicits responses, and one person acts as a scribe to write the ideas on a digital display or a flipchart. The one rule in brainstorming is that any idea, no matter how wacky, gets displayed. Later, the group sorts through the ideas to come up with those that are possible, most effective, and within budget. It can also be helpful to have an audiorecorder running during these and subsequent meetings so everything that is said is recorded in some way.

If you have a budget to allow for it, see if you can conduct a focus group to further your research for the script. A focus group is similar to a brainstorming session, but the group leader focuses the participants' attention on the details of the project. Participants in a focus group are chosen based on the demographic of the video's audience. Marketing departments in many corporations use focus groups for research, so it should not be a tough sell to obtain the needed budget for this powerful tool. Prior to the focus group, the writer and producer meet with a focus group leader to discuss the objectives and different aspects of the proposed video.

They develop an agenda for the one- or two-hour meeting with the group. They may write a list of questions that they will want the participants to answer and discuss. They may create some keywords or phrases, or even show images and ask participants their opinions of them. They might extract some important topics that the video could address, and they'll watch the reactions of the participants. Frequently a video- or audiorecording is made of the focus group for later evaluation. The reactions of typical audience members are valuable research data to shape your video script.

Facts + Frameworks = Concept

In addition to discussing ideas in a focus group, a brainstorming session, or a less formal meeting, the writer can explain different frameworks to present the information. Frameworks are the presentation styles of the video—the methods you use to present the facts and ideas. Your research has uncovered the facts you wish to present. Now you can select frameworks to best show those facts. Frameworks could be demonstration, comedy, dramatic vignette, animation, and more.

The following are examples of frameworks:
- Animation or graphical
- Demonstration
- Tour
- Documentary/subjective camera POV
- Drama
- Parody
- Interview
- Montage
- On-camera narrator
- Newscast/panel discussion
- Photos, stock footage
- Talking head

In her book *Corporate Scriptwriting*, Donna Matrazzo explains, "The framework should intrinsically evolve from and integrate with the facts you want to present. The framework should make the facts more memorable." Combining facts with the frameworks yields your concepts—the backbone of your treatment and script. Effective concepts are what make your script and the resulting video captivating, exciting, and motivating.

You'll also need your manager or client to approve the concepts early during the planning stage. Then, when you present your script draft and they suddenly want a different concept, you can refer to their approval of the initial concepts. Certainly, if their ideas have merit and they have the funds, they can increase the scriptwriting budget. Then you can take more time to perform additional research to come up with more facts. As you did with the initial material, you will select the appropriate frameworks to craft the concepts.

Concepts may be combined to deliver a script with enough variety to maintain the interest of even those viewers with attention deficits. For example, the video could start with actors dramatizing an employee-supervisor meeting. The next scene could incorporate an affable on-camera host who speaks to the camera. Later scenes could use a documentary framework with interviews and a voice-over narrator. Another concept is an actor or a manager guiding the viewers on a tour. A simulated news program is an approach that could incorporate an on-camera host, interviews, and a tour. An effective and attention-getting concept in the corporate world is one that presents a problem, shows the unintended consequences, and then demonstrates modeling behavior to solve the problem. Whenever you can elicit emotion in the viewer, you have him or her hooked!

Avoid creating frameworks first, or the medium could become the message. Perform your research to uncover the facts; then select the appropriate frameworks to present those facts. Otherwise, viewers may recall only that they saw amazing graphics or remember a joke, but they may forget the message.

The Audience

Corporate videos are unique in that the audience usually gets paid for viewing your video. They may prefer to be paid for other work tasks—work that may have to be put aside when their manager assigns them to watch your video. In some cases, employees need to view the video on their own time, perhaps online from home. The screening environment and the attitude of your audience at the onset of viewing the video are important considerations when writing the video script.

What if your viewers are required to watch the video during their break? What if they are watching it in a dark room after lunch? Are they left to view it at their own workstation while they may be concurrently doing other work? The viewing environment can dictate just how much eye candy and upbeat music you may need to inject into the video to maintain the attention of your audience.

What do the viewers already know about the subject? What are their attitudes about it? You want to be able to explain the subject to them, but you don't want to confuse them or talk down to them. The writer needs to keep in mind the viewing environment and the demographic of the audience with each scene he or she writes.

The Treatment

Once the audience has been identified, the frameworks have been selected, and the concepts have been developed, the writer is ready to start the scriptwriting process. The first step is to write a "treatment." The treatment is a document that describes the concepts of the video and details sequentially the scenes the viewer will see. The scriptwriter explains how he or she plans to treat the subject by outlining, usually in paragraph form, what the viewer sees and hears first, what happens next, and so on. The treatment incorporates the research that the writer conducted, combined with the ideas that came from a brainstorming session. The concepts are written with visual details, and keywords and facts are included. The writer presents the written treatment to the producer or manager for approval.

You may wish to divide your video script into acts or scenes, especially if there are segments taking place at different locations. Describe the locations with as much detail as necessary. You want the people who read the treatment to be able to visualize what you have in mind so later, when they read the script, they won't be surprised.

Present each segment chronologically. What do we see first? How do we introduce the viewer to the setting? What action takes place? What do the people look like? What will they be saying? Include key phrases and particular facts that lead to fulfilling the objectives. Be sure to include transitions from segment to segment.

Then look at your treatment and refine it. If you have the luxury of putting it down for a few days, that will give you the benefit of looking at it again later with fresh eyes. Visualize the actors and the activities, the sounds, the graphics, and when the music comes in and out. Does it explain what you have in mind? Are all the objectives targeted? Are there any segments that move too slowly? What areas need work? You may wish to read it aloud to yourself or into an audiorecorder for later playback. This is the creative process, so take your time to refine—and refine some more.

Writing for the Visual Element

Video is most effective when the visual element of the medium is used to its fullest advantage. According to Ms. Matrazzo, "If a program is well produced, you can turn off the sound and still understand the story." Imagine writing a script for a silent movie, where the visuals must tell the story. Will the reader of your script be able to read just the descriptions of the visuals and get the message?

Ms. Matrazzo suggests, "You should write the spoken words last. Use your visuals, nonverbal messages, sound effects, and music to say as much as possible. Then, let the spoken words complement them." She cautions against writing the words of the script first and filling in the blanks with visuals because it becomes "a dreadful, confusing amalgamation of pictures with no visual continuity and no feeling."

An effective way to open a corporate video is to use the technique called "montage." The opening shots are paired with music to introduce the viewer to the program and to set the tone for enjoying the video. Sometimes these are quick shots with beautiful compositions, or they may include phrases of text displayed in an artistic fashion. Frequently the video concludes with a similar montage. There is no reason not to incorporate montages in the body of the script, too.

Writing for the Spoken Word

Did you get an F in grammar? Not a problem. Scripts are meant to be heard but not seen. The video viewers will never read the script. It's more like a music score: listeners never see the sheet music, but they hear the performance of those notes. You have loads of latitude when writing for actors or for a narrator—whether an on-camera host or a voice-over narrator. Similar to speech writing, video scripts need not be written in complete sentences. Think of writing a newspaper headline. Choose words that catch the listener's attention. Get to the point quickly. Corporate videos frequently are brief. They are produced mainly to show a particular procedure or describe a concept in general, and website links or a printed manual provide the details.

Consider the sound of the words. Rhythmic wording is easy on the ears, and those carefully chosen words clearly slide off the tongue of the narrator. Did you write poetry or songs when you were young? Now is the time to rekindle the romantic writer inside you. Dust off that poetic license to reveal a panoply of metaphors and similes, alliterations, and onomatopoeias. Your rhythm and pacing can correlate with camera moves, edits, and music to create a symbiotic soup—a synergy of sight and sound to stimulate the senses and lift the spirits.

As in poetry, you may repeat a phrase or a word to emphasize its importance. Repetition is a tool to emphasize the importance of a particular fact or concept. As you structure your stanzas ... er ... your *scenes*, think of ways you can use repetition to make certain the viewer really understands an important message. Repetition helps with learning, so consider repeating important information to make your message more memorable.

Read aloud some of your scenes. Consider recording and playing it back so you can hear what your scenes sound like. Avoid tongue twisters such as this one that slipped through into a hospital training video I directed: "preschool speech screening exams." The narrator nailed it, but he gave me the stink-eye from the booth.

Names or words that may be mispronounced by a narrator need pronunciation spelling. For example, "Givenchy" would be written as it is correctly spelled followed by "pronounced Gee-von-she." If a syllable needs to be emphasized, you would write, "Ralph Lauren (pronounced LORE-in)."

Some corporate scriptwriters try to limit their sentences to fewer than 15 words or less than ten seconds to read. Some will edit out at least 20 percent of what they have written after the script is complete. You want the visuals to tell the story, and you want to avoid the dreaded "talking head."

Describing Visuals

Effective videos incorporate a diverse array of visually exciting images and sequences. While the director may wish to choose his or her own visualizations for the scenes you write, go ahead and write them as *you* see them. A good video script uses sights and motions to tell the story. Write descriptions of the scenes with as much detail as you can imagine.

When camera angles are germane to telling the story, write cues like "Zoom from MS (medium shot) to CU (close-up) of Jack installing the bearing." The camera cues help the reader to visualize what the scriptwriter has in mind. Creating juxtapositions of elements in your shot explains how the different objects or people relate to one another. Write "Pan right to left from the two-shot of Taylor and Mike to show Connie staring at them from behind her newspaper." Visually you have implied the characters' relationships without them having said a word. You don't need to specify camera angles all the time; the director may choose his or her own interpretation of the scene.

In addition to stating the situations, describe the emotions and the expressions on your actors' faces—for example, "Derrick is a male supervisor who has been accused of sexual harassment, and he is acting nervous. Alan, Derrick's manager, is explaining to Derrick the company's policy on sexual harassment. Rather than make eye contact with Alan, Derrick looks away." Certainly the director and actors may interpret the scene as they wish, and the actor playing Derrick may choose another way to express his nervousness. As you write, keep asking yourself, "What does the audience need to know to achieve the video's objectives?"

Script Formats

It doesn't matter if you choose to write your script in two columns (split page) or straight across the page, sometimes called "teleplay." When looking at a script, the director, editor, and actors need to be able to clearly distinguish between the audio and the video. They need to know which audio is on-camera (OC) and which is voice-over (VO). They need to know the difference between the scenes that were written with camera or editing cues and the scenes for which the director chose his or her own cues.

If you choose to write the script in columns, usually the visuals are on the left and the corresponding audio is on the right. Add visual directions when needed, such as effects, graphics, camera moves, and juxtapositions. If you are writing across the page, then capitalize the video, print the audio upper- and lowercase, and indent the audio. That makes it easier to read. Even split-page scripts frequently are formatted so the visual cues are in caps and the audio is upper- and lowercase. The format of the script is not as important as the content. However, keep in mind that the director, actors, and editor need to clearly understand your intentions.

You can purchase script software, such as Final Draft, Movie Magic, and Scriptware. Final Draft AV is designed for those who prefer to write in a split-page format. Software packages such as these let you move scenes around while maintaining alignment. They automatically number scenes as you add and rearrange them, and they let you add several shots to a particular scene. They autotype characters' names, let you add your own notes, and are nimble enough to allow for changes even during production.

Microsoft Word and other word processing applications have column tools as well as tables where you can set up scene numbers and use blocks to indicate audio and video. Some word processors have templates that you can customize, and you can use macros and other tools for automation.

Writing Dialog

Scripts incorporating dramatization bring out the storyteller in you. Here you can work with plots, tension, and resolution.

Frequently, training videos start by dramatizing how *not* to perform a particular procedure, including the disastrous consequences. Then the correct method is explained or performed.

Well-written and well-acted dramatic scripts help draw the viewers in by giving them characters they like or dislike. This leads the viewers to feeling emotions—the best hook of all! A poorly written script with unrealistic character development leads to a video that is not believable. Writers and directors go for the "suspension of disbelief." You want your audience to forget they are watching a video and become part of the vicarious setting you have established.

Create characters based on people you know. Write for their particular personality traits, and keep their words consistent with the character. If you study people's speech patterns, you'll notice that they don't always talk in complete sentences. Craft your dialog with interruptions and distractions, and your characters will come off sounding as if they were in a real conversation.

To come up with dialog ideas, think of a problem to build up tension in the viewer. Perhaps two employees are disagreeing with each other, and one of them starts lobbing criticisms. Then show the other character's reaction. The disagreement could escalate. This gets the viewers' attention and draws them emotionally to the characters.

Pauses and silence can frequently speak louder than words. An actor's silent stare at his or her coworker can have a piercing, emotional impact. Borrow from Hitchcock and build up suspense with an extended period of silence. Perhaps you can fade in music during a silent portion. Music can fade out just as an actor or narrator makes a poignant statement.

Writing Documentary Scripts

While a documentary may consist mostly of interviews, it usually includes a voice-over narrator—at least at the opening and closing, and perhaps at transitions between different segments of the doc. When writing scenes for an on-camera narrator or for the voice-over segments, use an informal writing style with easily understood words. Write in the second person, so the narrator is speaking to "you." Remember that viewers have only one chance to view a video; they can't reread a script because they never see a script.

Pre-interview those who will appear on camera, and create a list of questions. These, together with the expected answers, are part of your script. To ensure that the interviewee doesn't look like a talking head, list B-roll shots or still images that illustrate what the interviewee is talking about. Remember to add transitions between scenes so they flow well from one to the other.

Documentary segments may be peppered into training or marketing videos. In addition to interviews, documentary frameworks may be used to show procedures, personal interactions, and a tour of the facility. The script would specify the visual elements in the scene, together with the voice-over narration.

Script Drafts

Write the first draft as if it were the final one. Consider not printing the word "draft" on your first script. Plan to have a script meeting with the content specialist, video manager, or other executives. You might wish to read the script aloud to them. If people suggest changes beyond the scope of the treatment, you'll need to decide if these changes will improve the video, and if you are a contractor, you must decide how much more you will charge for writing in these changes.

Invest enough time to put down the script for a few days and then look at it with fresh eyes. Ask yourself the following questions:
- How can I shorten this?
- What have I left out?
- Do the visuals tell the story, even without spoken parts?
- Is the script meeting the objectives?
- Does it speak to the target audience?
- Is it understandable?
- Will it elicit the desired emotional response?
- Will the director, actors, and editor be able to understand my intention by reading this document?
- Will they be able to create the video I have in mind?
- Is the script detailed enough that the producer can come up with a reasonable estimate of the budget?
- Are the scenes numbered well enough to break down the script into a shooting schedule?
- Is there a clear structure with an attention-grabbing opening, a well-flowing body of the program, and a killer ending?
- Have I written the best script I can?
- Can it lead to an award-winning video production?

The script and the resulting video may have a lasting impact on employees and the viewing public. Remember to write drafts for yourself and revise. Then revise some more.

You don't need to start writing at the beginning; write any scenes that come to mind and reorder them later. Frequently, the introduction and conclusion are written after the body of the script. The script is your way of telling a story, of using your creativity. As you write, keep asking yourself what the audience needs to know to achieve the objective. Remember that the script is the blueprint for the video, and the corporation's literal image is on display. And, even more important, *your* name will be in the credits.

Scriptwriting Terms

Angle: Position of camera during a shot. Normal angle is eye level. High angles or low angles refer to the position of the camera.

CU: Close-up (includes the head and shoulders).

Cut: A direct change from one shot to another, as opposed to a dissolve or other transition.

Dissolve: One shot fades out and blends into the next shot.

Dolly or truck: Camera moves on wheels.

Dutch angle: Camera curves during the shoot, usually handheld.

ECU: Extreme close-up (usually cuts off the top of the head).

Establishing shot: A very long shot showing the entire setting.

Fade in/out: Screen gradually goes from black or to black.

Freeze: Still shot, usually accomplished in postproduction.

FX: Effects, usually visual effect created in postproduction.

LS: Long shot.

Master shot: An establishing shot or long shot used to reorient the viewer to the setting.

MOS or Motor Only Shot: (sometimes whimsically called "Mit Out Sound") meaning without sound.

MS: Medium shot.

Music up, down, or out: Mixing audio in relation to live sound.

OC: On-camera. The viewer sees the person who speaks as opposed to a voice-over.

POV: Point of view or subjective camera. Camera becomes the eye of the viewer.

Scene: Action that takes place in a single setting.

SFX: Sound effects.

Shot: One uninterrupted picture. A scene may be made up of several shots.

SOT: Sound on tape. Live sound recorded with the picture; may be recorded on a drive or any recording device.

Take: Each time a shot or scene is recorded, it is called a "take."

VO: Voice-over. The narrator is heard but not seen.

LEGAL CONSIDERATIONS

Introduction

As a video producer working for a corporation, you need to protect your company from liability in several areas. These areas include violation of copyrights and rights of persons appearing on camera, protecting the corporation's own intellectual property rights, avoiding liability for personal injury when filming on location or in the studio, and following laws regulating classifications of personnel as employees and independent contractors.

Corporations are thought to have deep pockets, and they are vulnerable to litigation-happy individuals who may want to sue to make an easy buck. In some cases, an individual or a group may have a political issue with the corporation, and they could create a legal action around the violation of their rights or some kind of injury they claim to have received. By following proper procedures throughout the production of the video, you may help avoid such suits and minimize liability.

Your manager and the company's legal department are your primary sources of legal advice; we are not providing legal advice here. Each state has its own laws, and an agreement that is fine in one state may not hold up in another. This chapter discusses the legal considerations in video production and how to protect your corporation and yourself from legal liability.

A legal entanglement can divert your attention from producing exciting and motivating videos. The last thing you want is to have to spend hours with the legal staff or have to appear on the other side of a video camera testifying under oath in a legal deposition. Learning about how the law applies to copyrights, contracts, filming permits, and working with the cast and crew will not only help you to stay out of trouble, but the management team at your company will appreciate that you know the law.

Trade Secrets and Nondisclosure

Corporations work hard to protect their brands, their intellectual property, and their reputations. The video producer, in the course of researching a script, could inadvertently reveal some sensitive information to someone outside of the company. Your organization may have some established policies about trade secrets and nondisclosure, and it is important that you familiarize yourself with them.

Freelance video crew, an outside scriptwriter, talent you hire, and even student interns all need to sign a confidentiality agreement to protect your company's patents, trade secrets, and other intellectual property. Check with your manager or legal department, but you may be personally liable, not just the corporation, if intellectual property gets into the wrong hands. You want to protect yourself from being accused of trade secret theft if the company deems that you made a disclosure in violation of the trust the company had in you. Even if it was an accidental disclosure—say, one of the freelancers passes on the information to others—you may be held responsible. Discuss this with your manager to make sure that you limit your personal liability and that you comply with company policy.

You should review your work carefully during the editing stage to make sure that you do not inadvertently violate either company policy or some third party's trademark rights. Perhaps you are editing a video that was shot on location, and you happen to notice, in the best take, that in the background a truck drives by with a logo of a competing brand. Certainly, you would blur out that logo. But what if you didn't notice that logo and the video got into circulation?

Contracts

Whether you are an in-house video manager or a freelance producer, you need to have a contract for services. Some people call it a "letter of agreement." No matter what you name it, a contract states what the two parties agree to, and it includes the "consideration" or the money paid for the service. Contracts usually have a fixed duration of time and can include the times and locations of filming and even deadlines for delivery of the finished script and video. In many cases your attorney can create a contract template, and you can fill in the details for each production.

Some video producers, both independent and in-house, use a two-step production contract. This is more common when an outside producer and the corporation are entering into their first agreement; they may not want to make a commitment for the entire production. The first contract is for writing a treatment and script. It includes the producer's research time, and a tangible product—the script—is the final result. The "consideration" may be a flat rate for the script or an hourly rate for the research and writing.

If the company likes the script and the freelance video producer feels good about working with the company, then both parties may proceed to a second contract that will cover the production. That contract could be at a flat rate, or it may be itemized by time and materials. If either party does not want to continue, then the company may keep the script and find a different producer to film and edit the video.

With subsequent productions, the independent producer and the company are probably comfortable enough with each other that they could develop a single contract covering both scripting and production. Should the client want changes to the scope of the contract, they can include a clause that explains the process for both parties to agree to the change and what consideration (additional money) would cover such changes. For example, additional scriptwriting, filming, or editing could be billed at a specified hourly rate.

The video production process is a creative one, and you want to have a built-in mechanism to allow for changes. Sometimes a corporate executive gets so excited at seeing a well-written script that he or she wants to expand upon it. At times, after the video is shot, the manager may want a version for a different market. A contract with a built-in mechanism for changes can foster added creativity and enhanced video productions.

Safety Issues

You have assembled a cast and crew and are filming on location. The deadline is tight and the pressure is on. One of the crew members, a freelancer, has a minor accident and has to leave the set to go to the ER. Do you have a policy in place to make sure the worker gets appropriate treatment and the corporation is shielded from liability? It is essential that the production and the corporation have liability insurance in force during the shoot. For freelancers, there is a standard policy called a "producer's package" that covers most risks involved in a production.

Your company has workers' compensation insurance that covers employee injuries, but it probably does not cover freelancers. Sometimes a crew member may be classified as an independent contractor for employment tax purposes but still be considered an employee for workers' compensation insurance purposes. You need to have a written agreement that specifies how the freelancer will be paid, that it is a "work for hire" under U.S. copyright law, and that all of the work done belongs to the company. Ask your manager how the company protects itself from liability from injury to nonemployees and contractors.

If you are producing a video that could affect the health or safety of the employees or viewers, it is a good idea to preface it with a disclaimer. You may be filming a process as simple as ergonomics or body mechanics, or you could be producing a video demonstrating the method for handling hazardous materials. If someone performs one of the procedures and is injured, his or her health insurance company may subrogate, which means they may seek damages from your company.

A disclaimer, however, may not be enough to shield the company from liability. The company should have insurance in place to pay for the cost of defense and any liability that a court or jury might find. Your company's legal department should be consulted on the wording.

Permissions, Releases, and Permits

It is essential to obtain a signed permission from anyone appearing on camera who is not a full-time employee. This includes professional as well as nonprofessional talent and even a crew member who might be visible in a shot. As for employees at the company, check with your manager, since employees may not be required to sign one for each production. At some companies, the nature of employment allows the organization to use an employee's image and voice for corporate video productions. However, it is a good idea to get permission even from employees.

To develop your own form, you can start with a stock permission/release form, such as one downloaded from www.video maker.com/ftp/pdf/model_release.pdf or from other sites, but have the company's legal department read and modify it. Don't rely on any permission form or any document that has not been evaluated and customized by your legal staff. Ask your actors to sign the form prior to filming; you don't want them to want to take it home for scrutiny. The permission forms usually give all rights to the company, including the rights to modify and edit the performance as they see fit. Plan on including a clause that lets you use still images from the video and production stills you may wish to take during filming. Make backup copies of the signed releases, and store them offsite.

The best practice is to get releases signed by everyone who appears in front of or works behind the camera. Check with your manager or legal department, but if you are filming outside in public, you probably don't need to obtain releases from people walking in the background. Most states' laws recognize that a person in public has no reasonable expectation of privacy. However, if you will be focusing on one or two people in your shot, and they see themselves in your film or TV show, they may demand payment; they could also force you to edit them out. If you plan on distributing your video or selling your finished show to a distributor, the distributor will ask for the permissions from all those appearing on camera. Before final editing is done, the entire work should be reviewed by legal counsel, either in the company or outside counsel, to evaluate any potential risks.

When you are filming at a large gathering, such as a festival or sporting event where audience members probably will be in a shot, it may be sufficient to post a sign visible to participants. The sign would state that filming is taking place and that by entering the area participants agree to be filmed. You would need to document that the sign is there and keep the evidence. You should check with counsel prior to the event to create a strategy for how to approach the shoot.

If you are shooting a conference, the speakers should sign the releases. If you are a freelancer hired by a company or by another producer, that entity would probably be the one providing the releases, and the rights will go to that company or producer. You may also need permission to film the conference from the organizers of the conference and possibly from the venue itself.

A permit usually refers to a document that lets you film at a particular location. If your company does not already have a form that permits someone to film at your facility, you can help them draft one. The permit may not be only for filming; it could be a general permit such as when an outside organization uses the company's conference room. Sometimes the permit asks for an insurance certificate that names the facility as the loss payee. If the permit or form would be used when a television news crew wants to perform filming at the company, you could require a copy of all the raw footage, as well as the option to use it for your own corporate video productions.

Some private business developments, such as the management of an office building or a shopping mall, require you to obtain a permit, sometimes at no charge. The facility will want you to sign a release of liability form and probably will want a certificate from your liability insurance company. If you want to film in a public park or on municipal property, you need to obtain a permit from the city clerk's office, or if you are filming in a large city, the city's film commission would issue the permit. Be sure to get a copy of the blank form well in advance so your manager and legal department can review it.

Many years ago, my company shot a commercial for a sports car manufacturer. We compiled a small crew and filmed on a road overlooking the ocean near San Francisco. We chose this location because we had learned it was popular with ad agencies because of its winding roads framed by ocean landscapes. Just as we were wrapping for the day, a county patrol officer drove up and asked for our permit. We had none. The officer explained that the county relies on film permits for much of its revenue and that we could have obtained a permit quite easily.

Copyrights

Generally, if you are a full-time employee creating the work in the course of your employment duties, the company owns the copyright for the script and video you produce. On the other hand, an independent contractor may own the copyright by default. In order for your company to be protected, you need to have an agreement signed by the independent contractor that recites that the work is a "work for hire" and that the company owns the work.

If you are an independent contractor hired by the company to produce the work, you need to get this issue clear with the company, and part of your responsibility to the client company will be to make sure that the work you produce for them can be legally used, which means having written agreements with all who work on the project. An alternative to giving up the copyright to the client would be for you, as an independent contractor, to provide an exclusive license to the company for a set number of years.

The copyright for an individual lasts for the duration of his or her life, and the heirs to the estate own it for 70 years after the author's death. For works made for hire and for anonymous works, copyright lasts for 95 years from publication or 120 years from creation, whichever is shorter. If you are going to do this, you still need "work for hire" agreements from everyone who works on the film, including employees of the company, making it clear that you are the copyright owner.

Check with your manager or legal department to see how they handle copyrighted online documents and print materials. That can serve as a model for copyrights at your company. They may want you to include the copyright notice in the credits of the videos you produce. While the notice may not be required for copyright protection, the symbol inhibits a potential copyright violator from saying he or she didn't know the work was copyrighted. Certainly check with your legal department on the wording and punctuation with the use of the symbol. Focal Press uses the copyright symbol in the following manner:

Copyright © 2010, Stuart Sweetow. All Rights Reserved.

You may also register your work with the U.S. Copyright Office. While registration is not required to protect your copyright, Philip H. Miller, author of *Media Law for Producers*, says that registering your video with the Copyright Office establishes a public record should there ever be a dispute. According to Miller, "If someone has violated your copyright, you need to register the work before you can bring a suit for copyright infringement before a court of law. Although it is possible to register the work after the infringement has occurred, this will limit you to suing for monetary losses that you can actually prove." Prior registration also lets you sue for attorney's fees and statutory damages.

You may register your copyright online with the Copyright Office. Go to www.copyright.gov and click on Electronic Copyright Office (ECO). The office accepts most video file formats, including uncompressed .avi files. You can pay the fee online, too. Online filing is the fastest, but it could take up to nine months to receive your copyright certificate.

If you wish to mail a DVD of the video, you can complete the Copyright Office form online, or you can download the form and mail it with the DVD. The instructions are at www.copyright.gov/forms/. The office states that if you mail your materials to them, it can take up to 22 months to receive your certificate.

If you wish to use an old film clip that is in the public domain or classical music whose copyright has expired, it is best to confirm that the copyright has not been extended. This is one of the difficult areas of the law, and it is best to consult with your legal department or legal counsel. Some copyright holders have applied for extensions for expired copyrights, and while we wait for a determination from the Copyright Office, copying the work may expose your company to infringement liability.

Another gray area is the use of a short portion of a copyrighted film or other copyrighted work covered by what is referred to in the United States as the "fair use doctrine." Section 107 of the U.S. Copyright Act defines the doctrine of fair use of copyrighted works. This doctrine allows use of copyrighted programs by news reporters, schools, researchers, and for parodies. According to the U.S. Copyright Office, "The distinction between 'fair use' and infringement may be unclear and not easily defined. The Copyright Office can neither determine if a certain use may be considered 'fair' nor advise on possible copyright violations. If there is any doubt, it is advisable to consult an attorney." "Fair use" is a defense to an infringement action. What this means is that since you have not obtained permission to use a copyrighted work, when the copyright holder sues the company or you for infringement, fair use is a defense. Before relying on fair use, you should have the work reviewed prior to publication or dissemination of the work, either with your company's legal department or by an attorney who is knowledgeable in this field.

If you wish to use music in your video, be certain you receive a license from the musician or the music library that grants you the rights. In some cases the rights have some limitations, such as the distribution methods or the duration of the license.

The Center for Social Media (www.centerforsocialmedia.org/) is a good source of information on the area of fair use. They have developed publications on best practices that assist media and legal professionals in determining what is considered fair use. Insurance companies are starting to accept these practices as guidelines.

You should check with your legal department regarding errors and omissions insurance. Depending on what the plans are for the work you are creating, such insurance may be necessary. In order to get the insurance, you will have to disclose to the insurance company the practices you have used to clear your work and any footage that is not cleared. A letter from counsel that describes the work you want to use without permission, the proposed use, and how it applies to the principles of these publications is often accepted by insurance companies.

Distribution Agreements

If your video section is producing materials that could be distributed via DVD or online downloads, you'll need to know about distribution agreements. This is something that the legal department may or may not know, so you may need to take responsibility to research the distribution business and its legal aspects.

You have a choice of self-distribution or contracting with a professional distributor. Some distributors want to have exclusive rights to market your video, while others are nonexclusive and act more as wholesalers.

Miller says that a distribution agreement, like most other contracts, consists of an offer, the financial consideration, and the terms of acceptance. If it is an exclusive deal, you'll want to make sure the contract puts limits on the duration of the agreement so the rights will revert back to you, or if the video is selling well through the distributor, limits the time to renegotiate the contract. You should include a clause that allows you to terminate the agreement if the distributor does not sell a minimum number of units within a specified time.

Miller recommends that you consider the distributor's contract as a draft, and he adds that distributors expect "producers to negotiate some of the financial terms." He recommends that you have your lawyer review the terms of the contract and help you better understand the terms and legal jargon. One clause Miller suggests you avoid is an "option on next work" clause. This gives the distributor the right of first refusal for your next production. According to Miller, "distributors almost expect to have the contract returned with this clause crossed out. Do not disappoint them."

Legal Considerations If You Are a Freelancer

As a contractor or freelancer you probably will have a written contract for the services you perform for your client corporation. Each production is different, and frequently video producers modify some contract terms for specific projects, based on the advice of their attorneys. It is probably a good idea to meet with an entertainment lawyer or an attorney who specializes in intellectual property to draft a basic contract and modify it for specific productions as they come up.

If you are writing a script or if you are producing a video that represents your creative work, you may want to consider licensing the video to the corporation rather than giving it to them outright. This may not fly with some companies, and you will have to decide for yourself whether you want to transfer the copyright to them.

When you give the entire work to the company, you enter into a contract clause called "work-made-for-hire." That is the same arrangement you would have if you were an employee; the copyright is transferred to the corporation, and you have no rights to it. According to Section 101 of the U.S. Copyright Act, "The parties expressly agree in a signed writing that the work is to be considered a work-made-for hire."

Video producers and videographers who would like the option of selling their video clips to stock footage agencies or who want to use the footage in an educational or documentary program should think twice before signing a work-made-for-hire clause. All the footage, even outtakes, becomes the property of the client. If the videographer happens to capture a beautiful scene worthy of selling to a stock footage firm or a mishap that could be put on a "funniest home videos" TV show, the work-made-for-hire clause could prevent him or her from doing so.

You can protect your rights when you, as the in-house producer, subcontract to a freelance videographer by stating in writing that the materials the freelancer provides you with are works-made-for-hire under copyright law. Miller says, "It is advisable to go further and specify that in the event that the materials are ever deemed not to be works-made-for-hire, the agreement constitutes an assignment of all ownerships in the materials."

Understanding the law regulating video production will help you and your corporation stay out of trouble. If you hire crew members for your shoot, you need to know about employment law. If you are an independent producer, you need to know about the work-made-for-hire clause in the U.S. copyright law. The laws regulating intellectual property can be complicated, but the video producer needs to be familiar with them. Talent releases, permits, and permissions are documents that you need to have on hand. You or your company may even be involved in developing distribution agreements with other parties.

While you can read about media law in this book and others, your company's legal counsel or your own attorney is the person you need to consult about any legal issues. Rather than copying a boilerplate contract, ask counsel to develop one for you. Have him or her review any agreements you sign and the licenses you receive, including those giving you the rights to use stock footage and music.

The laws vary from state to state, and if your videos will be distributed in other countries, additional legal considerations take place. Most of the laws are clear and straightforward; others may be subject to interpretation. Your legal counsel is your best consultant with any of these issues. You want to spend your time as a creative video producer, rather than someone embroiled in a legal battle.

TALENT: WORKING WITH TALENT, COACHING THE EXECUTIVE, AND APPEARING ON-CAMERA YOURSELF

Introduction

The literal image of the corporation is reflected in the videos the company produces. The video manager is responsible for ensuring that anyone appearing on-camera appropriately reflects the image of the company. Department managers may have experience in public speaking and feel confident they will perform well on-camera. However, when the studio lights are on, when the cameras roll, and when all eyes of the crew are on them, their confidence can fly out the window. The executive may try to convince the video producer that he or she can wing it when the cameras roll, but the producer will be doing the exec a favor by insisting on a practice or rehearsal.

In Chapter 6 we discussed auditioning and hiring professional talent. We discussed a style of directing that lets the talent interpret the script and the character he or she is playing. We also discussed "shooting the CEO" and directing employees as actors. In this chapter we present some thoughts about the video producer as a talent coach. How can you buoy the confidence of employees who reluctantly agree to play themselves in a video? How can you elicit the best performance from a professional narrator? How can you be an ally and a coach to the inexperienced on-camera presenter?

In addition to coaching the inexperienced on-camera presenter, this chapter discusses working with actors, including voice-over narrators. It expands on the discussion about the director's role in the enterprise. Customers and employees who view corporate videos compare them to television—a medium they have plenty of experience with. The video producer needs to make sure the performances do not disappoint.

If your assignment is to film the department manager, it is your job to coach that exec *before* the on-camera appearance so he or she is relaxed and confident; the message should come across clearly, smoothly, and without anything that could distract the viewer. This could be a tall order for the video producer who may feel intimidated by the person who signs her paycheck. However, learning some talent coaching techniques should restore the video producer's confidence as well as the on-camera executive's confidence in the producer. Most important, it could prevent a potentially embarrassing on-camera performance.

In some organizations, the video producer (you) is asked to be the on-camera spokesperson or host. If you were not informed of this in advance when you interviewed for the job, it could make for a frightening experience. The coaching techniques discussed here will be ways that you, as the video manager or producer, can develop your own individual on-camera presentation skills. Then you can effectively represent your company while appearing as cool as you do from the other side of the camera.

Coaching Nonprofessional Talent

Certainly, you are a talented professional video producer. That is what you were hired for. However, some organizations ask that the video producer also act as a TV reporter or as an interviewer on occasion. If you have no experience with on-camera performing or stage acting, consider contracting with a talent coach, and include that in the production budget. This could be a speech or drama teacher from the local college, a television news reporter, or another video producer with directing experience.

The coach will act as your consultant and could be retained on an hourly or per-production basis. The coach can show the exec how to read from a teleprompter, or the coach can work with employees who may need to act out a segment in the video. Sometimes, employees who just play themselves on-camera can freeze under the hot lights of a shooting set and the glare of the cast and crew watching them.

The coach works with individuals to help them to relax and be realistic. Many untrained actors, in their eagerness to provide a good performance, tend to overact. The coach will help them find their own comfortable level of energy. Other nonprofessional talent, faced with scenes they need to memorize or read from a teleprompter, get stiff and speak in an unnatural way. The coach can help them to be a part of the action and draw from their individual presenting strengths.

On-Camera Reporters and Guests

The video producer may be involved with producing a live show with a guest located at another city. Using satellite or Internet transmission, the producer will be responsible for at least the home office camera feed. The on-camera executive will probably wear an IFB earpiece as well as a clip-on microphone. IFB stands for "interruptible feedback," and it refers to an intercom system that connects the host and guest mikes to the earpieces they each wear. They also hear the director. It is best to ask all on-camera persons to angle themselves just slightly to hide the earpiece.

Your script may call for an executive or a professional on-camera narrator to talk to the camera. If this is shot out of doors, an IFB system can help the director communicate with the talent. Certainly the director should not talk through the IFB system while the talent is performing.

If the talent will be walking and talking on-camera, the crew should block or "map out" this action so the camera operator can plan for the movement. This is a common reporting style in documentary-style news programs, and it adds a dynamic feel to the scene. However, the exec who thinks he can pull this off easily may need some coaching. The movements need to be minimal, and the scene may be divided into two or three separate shots, rather than taken all at once. Walking and talking can be difficult for some people, so the producer/director should be flexible and be able to find an alternative if this movement is not working.

The Floor Director

Just before filming begins, the floor director explains to the talent and guests where the cameras are and what signals he may use to direct their attention to a particular camera. This is the time for the floor director to check the appearance of each person who will be on-camera. Is there a shine on someone's face or head that needs a touch of powder? Is there a dangling necklace that might bump the clip-on microphone? Is someone wearing a shiny pin or watch that could cause reflections or flares?

Clip-on mikes are popular in corporate video productions, but sometimes a shotgun mike on a boom is used. The floor director will notify the on-camera personnel not to be alarmed if they suddenly see a long mike hovering over their head. Clip-on mikes can be attached to the lapel or tie by the floor director, but only after he or she asks permission. Then the floor director should ask the talent if they could hide the cable in their clothing. The floor director may perform this task, but if it isn't done discreetly, it could upset an already-nervous on-camera presenter. Sometimes, the presenter can use a restroom to privately hide the cable and attach the mike to the belt pack. The floor director needs to confirm that the mike is turned on at this time.

The floor director signals to the talent when there is a camera change. He or she usually stands near the on-air camera and performs a sweeping underhand arc pattern toward the newly selected camera. If you are the host during an interview show, the floor director should wait until the camera is not on you before giving you a cue. It can be distracting trying to speak on-camera while looking out of the corner of your eye at the floor director. Of course, if the director is taking a two-shot, you may have no other choice than to use your peripheral vision.

Professional Narration: On-Camera and Voice-Over

As discussed in the chapter on directing, an actor hired to play the role of the on-camera spokesperson for your company needs to look and act the part. Make sure your manager participates in the audition process and approves your choice for talent.

You may want to consider having a noncompete contract with the host stating that he or she cannot work in a similar capacity for other companies in your industry. Similarly, you may want a clause that states that for a certain period of time, your spokesperson will not portray a character in a movie or television show that could make your company look bad. For example, if your company manufactures toys, you don't want your host appearing as a drug dealer in a soap opera.

Make sure the talent knows how to pronounce all the words in the script correctly. We are so familiar with the names of our products that we may forget others don't know the correct pronunciations. Spell them out phonetically in the script.

Many budgets include time for talent to learn the script and rehearse their lines. They should be camera-ready on filming day. You may want to spend some time rehearsing with them and helping them to emphasize key words and phrases.

Voice-over narrators frequently mark up the script with slashes for pauses and underlining for emphasis. Since they will be reading from a script, they may mark it up all they want. You as director should attend the voice-over narration session to direct their delivery. You may want to record alternate takes with different emphases and perhaps different copy to give you more choices in the edit suite. Bringing a narrator back to the studio to read only a single new sentence requires a hefty minimum fee.

While teleprompters are the best way to go for on-camera narrators, if you are on a limited budget or shooting on location, consider hiring a narrator who can work with an ear assist. The talent wears an earpiece that plays back the script from an MP3 player in his pocket. The host records the script scenes into the MP3 player and repeats, on-camera, what she hears. The narrator stands so the earpiece is outside of camera view. This takes practice to perfect, and sometimes the delivery can come across as unnatural. However, for a low-budget production, it is an alternative to holding cue cards.

Actors for Dramatic Roles

In Chapter 6 we discussed encouraging actors to feel the emotions of the characters they are playing. This comes from the "method acting" approach developed by the Russian theater director Constantin Stanislavski in 1897. The method involved actors experiencing in their minds the roles they would play, and it is a popular acting technique to this day.

The director asks an actor to think of emotions connected with past experiences that would relate to the scene. For example, if you were acting in a scene where you had an industrial accident, and you experienced an injury as a child, you would bring up the emotions you felt at the time. The ability to call up that experience and the associated emotions is a skill that stimulates a realistic performance.

Another concept in method acting is developing such a high level of concentration when performing the scene that the actor is not aware of the cameras and crew. Understanding the motivation for the scene is another technique for helping talent to perform realistically in their roles and to develop their own interpretations of the action.

When you give the actors their copies of the script, include descriptions of the characters they are to play. Demographic information such as age, ethnicity, home town, level of education, and their job function helps talent to behave like the character they portray. Describe the emotional disposition of the character and the person's physical characteristics. How does that character relate to others? This is all information that will help the actor feel like the character he is to become.

Wardrobe

Some colors and patterns work better for on-camera reproduction than others. Solid white may be difficult to reproduce, and it may contrast with someone with a dark complexion. Herringbone and tight stripes may cause shimmering when played on some monitors. It is a good idea for on-camera talent to bring at least one alternate outfit so the director has some choices.

The background and the set colors also play a role in wardrobe choices. If you are going to use a green screen, the talent should not wear anything green—even something as simple as an accent pin or earrings. If the set is pure black and the talent wears all black, it could require that the gaffer or lighting technician provide additional illumination to show the clothing texture.

Some fabric textures should be avoided. Satin can appear too shiny for the camera. Chiffon may be too sheer and revealing under a bright light. Any metallic-looking fabrics or those with beads or sequins should be avoided. Natural fabrics such as silk, cotton, and wool, as well as fabric blends, make good wardrobe choices. Clothing should fit properly. A suit jacket with sleeves too long could make a man look like a boy wearing a man's suit. Pant legs should be long enough and socks high enough that a man's legs are not exposed when he sits.

On-camera presenters should be instructed that they will be wearing a clip-on microphone; they may need a collar to attach it to. If they will be standing, they should have a waistband or a belt to attach the transmitter pack. A collarless dress with no waistband creates a nightmare for the sound technician.

Makeup

In the old days of standard-definition cameras, the resolution was low enough that slight wrinkles and blemishes might go unnoticed. Thanks to high-definition, however, skin imperfections are reproduced all too accurately. The corporate video manager should consider writing into the budget funds to contract with a makeup artist. The makeup artist should have experience with television makeup, which is a very different process from makeup for the stage or still photography.

Television works best with a natural look, and TV makeup artists like using pancake makeup. It creates a smooth look to the skin. They add powder to create a matte texture that avoids reflections from lights. Concealer is used for individual blemishes, and a little blush helps add color, especially to light-skinned talent. This works for both men and women.

Women usually can apply makeup at home, and they may bring some materials to the set. Men rarely wear makeup, so if a man will appear on-camera, that is a reason to hire a makeup artist. In addition to pancake makeup and concealer on a man, sometimes the makeup artist will add a subtle touch of eyeliner and even a bit of lipstick. The trick to any makeup application is to make it unnoticeable.

When working with makeup, wardrobes, and actors in corporate videos, it is important to not overdo anything. Too much makeup or unusual attire can backfire just as badly as overacting.

On-Camera Training and Presentation Skills

Chapter 15 discusses "media training," which is the process of preparing company spokespersons to speak to TV news journalists about their organizations. This includes handling questions about crises and perhaps even an ambush interview by an overenthusiastic reporter. The video department can collaborate with the communications department to train execs and other personnel to present themselves well in front of the camera.

The personnel do not need to learn how to be actors; they should just be themselves and appear relaxed in the midst of the lights and the crew looking on. The television camera is the avenue that the CEO or division manager can use to communicate with employees, customers, and the general public. If he or she appears awkward or stiff, the results can be disastrous. The viewer becomes distracted by nervous gestures and loses focus on the message.

This is why is it important for the execs to learn to be effective on-camera. Whether they are talking into their Flip camera from outside a convention center, speaking live from the in-house studio, or appearing in an interview with TV news media, it is important for the presenter to connect with the audience. Actors learn the techniques of developing this rapport by being believable and confident on-camera, and company execs can learn them as well.

Becoming familiar with the material and plenty of practice are ways for on-camera spokespersons to relate to the camera and make the process look effortless. The exec should read the entire script to get an understanding of it as a whole. Then, when alone, he or she should practice reading his or her individual portions aloud several times. They may use a mirror or a video camera to practice their deliveries. If time allows, the person should practice every day prior to the filming date.

If you conduct a class to train employees to appear on-camera, the class should be small—perhaps only two or three students at a time. You want the class to be more like individual coaching sessions but with the added benefit of interaction and group critique. These may be taught by the video manager or by an acting coach or consultant who provides media training.

One of the qualifications of the instructor is that he or she be patient and supportive. With the camera and their colleagues looking on, the students are put in a vulnerable position. The instructor should focus on the students' strengths and provide mainly positive feedback, at least during the initial segments of the training.

Later, he or she can take time to give negative feedback. These criticisms should focus on specific behaviors that can be improved, and the instructor can soften the criticism by adding that it is his or her subjective response. For example, the instructor could say, "My attention drifts when I see you fidgeting with your wristwatch as you speak. Try putting your hands to your side, or use your hands for gestures."

While executives in the firm will benefit from this training program, it is also suited to the employees who may be asked to play themselves. Training in presentation skills can be a boon to sales staff. They receive training in product features and sales techniques, and can benefit from learning how to present themselves with panache. Throughout the training, keep in mind that all individuals express themselves in their own unique ways. This training and coaching should recognize existing presentation skills and build upon those individual strengths.

Conducting a training program such as this not only helps improve the individual's on-camera presentations, but it may also add to the visibility of the video unit. Some video departments charge other departments for taking classes such as these, and it could help generate revenue.

Whether you are working with executives who must develop their presentation skills, employees who need coaching on how to act natural on-camera, or salespeople who want to wow their customers, the basics of good acting apply: Let your own personality shine through rather than trying to be someone else. Find your individual skills and build on them. Practice, rehearse, and know the material thoroughly; don't try to wing it. Learn to relax, either by doing some relaxation exercises or simply by being prepared.

With each successive opportunity to perform on-camera for video productions, you will develop greater confidence to tackle the next shoot. You may be one of the spokespeople for your company, and your fellow employees and customers will enjoy seeing you on-camera.

LOCATION SHOOTING

"Anything that can go wrong will go wrong."

—Murphy's Law

Introduction

In my humble opinion, nowhere is Murphy's Law more apparent than during location shooting. Mean Mr. Murphy lurks under the conference room table as you interview the CEO. He peeks from behind the curtains in the auditorium as you stream the shareholders meeting. He turns on the refrigeration unit in the soda machine just as you are completing the best take with your on-camera narrator.

Location filming is rife with nuisances just waiting to happen. Through a combination of superb planning, a gaggle of backup gear, and sheer good luck, you can keep Mr. Murphy at bay. Well, maybe at least until you complete most of the day's shots.

However, most likely one or more things *will* go wrong on location. In addition to backup equipment, you will need to have backup plans and a big bag of tricks. If the office doesn't have enough power for the gaffer's deluxe lighting design, perhaps you can shoot the scene with fewer lights. If the noise level coming through the window of the conference room is too high, maybe you can shoot your scene in a room without windows. If the CEO has a shiny pate, you can have a makeup kit or makeup artist at hand.

There may be times when even backup plans don't work. That's when the video producer/director needs to stay cool, calm the client and crew, and make some decisions. The office staff has limits on how far they will go to accommodate your video needs. You may, at some point, have to tell everyone to take a 20-minute break while you sit quietly alone to clear your mind.

divide the power. A licensed electrician may be employed to tap into the power main. You could also consider renting a portable generator; just be sure you know how to operate it and keep it outside.

A director I know had a studio full of cast members assem-

Arrange for one or two rooms to store equipment cases and backup gear during the shoot. One of the rooms can also be used for the cast members to gather between takes and for the crew to hang out during breaks. Some producers will want an additional room to provide coffee and snacks; it also acts as a distraction for the office staff during equipment setup.

Logistics on Location

Corporate videos shot on location present their own special set of logistical issues. If you are shooting in an office building, you'll need to get permission to bring equipment in and out through the loading dock. Certainly, you'll make sure your grip truck does not exceed the height of the entrance to the dock. Check if there is a building manager or director of security. Depending on the company, security could be tight or tighter.

Keep in mind that many companies want to restrict visitors to certain areas. Large crates and strange people moving around in the corridors sometimes makes people nervous, and companies need to be concerned about the general safety of their employees. The security office may also be vigilant about protecting the physical surroundings, such as the crew not scratching tile flooring or doorways. Plan on using the freight elevators only; don't bring equipment through the passenger elevators unless told to do so. Obtain permission before you get a shot of the company logo or any other intellectual property.

Plan to obtain a permit to conduct business on the property. The permit may require that you provide an insurance certificate, and your crew and cast members may need to bring driver's licenses with them as identification. Your host at the building or the security section can provide this permit; make sure you get this completed well in advance of the shooting day. Inquire if there also is a special form to use to remove your equipment from the building. Some facilities have a "building pass" or an "equipment removal pass," where each item of equipment is listed. This protects your equipment as well as theirs.

Food, water, and bathrooms are hardly part of the creative process, but they can certainly hinder it if someone doesn't have access to them. Some companies have their own cafeterias; if so, make arrangements for your crew and cast to

Figure 11.1 When filming on location, your crew may need to squeeze into the corners of a conference room. While limited space may preclude your getting the best lighting, plan on illuminating the scenes with your lighting instruments rather than relying on room lighting. Photo courtesy of Richard Cash.

use them at your expense. Companies that lack their own kitchens probably have lists of local restaurants. While most production managers like to feed their staffs on-site, when shooting at the office, it is okay to let the crew take an hour off to eat off-site. Unless the company has an arrangement with a catering service and a room to serve meals, the corporate conference room probably is not the best place to have lunch.

And it may not be lunch; it could be dinner and late-night snacks. Many corporate videos are shot in the evenings after the employees have gone home. You have the building to yourselves, and sometimes it is easier on everyone if you plan the filming during off-hours. Make sure that you have arranged with housekeeping in advance, lest vacuum cleaners start rolling when you are trying to record sound.

If your location shoot will be outside, try to scout the location at the same time of day as the shoot. Listen for airplanes, traffic, lawnmowers, and other sources of noise. Is there a likelihood of the sun being directly overhead? If so, you may need to rent a silk with frame and stands. How about lawn sprinklers, street repairs, or barking dogs? Do you have a plan for inclement weather? Is there room to park your production vehicles and those of the cast and crew? If you will be using a generator, is there a suitable exterior location for it? Have you made arrangements to safely transport its fuel?

If you're shooting on private property, you'll need permission and maybe a permit from the owner of the property. Private property includes such locales as shopping malls and possibly even some of the space in front of a building or store. Public property such as a park or the sidewalk is usually regulated by the city. Contact the mayor's office to learn which department handles such permits. That office will probably want an insurance certificate, as well as a check to cover the permit fees and possibly costs for parking or police. Many cities welcome film crews, since their need for lodging and meals adds to the local economy. If you need to block off a street to film, you may need to pay only for the lost parking revenue and police officers' time.

Nondisruptive Equipment Setups

Back to the inside job. The permits are in place, the equipment is rolling in, and catering has been arranged. As you plan the shooting day, think of the look on the office manager's face as your crew arrives and starts assembling the gear and rearranging the office. He or she may feel panicked as the neatly organized workplace is turned into a shambles. Light stands appear where there once was a desk, cables are routed everywhere, chairs are stacked in the hallway, windows might be getting gels.

The first hour when the crew arrives and begins setting up their equipment can look chaotic. Consider staging all the gear into a room separate from the filming room. Then crew members can bring out each item as needed. The production coordinator could create a drawing of the shooting room with the setup sketched out so the gaffer and grip know exactly where to place the lights. A crew that has been briefed on the setup and knows what they are doing can work together well. Remind your crew that they are guests at the office building and that they should try to keep the rooms as neat as possible as they perform their tasks.

Depending on the employees' attire at the company, you may want to ask your crew to go easy on the exposed tattoos and piercings. Jeans and t-shirts may be appropriate for a filming crew, but torn or ragged clothing may send the wrong message. Clothing with offensive language or logos should be left at home, and the producer needs to let all the crew members know that in advance.

Make sure your crew knows that when they leave, everything must be returned to their original locations. Some production coordinators will take photos of the room so the crew knows where to return things. During the setup time, a producer might meet with the office manager in a conference room away from all the pandemonium. The director could be rehearsing the cast in a different room or to the side. The camera operators should be able to set up their gear without interfering with the employees working there.

A production assistant could be assigned to make sure everyone has water or coffee and knows the locations of the bathrooms; that way, no one bothers the office staff. That PA could also attend to the curious staffers who may have endless questions and, perhaps, a secret desire to be part of your cast or crew.

Safety is a major concern when there is a combination of equipment and personnel. Bring sandbags to secure light stands. Be careful that no lights are positioned near sprinkler heads. Tape down all cables that might be where anyone may need to walk. Use gaffer tape, not duct tape. Make sure you bring your own stepladder so a gaffer doesn't need to stand on any furniture. Be careful that no equipment carts bang into doorways or walls. If you are performing any handheld walking shots, arrange for a production assistant to guide the camera operator so he or she doesn't walk into anything or anyone.

Try to avoid nailing or taping anything to walls. Even gaffer's tape can peel off paint, so test it on an inconspicuous area first. Be careful with fragile and delicate objects, and make sure the crew or cast uses coasters for their drinks. Some conference rooms have expensive wooden tables that are susceptible to damage from a soft-drink or a hard piece of equipment.

When the shoot is over, remember to put everything back where it was, empty the trash cans, and turn on any refrigerators or other equipment you may have needed to have unplugged during sound recording. While the crew is striking the gear and cleaning up, you may want to set up a monitor to view the day's rushes, and this could be a time to invite office staff to enjoy the viewing, with the approval of their manager. The chaos of the location production suddenly subsides as the viewers see the fruit of your labors and get a better appreciation for all the work it takes to pull off a location production.

Client Guide for Location Filming
by Stuart Sweetow of Audio Visual Consultants

This is the location filming guide my company sends to clients in advance of filming. A little planning can keep the process smooth and productive.

What to Wear On Camera: Please refer to the *AVC Client Guide: Looking Your Best on Camera* at http://avconsultants.com/avc-guides/looking-your-best-on-camera. Muted colors work best, and avoid fine lines and checks such as herringbone cloth.

Building Entry and Parking: Try to secure a parking space as close as possible or arrange for access to a loading zone. The easier we can get equipment into the building and the room in which we are shooting, the less time participants will have to wait. Please make any arrangements with the security department, and secure permits if needed, including any that might be required to remove equipment from the premises.

Electricity: AVC crew will want to use electricity at the location. We usually use professional lighting equipment and don't want to blow any circuit breakers. Please try to have electrical outlets available that are not shared with coffee makers or other devices that draw a lot of electrical power. Please identify the location of the circuit breaker box, just in case we do blow a breaker. Advise office personnel to back up their files frequently in the unlikely event of a blown breaker. We all hope for the best, but it is a good idea to have a plan for the worst.

Microphones: If a presenter will be speaking on-camera, we usually ask that he or she wear a clip-on wireless microphone. The mike clips onto a collar, so ask the presenter to wear a top with one. Also, the mike comes with a belt pack, similar in size to a cell phone; the presenter will need a waistband or belt onto which the pack attaches.

Setup Time: The producer will let you know how much time is required to set up the lights, mikes, and camera, but figure about an hour of time. If the crew needs to film in more than one room, there will be additional time to take down the equipment, move it, and set it up in the next room.

Ambient Sound: Please try to keep noises to a minimum. Notify the producer in advance if there will be any construction or other sources of noise in your building or your neighbors' buildings. During filming, cell phones and desk phones will need to be silenced.

Additional Visuals: The crew may wish to shoot B-roll or auxiliary shots of people at work, shots of buildings, and other interesting visuals. If you have photos, flyers, artwork, logos, signs, or anything you think might enhance the look of the final video, tell the producer.

We look forward to keeping the filming a fun and enjoyable process. A little planning goes a long way to ensuring that goal.

Your Murphy Bag

These are a few items to carry with you on location shoots. You probably will want to customize this bag with additional items. Don't show this to Mr. Murphy!

Adapter plugs and spare cables
Backup equipment
Business cards
Cable ties
Cell phone charger
Clipboard
Clothespins
Duvateen or black cloth
Earplugs
Electrical tester
Extra cash
Facial tissues
First aid kit
Flashlight or two
Gaffer's tape
Gloves
Hand sanitizer
Hat
Headphones
Knife
Lens cleaner
Log sheets
Makeup kit
Maps
Marking pens
Menus from local restaurants
Paper towels
Pens
Permissions
Personal Items
Phone numbers of everyone involved
Pocket tool
Production notes
"Quiet" signs
Release forms

(Continued)

Your Murphy Bag (Continued)

Script
Sewing kit
Shooting schedule
Spare batteries for every device
Spare lamps
Sticky notes
Stopwatch
Tools and more
Trash bags

Site Survey Checklist

Contact Person: Cell phone, alternate phone, alternate contact.

Facility: Address and directions, hours open.

Parking: For production vehicle(s) and cast and crew.

Equipment Loading: Location, path clear of obstructions, any stairs? Any restrictions for wheeled carts?

Security: Contact name and phone, need permissions or forms, including removing equipment. Can we have keys?

Storage of Equipment: Need separate room that can be locked.

Production Room: Need access in advance to setting up equipment and afterward to strike equipment. If office, can the CEO or resident be away during setup time? Are there drapes or window covers?

Furniture: May we move facility tables and chairs? Where should we store furniture?

Electricity: Where are the circuit breakers? Will there be a coffee maker or microwave on the same circuit? May we run long extension cords to adjacent rooms for different circuits? Can an electrician provide us with more power if needed? Can we set up a generator outside and run cables?

Noise: Visit at approximate times to determine construction noise, flight paths, and so on. Will there be telephones ringing, ventilators going on and off, and other ambient noises?

Location Personnel: Who will need to be on the set? Will there be any decision makers or technical staff arriving whom we have not met?

Other: Restroom locations, drinking water, nearby restaurants, nearby Radio Shack, local AV rental, and video production companies.

THE INTERVIEW FORMAT

"A skilled interviewer can ask questions in such a way as to draw out information from even the most reticent person. The well-prepared and personable interviewer can create a lively dialog, even from dry material."

—John Craft, professor at the Walter Cronkite School of Journalism

Introduction

A corporate video can be produced in a documentary format based entirely on interviews. Alternately, the interview segments can be part of a larger production that includes a host-narrator, demonstration segments, and even dramatic scenes with actors. Interviews are popular in corporate video production because they offer a platform for experts to be shown in settings similar to that of commercial television broadcasts.

Budgets can be minimal because interviews need relatively less planning than other formats, and they require only limited scripting. Since there are no actors, and perhaps not even a set or props, interviews can be completed in short turnaround times. However, they require diligent research, a reasonable amount of time to prepare the interviewees, and the selection of a host with experience conducting an interview.

While the corporate video producer may not be in a position to choose the interview host and guests, it is important for him or her to have as much influence in their selection as possible. They can justify this by explaining to their managers that selecting the right interviewer and appropriate interviewees will enable the video to adhere to the stated objectives and the needs of the audience.

Both the host and the guests need to speak to the audience at their level and not appear to be slick television personalities.

The producer may need to help his or her superiors understand that while the organization wants an expert to be interviewed, the expert who is too savvy or smooth may be more appropriate for commercial television than for corporate video. Additionally, you don't want the guest to appear to have been coached or have rehearsed the interview. The answers could appear to be stock sound bites and could result in a meaningless interview. The video producer needs to walk a fine line to select the expert who is tops in his or her field and performs well on-camera but does not have such a flamboyant personality that it could become a distraction for the viewers.

In some corporate videos, the interviews and documentary-style video segments serve as the armature of a production onto which the other elements, such as a facility tour, an on-camera narrator, and demonstration segments, are attached. The script can be written so the host can transition away from the interview to introduce such segments that visually express what is discussed in the interview. Then they can cut back to the interview as other subjects are presented and illustrated.

This visual variety may be facilitated with B-roll as the guest speaks, or it can be scripted and narrated by the host or another narrator. Magazine television shows such as *60 Minutes* serve as a model for this type of corporate production. You want to avoid boring your audience, and B-roll best illustrates what your guest is discussing. Be certain to write a good introduction and conclusion to the interview segment so the viewer knows what to look for and is reminded at the end what key topics were discussed.

Interviews frequently start with the host looking at the camera and speaking to the viewing audience. Then he or she may turn toward the guest and ask the first question. At the end of the interview, the host may thank the guest, turn to look at the camera, and state his or her concluding remarks. Some formats may have a set time length; others may be flexible with time. Some will include music or graphics at the opening and close of the interview.

The background should be appropriate for the setting, and lighting should not be so harsh as to cause discomfort to your guest. Bald men may look better without a back light or with one that is highly filtered. The chairs should be stationary; you don't want a nervous guest swaying back and forth in a swivel chair. While preparation involves minimal scripting, the producer needs to handle myriad details that can make or break the impact of the interviews.

Preparation

The producer should research the topic of conversation as well as the background of the guest. If the guest has written a book or journal articles or has appeared in news stories, try to read or view what is available. Provide the host with a relevant but brief synopsis of the research. The guest will appreciate that the host has done his or her homework. This could help the guest to be more open to a lively conversation, and it avoids the chance that he or she could feel on the defensive.

Either the host or the producer will write the questions for the interview. The host's knowledge of the subject will not only help develop rapport with the guest, but it will let the host stray from the prepared questions if the conversation warrants it. In the corporate setting it is common to provide the guest with the list of questions in advance, but if you rely on only those questions and answers, the interview could seem staged. Encourage both the guest and the host to move the conversation into interesting and relevant tangents.

If your background is in television news reporting, try to hang your inquisitor's hat on the rack, and remember that the intent of the corporate news story is to show the corporation and the interviewee in a positive light. Corporate videos are not news reports; they exist to promote the company's point of view. There is no need for balanced reporting. However, it is useful to include some questions that are controversial or might be on the minds of the skeptics among your viewers.

Shooting an Interview Sequence

Rather than shooting an interview in a conference room or an office, try to find an appealing or relevant location, such as in front of an architecturally attractive building, inside a laboratory, or next to particular equipment. These settings help give context to the interview as well as visual appeal. Just be careful that the background does not become distracting.

Talk shows are usually shot with three cameras. One captures a wide, establishing shot of the host and guests, one gets close-ups of the host, and one gets close-ups of the guests. Generally the viewer sees the establishing shot first, then some medium shots (MS), followed by plenty of close-ups (CU). When appropriate, later in the conversation, the director chooses the establishing shot to reestablish for the viewer what the whole scene looks like.

Figure 12.1 When conducting a video interview, the interviewer should sit near the camera lens. That way, the viewers see the guest completely rather than in a profile. Photo courtesy of Richard Cash.

It is possible to perform a three-camera interview shoot with only one operator. Camera-one is the wide shot and is static on the tripod. Camera-two is also static, but it is focused on a MS of the host. Camera-three is controlled by the camera operator. It zooms in for CUs of the interviewee. The three shots are combined together in postproduction.

Two cameras can simulate the three-camera shoot. Camera-one gets the establishing shot, while camera-two focuses on close-ups of the interviewee. During a camera-two take of the interviewee, camera-one may be zoomed in for a close-up. You can shoot the interview sequence with live switching or with camcorders, where each camera records to its own media, hard drive, or tape. The sequence is then compiled together in postproduction.

Consider putting camera-one on a dolly or curved track, and slowly arc the shot to give the scene a dynamic feel. Wait until the camera stops moving before cutting to the other camera's static shot; otherwise the effect could be jarring and distracting.

The Single-Camera Interview Shoot

If you are shooting the interview with only a single camera, try to avoid a situation where both the guest and the host sit facing each other. You will end up with two profile shots; it is best when you can see both eyes of the person who is speaking.

Also, try to move the chairs close to each other. That way, when you show a wide shot, there isn't too much blank space between the two people on-camera. The camera can then zoom in close, enabling detail on one face.

To accomplish a single-camera interview, try this sequence of filming:

1. Introduction with a wide two-shot as an establishing shot.
2. Reposition the camera to film an over-the-shoulder (OTS) shot of the host. This camera can get a wide shot, showing the host's shoulder and side of the head, as well as medium shots and close-ups. As a first pass, shoot all the questions from this angle.
3. Write down all the questions that the host asks.
4. Reposition the camera to the previous wide shot, and ask the host to repeat the questions.
5. As an option, shoot all the questions of the host over the shoulder of the guest, so the viewers see both eyes of the host. This can even be shot as CUs of the host after the guest has left. If that's the case, consider having a crew member sit in so the host has someone to look at when asking the questions.
6. Shoot some "noddies" where the host is nodding in reaction to the statements. Get shots of smiles, intense looks, and neutral reactions. These can be used to cover cuts in editing and to add visual variety.

Employing Composition and Continuity in Interview Filming

Whether you are shooting with a single camera or with multiple cameras, employ some rules of composition to make the sequence as visually interesting as possible. An OTS shot helps create that illusion of depth by including a little of the back of the head and the shoulder of the host in the foreground—out of focus—while the guest is highlighted and sharp. The sequence starts with the establishing shot, showing the two facing each other. Then it goes to one OTS shot focusing on the guest, followed by another OTS shot showing the host, followed perhaps by a reestablishing shot. The cameras shooting the OTS shots can also zoom in for close-ups.

Be careful to employ the 180-degree rule by not crossing the imaginary line that goes across the interviewer and interviewee. You want to make sure that the two subjects look at each other in the same direction in the establishing shot as they do in OTS and close-up shots. Chapter 13 discusses the 180-degree rule in more detail.

Close-ups are the intimate shots that help the viewers feel closer to the action; they give them an opportunity to clearly see facial expressions and eyes. When videos are viewed on desktop computer monitors, perhaps in small windows in the monitors, you'll need plenty of close-ups. Make sure you have some headroom at the top of the screen so you don't cut off the subject's head.

During the interview, it may be appropriate to capture the extreme close-up (ECU) where the camera gets so tight that you don't have to worry about cutting off the head. Documentaries and TV news sometimes employ this technique when they want to create an emotional connection between the subject and the viewer. The image may be cropped so close that the frame shows only the mouth and eyes. You'll need to employ a skilled camera operator using a good fluid-head tripod with a remote zoom control to pull this off smoothly.

Your guests are already nervous, so let them relax while the crew sets up the gear. Use crew members for lighting and mike checks, waiting until you really need the subjects on the set. Make sure your guest is not wearing glasses with transition-type lenses that darken when exposed to light; you don't want them looking like a rock star with shades. Avoid multiple takes, unless necessary. Often, the first take is the best.

Figure 12.2 This subject is filmed with windows behind him. Diffused HMI lights act as key and fill lights. A quartz backlight with a blue filter illuminates the hair, and another quartz light below the subject is another fill light.

Consider employing the skills of a set designer to create an interview set that is aesthetically pleasing and includes the company's branding elements. Depending on the objectives and audience, you may opt for a background with bold, geometric elements, or you may want a softer look with plants and flowers. The set could have artwork in the background, intentionally kept out of focus, or the background could be completely black. The set should complement the image of the company and not be distracting.

You can create a dynamic look to your interviews by filming in the field with the host walking and talking with the guest. Ideally, both interviewer and interviewee should wear clip-on mikes, but sometimes you may need to record with a handheld mike. With a hand mike, the interviewer maintains ultimate control of the conversation; only when he or she points the mike at the guests will they speak.

If you are the interviewer, hold the mike a little closer to the guest's mouth than you may think is comfortable. Try to hold the mike under your guest's chin so it is not visible to the interviewee. Position yourself facing the guest and with your back turned somewhat to the camera so the viewer can see both of the subject's eyes. Avoid the common mistake of talking loudly and closely into the mike yourself and holding it too far from the guest to hear her well on the soundtrack. Be careful for the guest who starts talking too loudly or too quietly; he or she may change the amplitude and cause distortion or a weak signal on the soundtrack. Watch out for mike-handling noises; that is one reason not to let the interviewee hold the mike. If you are outside, use a windscreen. If budget allows, have a separate audio technician monitoring the audio with headphones. Frequently the camera operator (which may be you) will be doing this.

Notes to the Interviewer

The producer may have prepared you in advance with a briefing on the subject and may have provided interview questions. You may be both the host and the producer. Either way, you may have had a chance to read some material that your guest has written or, ideally, seen him or her in a video clip. That clip will help you to understand how the guest appears on-camera and at what point he or she has developed rapport with the interviewer.

If you didn't write your interview questions yourself, rewrite the questions so they come from your own voice. Consider creating some of your own questions. Prepare follow-up questions to the initial ones; they help the conversation to move along. Avoid any questions that may be answered with a simple "yes" or "no," especially at the beginning of the interview.

If you have a chance to meet with the guest in advance, and with his or her agreement, offer a little coaching on how to answer questions in complete sentences. Explain that in postproduction your questions may be removed, and the guests' answers need to stand alone. It is best if they start their answer by paraphrasing the question or answer in a complete sentence that includes the content of the question. Encourage them to think of an attention-getting opening to one of their early answers. Ask them to avoid technical terminology unless the viewers will understand it. Show your interest in the topic; it can set the tone for the guest to express his or her own enthusiasm.

If you have a chance, before you both walk onto the set, try to loosen up your guest with some small talk. Make sure the crew has offered him or her a noncarbonated soft drink or a light snack. Confirm that the guest does not have a crooked tie or that hair is out of place. Do what you can to help him or her feel comfortable.

At the start of the interview, you may have an opportunity on-camera to introduce the guest and the topic of discussion. Rehearse this prior to the scheduled time of the interview and before the guest arrives; you don't want to draw attention away from your guest. Let the guest know in advance that you will start the interview by looking at the camera and introducing him or her. Explain time constraints, if any, and let the guest know if the interview will be divided into segments where he or she may take breaks.

Your first question to your guest could be a simple one or about an element of the subject that the guest is passionate about. He or she will enjoy answering that question, and it could help establish rapport. Gradually introduce more controversial questions or those that are more difficult to answer. Avoid any questions that are too long, too detailed, or are really two or more questions in one. Make sure your guest understands the question; if he or she appears confused, stop the camera and clarify the query. Offer to go to another question that he or she is more familiar with.

During the interview, try to maintain as much eye contact as comfortable. Rather than looking at your notes for the next question, listen to your guest, and use such active listening techniques as summarizing and restating key points, as well as nods and smiles. Your animated reactions to the guest's comments help make the interview a dynamic dialog that further involves the audience.

Whenever possible, ask open-ended questions—those that can't be answered with simply a "yes" or "no." This forces your guest to think and provide an in-depth answer. These answers may lead to other areas worthy of exploration. To share more details of the subject, start questions with such openings as "Tell me about ..." or "How do you think our employees feel about...."

If the guest gets too complicated with his answer, ask your question again, but insist on a clear and simple explanation. Think of the implications of some of your guest's answers, and be ready to depart from your list of prepared questions. Such a diversion could help flesh out the story and be more interesting to the viewers.

When appropriate, respond to a guest's story with a brief personal anecdote. This helps relax the guest and gives him a little break. If you show your interest and genuine enthusiasm for the subject, you can help bring out the exciting side of the guest. Be careful not to interrupt or monopolize the discussion with your own stories. If the guest pauses, don't immediately jump in; give the guest a little time to think. If it gets too long, you can edit out the pauses in postproduction.

When interviewing two or more people, it is best to start with the guests' names and then ask the question. This gives them a chance to be ready. For example, start the question with "John, I understand your department uses a new mobile display application. Would you tell us how that works?"

Remote Interviews

Just as broadcast television does with satellite technology, corporations that use an Internet protocol can create a live telecast with the interviewer and guest in different cities. In addition to cameras, mikes, and lights, remote interviews use special equipment to enable interaction. An IFP earplug lets the host and guest hear each other, and live monitors let them see each other.

In many cases the guest and the host need to look at the camera lens and imagine they are seeing the other person's face, but a monitor may be used so they can both see each other. If the guest is new at this, prep him or her by explaining that it will be like a phone conversation or teleconference.

Postproduction

As is done with documentaries, interviews may be transcribed so the producer can direct the postproduction. Some producers write the scripted narration after reading the transcribed interview. In addition to developing a concise story without unnecessary detail, it helps the producer develop appropriate segues and transitions between the narration and interview segments. The department manager or executive producer may wish to read the transcripts or approve the producer's selections before the video editing commences.

Many directors set up the editing session with each camera's files synched together on the timeline. The editor then runs all the files together, and the director calls each camera as if it were a live shoot. The advantage of switching in postproduction is that the director can change his or her mind, go back to the previous take, and insert a different camera shot.

A technique to combine interviews from two or more shoots is to parallel cut between the different interviews. Take each topic at a time, and show how different people have different opinions on the issue, as is done in news documentaries or magazine formats such as *60 Minutes*. Contrasting viewpoints displayed as different people and settings can add interest to a topic. In a corporate environment, two different guests may complement each other to better explain the topic.

When you have a limited amount of screen time or you just want to use a different style of producing an interview, remove the interview questions and put in just the guests' sound bites. This removes any attention from the interviewer as his or her questions are asked off-camera. One advantage of this approach is that the producer or director can be the one asking the questions; you don't need the same interviewer throughout the video. The program objectives will help determine if you will produce a short-form interview or a longer one with a more detailed conversation.

Well-produced and well-edited interviews help the viewers feel they are part of the conversation. Interviews in corporate video programs are a low-cost and effective method of introducing individuals who are experts on their subjects. While scripting and talent budgets are lower for interviews, several other considerations, such as selection of host and guest, location of the interview, and appropriate topics of discussion, need to be addressed to make the interview successful.

Diligent research of the topic, sharing that research with the host, and preparing the guest are all essential planning tools for a winning interview. Add B-roll or a roll-in, and you enhance the discussion with visual variety. A video program could be composed almost entirely of interviews in much the same format as a documentary. However, integrating the interview scenes together with other production segments such as demonstrations, dramatic vignettes, and facility tours adds to the visual variety of the video.

AESTHETIC CONSIDERATIONS

Introduction

In corporate video, sometimes attention is so focused on the message that the aesthetics of cinematography become relegated to a secondary position or are disregarded completely. The video producer or director should consider contracting with a director of photography (DP) who can add an artistic patina to imagery that will help maintain the attention of the viewer. An art director or a set designer can make certain that the scenes are crafted to reflect the visual style of the corporation. A lighting designer or gaffer can create a lighting scheme that complements the efforts of the rest of the artistic team. A graphic artist with experience in motion graphics maintains the high artistic standards in the postproduction process. The look of the company is projected in the videos it produces, so attention to aesthetics can boost the literal image of the corporation.

Together with creating a visually appealing video, attention to composition and continuity can help convey your message with impact and clarity. A well-composed image directs the viewers' eyes to particular portions of the frame. Proper use of continuity avoids confusion from shot to shot and helps maintain the suspension of disbelief.

We can't emphasize enough how the video producer influences the corporate image. The selection of talent, the use of colors, the background details, the graphic elements … all of these must match the look and feel of the corporation and contribute to the general branding that the company works so hard to establish.

Branding Complementation

Logos, color schemes, patterns, and packaging are some of the visual ways a corporation uses its brand. Phrasing, contextual use of the company name, and juxtaposing the name with certain buzzwords are ways the corporate video producer can effectively use the brand in the script.

In addition to the company name, there may be individual products that the company markets that have their own brand recognition. The producer needs to know his company's range of products or services and the corporate affiliations so she does not inadvertently provide product placement for the competition.

For example, a producer I worked for on an educational film removed Coke cans from the set of a party scene. She considered that a future potential distributor for her film could be affiliated with PepsiCo, and the presence of a competitor's product could nix that distribution deal. A script that makes a joking reference to Gatorade or Quaker Oats could also interfere with any possible relationship with PepsiCo, since they are part of the PepsiCo family.

Note the use of the term "family" rather than such terms as "owned by" or "acquisition." Depending on the corporate culture, a term such as "family" sounds much better in a script. Read the annual report and any press releases to learn the words and phrases your company uses. When planning your video, consult with the marketing communications or press relations departments.

The company graphics section or media relations department can get you copies of logos, color palettes, and other branding elements. They probably have particular standards on how these visuals may be used. Consider using company colors as part of the background set and in motion graphics in your videos. This subtle approach not only wows the execs, but it also provides a complement to the visual image of the company.

Creative Corporate Camera Work

With your attention to the aesthetic and your repertoire of skills, you *make* motion pictures, not just take them. With experience, you'll develop an eye for positioning the camera and placing the elements in your frame in ways that complement the message and enhance the visual appeal. Take the time to experiment with different camera positions and angles, and plan on shooting alternate takes to provide your editor with choices in postproduction.

Rather than positioning the camcorder always at eye level, try crouching down or even sitting or lying on the floor to get that dramatic low angle. Pop on a super-wide-angle lens, and

Figure 13.1 A wide-angle lens or fish-eye lens can add an exciting perspective. Expand your filming repertoire with a lens attachment or matte box. A matte box acts as a lens shade and accepts drop-in filters.

the shot becomes even more spectacular. Get up on a chair or table to capture a wide perspective on your scene. You can even tilt the camera a little to the side in what is called a Dutch angle. Do this carefully and rhythmically, and you'll add excitement to an otherwise routine scene.

Experiment with different ways of holding your camcorder, and you will open up new worlds of fascinating imagery and visual delights. Turn it upside down, and you can fool your viewer when you shoot the reflection of a building in a still pond. Hold it high over your head or mount it on a monopod to lift it even higher. Some camera-mounting devices let you get a very high angle, such as a tripod that can extend 15 feet or more into the air. Mount the camera on a skateboard or suspend it from a bungee cord. It is your video production, so take the time to experiment and come up with some dazzling imagery.

Consider using filters to enhance your imagery. The filters can be physical glass filters placed in front of the lens, or they can be digital filters added during postproduction. A polarizing filter should be used during most outdoor scenes shot in direct sunlight, or the colors can get washed out. It also minimizes glare and reflections off equipment and shiny surfaces during interior and exterior filming. A graduated filter adds a little color to one portion of the frame while keeping the rest clear. Sunsets frequently are shot with a graduated amber filter; the color is full at the top of the frame, and the filter gradually blends to clear glass at the bottom. Look online for samples of the various effects you can achieve with the amazing array of filters on the market.

Composition

Architects, painters, and photographers use the elements of composition to render works of art. There is no reason a corporate video cannot be considered a work of art. A beautiful video will capture the emotions of the viewer and have a lasting impact on him or her. Employing compositional tools such as balancing elements in the frame, using color, working with lines, and using such techniques as the "rule of thirds" can help you to create a stunning video that employees will enjoy watching.

To use the rule of thirds, mentally divide your frame in thirds vertically and horizontally. You can even create a template to overlay your monitor to display this tic-tac-toe pattern, as shown in Figure 13.2. Then try to place the most important elements at one of the crossings. For example, the upper right third of the screen is where the eye naturally moves to, and that

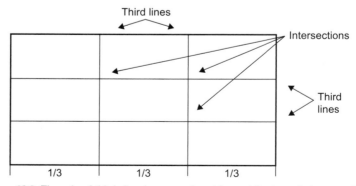

Figure 13.2 The rule of thirds has been employed by architects and photographers throughout the years, and it works for videographers, too. Try to place the main subject at one of the cross points. A secondary object can go at another cross point. Horizons and building lines could correspond with one of the third lines.

could be where a main character or object is located. The secondary person or object could be on the upper left third of the screen. The rule of thirds helps avoid a static shot where the main element is in the center of the screen.

It can also apply to filming a horizon. Rather than positioning the horizon in the center of the frame, for a more dramatic look, place it at the upper or the lower third of the screen. In many cases, this rule can be used to help you create appropriate headroom for a close-up of an on-camera narrator. Place the eyes or the nose at the top third level.

You can use this rule to create "nose room" or "looking space" where the subject directs his or her attention. For example, in a documentary-style interview, the subject is looking at the interviewer who is sitting just to the left of the camera lens. In your frame, position the subject just to the right of the center if he or she is looking at the interviewer. The space in the background between the subject and the interviewer could be used for an out-of-focus product shot, a bookcase with carefully selected titles, or simply a small piece of artwork.

The eye is attracted to movement and brightness, so try to keep the background at a lower light level, and avoid backgrounds with people or traffic unless there is a reason to do so. Be careful to avoid any vertical lines, such as the edge of a bookcase behind the subject's head; it could like something is growing vertically out of the head!

Until 3D television becomes widely adopted in corporate video, you need to create the illusion of depth within your two-dimensional screen. One way to create this illusion is by using diagonal leading lines to draw the eye into the frame. For example, if your subject is sitting at a conference table, consider placing the camera, with a wide-angle lens, next to the edge of the table so the edge creates a line leading to the subject. If you are filming a conference, an opening shot taken with a wide-angle lens from the back of the center aisle leads the viewers into the action.

Rather than shooting your subjects straight on, you can achieve a bit of a 3D effect by filming from an angle to the side. For example, a building takes on perspective and looks more dramatic if you shoot it from a corner. It takes a little more time and perhaps some creative thinking to make a static shot come to life, but invest a few moments to choose the ideal location for your camcorder.

If there is a doorway or window in a background, consider using it as a frame around your subject as another way to create the illusion of depth. Frame an exterior shot of a building by placing the camera below a tree or a bush that makes part of a frame above the building. Large indoor plants or flowers, carefully positioned, can be used to frame the subject being interviewed.

Framing, leading lines, and the rule of thirds are some of the guidelines of composition that will help you create aesthetically pleasing images that add zest to your videos and leave lasting impressions on your viewers. Practice them and refine them; soon they will become part of your production repertoire. You don't need to carefully compose every single shot, but employ these rules at least when capturing important shots, such as openings and closings of scenes. There is much more to learn about composition, and a good photography book such as *The Photographer's Eye* by Michael Freeman could help you develop this skill.

Continuity

Part of creating a successful training or marketing video is directing the movements of your subjects in ways that clearly tell the story. Continuity refers to action that appears continuous, even though shots were filmed out of sequence. You don't want to confuse the viewer if action does not flow continuously. For example, when your actor moves from left to right in the first shot, he should move in the same direction in the next shot. Similarly, if Elizabeth looks to her right to speak to Ben, she should be looking in the same direction each time she speaks to him.

One technique that directors of photography use to maintain continuity is the 180-degree rule. They imagine the actors on a stage with a line running down the middle of it. The camera or cameras stay on one side to avoid crossing the line. It is easy to forget and take a shot that breaks the screen direction. However, if you keep this 180-degree rule in mind, you maintain continuity of screen direction and eliminate any chance of confusing the viewer.

Another way to maintain continuity is to avoid the "jump cut." This occurs when you film someone, stop the camera, and then start again. For example, your actor is speaking to the camera and he makes a mistake. If you pick up the talk from where he left off, he will appear to jump a bit when you put the shots together in the edit room. One way to avoid a jump cut is to take the pickup shot with a wider angle and then alternate between medium-shot and close-up. The result will resemble a two-camera production.

You can cover up a cut with a reaction shot, also known as a cutaway (CA). If the person speaking makes a mistake, in postproduction you can insert a shot of the audience listening and then cut to the pickup shot. The viewer doesn't see the jump cut. This works not only when the speaker makes a mistake but also when you want to cut out part of a talk.

You can also shoot a single person speaking with two camcorders, placed side by side, each recording onto a drive or tape. One camera shoots the medium-shot, and the other shoots the close-up. You can then cut from camera to camera during postproduction. A similar technique can be employed when filming a dramatic vignette or nearly any kind of action. Spread apart two or more cameras, as if on the edge of a stage, and cut to the appropriate camera shot as needed. This placement lets you adhere to the 180-degree rule.

A cut-in (CI) is yet another device to cover a cut to maintain continuity, and it is used quite frequently in training and marketing videos. The video may start with a wide establishing shot or two, then perhaps some medium shots. Then the narration points to something specific, and the viewer sees a close-up of the action.

For example, an on-camera trainer demonstrates how to operate a piece of equipment. When he says "Press the start button," the viewer sees a close-up of him pressing the button. The CIs are filmed after the master shots. The director maintains continuity by making sure the trainer uses the same hand to press the button and that he or she moves toward the button at the same speed.

Clean entrances and exits are another continuity tool. Start the button-pressing shot an instant before the hand enters to press the button. When a subject will be walking into the scene, start the shot a beat before he or she enters. That way, the viewers have a chance to establish the setting in their own minds before action takes place. Similarly, when someone exits a room, perform the cut just after they have left it. Watch movies and TV to see this technique frequently employed. It allows for a comfortable, smooth flow of action.

Moving the Camera

Zooms are becoming overused. Effective use of zooming in (or "pushing in" in directors' lingo) focuses the viewer's attention on a central portion of the scene. Zooming out, or "pulling out," can be used to show the relative position of people or objects in the frame. It can also be used to reveal the larger context of the action. Zooming just for the sake of zooming only draws attention to the medium, distracts the viewer, and relegates the message to a secondary role. Zooming both in and out makes no sense at all. Move in one direction only, not back and forth.

Similarly with panning, when you pan back and forth, it's like spraying the garden with a water hose. Pans should be deliberate and should show the juxtaposition of elements in the frame, or they should be used to follow the action. When you follow the action, keep plenty of "nose room" in front of your subject as he or she moves. That gives the viewers a feeling they know where the subject is heading. Suspense movies do just the opposite to make the viewer feel uneasy.

Rather than panning or zooming, consider moving the camera through the scene to follow the action. Several steadycam-like devices are on the market that let the camera "fly" and "glide" with a smooth, fluid motion. These are great for POV (point of view) shots where the viewer sees the scene from the main actor's perspective. It's best to hire a trained person to operate a larger camera with one of these steadycam rigs; there could be a liability issue if an untrained camera operator injures her back on your set. However, steadying devices that are designed for the lighter-weight camcorders are available, and almost any camera operator can deploy them with a little practice. Some devices even let you move the camera at ground level for dramatic shots with a wide-angle lens.

A jib or crane lets you move the camera smoothly from a low angle to a very high angle. Mount one on a dolly, and you can combine the vertical elevation with a lateral movement. Add a zoom, and you can create an even more dramatic shot incorporating a combination of these moves. Hire a pro who knows the particular jib or crane, or purchase one and learn it yourself. You'll need a large area to set up the equipment, as well as careful lighting to creatively execute these dynamic shots without the lights getting in the picture.

Some directors of photography try to incorporate movement into every shot they take. Well-planned, dynamic shots create a fluid flow from shot to shot; that is the motion that makes motion pictures come alive. In some cases you may not want every shot to have motion. Viewers' eyes are attracted to movement, and perhaps you want to focus more of their attention on key shots. You will have to decide just how kinetic you want your video production to be.

The objectives of your video, the audience, and the corporate culture dictate whether the video will be edgy with lots of movement or more straightforward where the message is king.

Openings and closings to videos lend themselves to more movement and perhaps to a splash of the avant-garde. Experiment with different movements and camera angles; your viewers will thank you for it.

Art Direction and Set Design

Acquaint the designer with the company's culture, as represented with their brands and their logos. Show them web pages, brochures, and other graphic design products that the corporation has produced. Share with them the production planning results, such as the objectives and the audience.

Then let them employ their own creativity. Be sure you get drawings or a sample layout of the set and the background, and you may need to get these approved by your company's own art department. The designer may also be involved with the set construction and may work with the gaffer or lighting designer. A good designer will create backgrounds that not only complement the foregrounds and the company's brand but will be subtle and distinct enough that the talent and employees on-camera stand out.

With chroma-key green screens or blue screens, you can choose from libraries of stock virtual backgrounds or create your own. A good set designer or art director can help you select stock backgrounds, or they might create them. You'll need to make sure the architectural or interior design style

Figure 13.3 Soft lighting may be achieved by shining a light through a large diffuser. A light peach filter gives the subject a slight tan.

matches the look that your company identifies with. Foreground and background colors need to complement one another whether you are shooting chroma-key or not. Make sure your on-camera talent avoids green if you shoot on a green screen or blue if it is a blue screen.

Figure 13.4 When shooting with a green screen or chroma-key, make sure you have even lighting across the entire screen.

Figure 13.5 Green screen compositing enables the video producer to insert virtually any background behind the actor.

If you are conducting an interview or panel discussion, you will need to decide if the on-camera presenters will be sitting behind a table that covers their legs or simply in chairs. Generally, authority figures, such as judges and ministers, sit or stand behind some piece of furniture. If you have a wide shot of a group of people sitting at a conference table, consider using a tablecloth or just a black cloth hanging from under the front of the table to cover their knees. If your company prefers the more casual look, chairs facing the camera will work just fine.

With a larger-budget corporate video, you may be able to hire an art director. That person supervises the set designer and is responsible for the overall look of the video. In addition to set design, the art director oversees wardrobe, makeup, and other visual elements.

Wardrobe, Makeup, and Hair in the Corporate Video

The corporate culture dictates the daily work attire. You probably already have observed if men wear ties or t-shirts to the office. Your actors or on-camera employees are the ones who represent the company's image, so make sure they dress appropriately. Unless you have a wardrobe budget, if you have scenes with one or two key people on-camera, ask them to bring at least one change of clothes. Close stripes and tight patterns such as herringbone can cause a "moiré" effect that results in waves or vibrations occurring on the TV screen.

While many male corporate execs won't understand the need for makeup, when they see how good their colleagues look on a high-def screen after the expert application of subtle makeup, they should be won over. Video tends to create a high-contrast image, and high-def seems to display those slight blemishes and wrinkles as mountains and valleys. Makeup can create a smooth look to skin by creating consistent color and shading; it is like touching up a photo. According to Peter Utz, author of *Today's Video*, "Makeup is an important element in your talents' metamorphosis from 'average street person' to 'confident professional.'"

Women who are used to applying their own makeup can also benefit from a professional makeup artist. Dark eye shadow and dark rouge should be avoided because of the camera's tendency to add contrast. Glossy lipstick or lip gloss may add too much shine. Subtler tones work better, such as dark grays, light reds, yellows, and browns. Similarly, choose more subtle tones

Figure 13.6 Makeup is frequently overlooked in corporate video production. High-definition cameras reveal wrinkles and blemishes, but a good makeup artist can cover them up.

of green and blue eye shadow. Makeup for television generally should be chosen for a more subtle, low-contrast look than when going out on the town.

Balding men need to tone down that shine, and the makeup artist should stay on the set throughout the duration of the filming. Hot lights cause perspiration that results not only in shiny heads but in shiny cheeks and foreheads as well. Even men blessed with a full head of hair will perspire under lights. People with oily skin have a greater tendency to glisten a bit too much when the set gets warm. If you don't have a budget for makeup, take along some powder to dull the shine and some large napkins to protect the clothing.

Getting back to nonbald men, a slight receding hairline can be filled in a little with some feathery touches of an eyebrow pencil. Just be certain you're not going for an extreme close-up on these men. Nails should be cleaned and manicured if you will be showing close-ups of them in demonstration shots. Be careful when applying makeup to your talent if you are not a makeup artist. Don't use the same applicator with more than one person. Some people have sensitive skin and may be allergic to certain makeup.

Hair can become too shiny, or if it gets out of place, it can draw attention to itself and away from your message. When using chroma-key (either a green screen or blue screen), the edge of the hair should be neat, or you may incur some added postproduction time to touch up some of the green or blue that may peek through. Don't hesitate to tell the talent, even if it is the CEO, that he may want to comb his hair or that there are a couple of stray hairs in his beard. Let the talent excuse themselves to a restroom or a room with a mirror to fix the problem.

You may find that the corporate execs are not as stuffy as you think. In many companies, the video producer is seen as a creative person who could incorporate some of these aesthetic principles into his or her videos to bring excitement to the organization, if not help attract more customers. Some managers and company officers recognize the importance of creativity and allow some latitude as well as financial support to the artistic video producer. Try to add a creative team to your production budgets. An art director, set designer, makeup artist, and graphics designer can work together to boost the overall look of your video and complement the literal image of the company.

SHOOTING AND EDITING FOR THE ENTERPRISE: TECHNICAL CONSIDERATIONS

Introduction

Corporate video departments use a wide range of cameras, from the low-end Flip and Sony bloggie camcorders to the 4 K Red One and Sony Cine Alta. Managers who want to send quick videos to their teams don't need to schedule a shoot with the video department; they can just look into the lenses of their smart phones or pocket cams and record their messages. On the other side of the spectrum, departments that wish to produce a major presentation that will be projected on a large screen can benefit from the cinema-quality resolution of one of the high-end 2 K or 4 K cameras.

Most corporate productions use equipment that falls between these two extremes. While HD broadcast cameras with studio configuration options fulfill the requirements for professional video production, some video producers opt for some of the smaller "prosumer" HD cams that are portable, easy to set up, and produce spectacular imagery.

While corporations still maintain soundproofed studios with broadcast cameras, many organizations take advantage of the portability of smaller cameras to shoot in the field. Add a laptop with software applications for camera switching and audio mixing, and you have a complete compact location production package.

Some producers will use their laptops to edit the footage during their flight home. Postproduction bays in many corporations now include Apple's Final Cut Pro and Adobe's Premiere Pro, in addition to the higher-end Avid and Grass Valley gear. Organizations using video today benefit from Moore's Law: processing speed, memory, and the number of pixels in camera sensors increases exponentially.

Enterprise-Grade Cameras

Your company may have already purchased broadcast-grade cameras, and the video manager and producers should acquaint themselves with the features and capabilities of those imaging tools. If you are in a position to buy cameras for your company, you will want to know what to look for so you can provide the highest-quality video at minimum expenditure.

Some corporations will outfit their remote offices with prosumer camcorders with attached lenses. If you want to produce multicamera shoots, purchase three of the same brand and model to ensure that the colors will match. Miniature camcorders such as Cisco Systems' Flip, Kodak's Zi, and Sony's bloggie are low-cost incentives for executives who want to record spontaneous messages to their teams. They are designed for quick upload to the network or to YouTube. As convenient as they are, these little cams have major limitations. Some don't accept external mikes, so the audio probably will be subpar. And they may not have exposure and white-balance controls, so your department manager may not look as spectacular on them.

On the other hand, pro camcorders for the enterprise have a zillion manual controls so an engineer or technician can create

Figure 14.1 Even if your company does not have a studio, any large space can work, especially those with tall ceilings. Look for empty warehouse space, and bring in your own background or a green screen.

the perfect look. They store video on either flash cards, such as with the Panasonic P2 cards, or optical discs, such as with the Sony XDCAM series. In either case, you may want to bring a laptop and an external hard drive on location to transfer files. That way, you have a backup or you can reuse the cards or discs rather than having to purchase additional media.

The video manager who will be purchasing cameras should consider choosing a model that can be configured for studio production or multicamera location shoots. These features include time code in and out, genlock, remote camera shading controls, and a way to mount a small monitor on the camera for the director or camera assistant. Some cameras can be outfitted with a long viewfinder to make it easier for the camera operator to focus. Pro cameras have menu options to control colors, white levels, black levels, gamma levels, and detail. Gamma controls the midrange (gray) tone, and detail control helps dial down the contrast to reduce the reproduction of blemishes and wrinkles. Connection to external camera control units (CCUs) lets the technical director shade the cameras and match their colors with the other cameras.

Wireless lavaliere microphones, a shotgun mike with a boom pole, and a soft-lighting kit are necessary for professional location production. A pro camera sometimes comes with a slot in the rear for a wireless mike receiver, and some come with an Anton-Bauer mount for the camera battery and wireless receiver mounting. Another feature to look for is the capability to hotswap batteries and flash cards during recording.

Lenses

Generally, you can get sharper images from cameras that use removable lenses, such as Fujinon and Canon lenses. The lenses have more elements than attached lenses, and they usually have ways you can adjust the zoom and focus from remote controls mounted on the tripod handles. As you purchase or rent your second and third cameras, try to use lenses of the same type and brand as on your first camera; it will help to ensure consistency with such parameters as edge focus and contrast. Additionally, cameras with removable lenses let you attach a prime lens, such as a fisheye or super-wide-angle lens for dynamic shots. Make sure you know how to adjust the back focus each time you change lenses. A good investment would be the purchase of a "back-focus chart"—sometimes called a "Siemens star"—to adjust the back focus of removable lenses. It is also used during film or video shoots to help set the focus in special situations.

Pro camera chips usually are either 1/2 inch or 2/3 inch, and the lens must match the size of the chips. The cameras that operate in the 2 K or 4 K range use 35 mm chips and are the same lenses that motion picture cameras use. Even the 1/2-inch and 2/3-inch chip cameras can be adapted to use a motion picture camera lens. You can purchase or rent an adapter so you can use these cinema-quality lenses with almost any camera that works with removable lenses. These cinema lenses have very smooth focus controls.

Figure 14.2 The author provides IMag to project the images of the speakers on large-projection screens. This requires a long lens—in this case a 24X lens. Photo courtesy of Cleo Brown.

Cameras with pro lenses can be outfitted with a matte box and rails to hold the matte box. The matte box holds lens filters, and several filters may be combined together. The matte box also acts as a lens shade, but you can purchase a French flag to shade even more light. A French flag looks like a single barn door, and it mounts on top of the matte box.

French flags, matte boxes, and cinema lens adapters are also available for prosumer cameras with attached lenses. As corporate video crews expand their location filming projects, they want the same lens accessories that studio cameras offer.

Figure 14.3 When filming exteriors or in rooms with windows, camera operators like to have flags to block out light that could distract from their view from the camera's monitor.

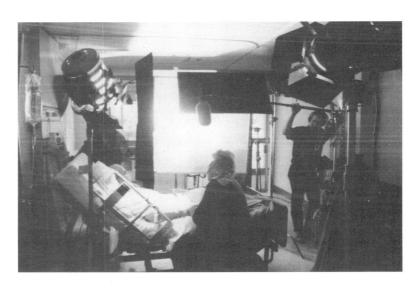

Figure 14.4 Many corporations put on the Ritz at meetings and trade shows, especially when they are rolling out a new product. These offer opportunities to produce spectacular footage that can be repurposed in future video productions.

Camera Support

Tripods should have good fluid heads that can be adjusted for balance each time you change lenses or add accessories. For example, when you place a smaller, prime lens on the camera or when you attach a monitor, the balance changes. A good tripod head allows you to adjust for these different accessories. A cool accessory that cinematographers use is a gear-driven head. It enables very smooth pans and tilts that help give your productions that professional look.

Pedestals are used for camera support in the studio because they can raise the camera up and down. They either have attached wheels or may be easily connected to a dolly. For shooting in offices, consider renting a "doorway dolly" that maneuvers around smaller spaces than a studio. The camera operator sits on a seat on the dolly, and the camera assistant pushes the dolly during the shot. During filming, when you pedestal up or down and dolly in or out as opposed to tilting and zooming, you create a sense of perspective for the viewer and help simulate a 3D space.

Figure 14.5 Nearly any office may be transformed into a studio. The back light illuminates the hair and shoulders. Notice the small light on the desk that acts as a fill light.

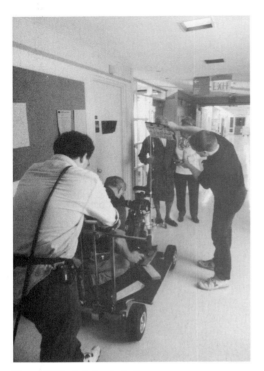

Figure 14.6 A dolly shot gives the viewer more of a sense of three dimensions as opposed to a pan or zoom. Rent a "doorway dolly" so it will fit into an office, and plan on hiring a production assistant to push it.

Steadycam-type systems are great alternatives to dollies, since their movements are nearly unlimited. Usually the video manager hires an outside contractor who provides and operates the steadycam device. Make sure the camera operators provide their own insurance; otherwise, the corporation may expose itself to injury liability. The vest-mount systems require special training; the wrong move with the rig could strain the operator's back. Small camcorders may be mounted on smaller handheld steadying devices. Several handheld systems are on the market, but users should know that they do put a strain on the arms.

Exposure Metering

When lighting for a shoot, consider using a light meter to give you the most accurate exposure. Most HD cameras operate at an ISO of 320–400 and shoot at 1/60 of a second. These parameters will help you to use a light meter and balance the lights for a smooth look without hot spots.

The camera operator who is used to working in film needs to know that, unlike film, video handles highlights well and does

Figure 14.7 We laid tracks for this exterior shot with a dolly. Notice we also set up a bright HMI light to fill shadows, and we connected it to a generator.

Figure 14.8 If your company is rolling out a new product, it may be worth it to hire a grip truck with several different lights and accessories. Discuss with your supervisor well in advance a strategy to propose a budget for a gaffer and even a whole crew. Rails to dolly the camera, flags, scrims, and reflectors can give your video that dazzling look that is sure to impress management.

not do as good a job with the darker areas of a scene. Therefore, the gaffer or lighting person should set exposure to the highlights first and then turn on a fill light to be able to show detail in the lowlights. A good program monitor that is properly adjusted will be the final look at the lighting in the scene.

The cameras should output to a waveform monitor and a vectorscope. These ensure that the lighting is balanced and that the colors coming from each camera are accurate. In studio control rooms, they may be hardware monitors, but they are also available as tools within software applications. Try to budget for a technical director to operate the waveform monitor and vectorscope. Using a vectorscope, the technician may want to make minor internal adjustments to each camera to balance the colors among them. Similarly, he or she will use the waveform monitor while adjusting the camera's white and black levels. This is called "shading" the cameras.

2 K and 4 K Cameras

If you will be shooting commercials or videos to be projected on a large screen, consider renting or purchasing one of the cameras with the larger 35 mm sensors that provide up to 4,000-pixel resolution. The Red One and Sony Cine Alta are two systems that use these large camera chips together with lenses designed for 35 mm motion picture cameras. These cameras usually need a camera assistant to finely adjust focus, and they require special hard drives for storage.

Figure 14.9 The Sony Cine Alta records in 4 K, which is the resolution of 35 mm motion picture film. You can mount 35 mm cinema lenses to this video camera, and it records onto HDCAM videotape or to a hard drive.

A lower-cost option for capturing video on a 35 mm sensor is using one of the DSLR cameras that provide HD recording. These cameras bridge the gap between image capture with a still camera and HD video production. Run times are limited with these DSLR cameras, partly due to card sizes and heat dissipation. Motion picture lenses may be adapted to work with some of these DSLR cameras. Camera support rigs are available to mount a monitor and other accessories.

One of the advantages of using these large-format cameras is that you can adjust their irises to create a very narrow depth-of-field. This enables the camera operator to create a scene to focus the viewers' attention to the foreground subject. When filming an interview, you can force the background to be out of focus. This is called "bokeh" in the industry, and when used creatively, it helps simulate a 3D effect in a 2D space.

Mobile Studios

An alternative to a fixed shooting studio is a portable studio, rack-mounted and in flypack cases. You may purchase a rack with a camera switcher, monitors, and accessories and build it yourself. Alternately, you may purchase a turnkey system with equipment already installed in the rack. The turnkey system providers will add the flypack, retractable wheels, and an airline-approved case for travel. Systems may be customized with such equipment as a character generator, hard drive recorder, audio mixer, and computer.

You can attach your own cameras to the system and, through an intercom, direct the camera operators using multiple monitors in the rack to view the shots from each camera. In some cases you can eliminate the camera operators by mounting the cameras on remote-controlled pan-tilt supports and using remote zoom controls. The director can sit at the switcher console and control three cameras without the need for camera operators. The systems require the technician or director to set up the cameras, run cables to each camera, and shade the cameras so they all output the same levels. Generally, one camera is locked down for the master shot, and the other two cameras may be used for close-ups, cut-ins, and cutaways.

Teleprompters

Teleprompters display the script for the talent to read. The text is displayed onto a clear glass panel that may be placed in front of the camera lens. Prior to filming, the text is entered into a computer that generates the display. The script is displayed as very large, scrolling text. A technician controls the speed of the scroll of the text.

Executives and nonprofessional talent who have never used a teleprompter should practice with one before the filming day. Otherwise, the delivery could come across as if someone is reading to the audience rather than talking to them. The teleprompter operator controls the speed of the text scroll to match the speed of the speaker, and the operator and speaker can practice a run-through prior to filming. The director can coach the exec to create some pauses and to emphasize certain words. Narrators sometimes use slash marks to denote pauses and underlines to emphasize words. These same symbols may be added to the teleprompter display.

Figure 14.10 The U.S. House of Representatives has a Mobile Studios portable system that controls three cameras. The director may sit in the hallway, and system options include robotic controls for the cameras. Photo courtesy of Mobile Studios, Inc.

Figure 14.11 A teleprompter connects to the camera (1) and uses a hood over the lens (2) to reflect an image of the script from a display (3). The actor appears to be looking at the camera lens, but he is really looking at an image of the script in a reflective glass (4).

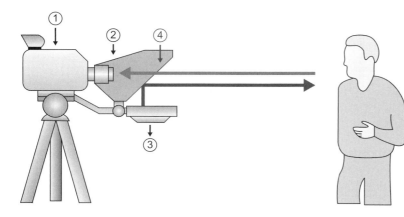

Figure 14.12 If the budget won't allow for a teleprompter, type cue cards and hold them above the camera. Notice that the print is large and each cue card is small enough so the host won't have to turn to look at a wide card.

Audio and Lighting Considerations for the Enterprise

The video manager needs to know that the FCC has mandated that as of June 2010 wireless microphones that operate in the 700 MHz frequency spectrum may not be used. Manufacturers stopped selling systems operating at that band, but your video department may still have them in inventory. As part of the digital television switchover in 2009, the 700 MHz spectrum is reserved for emergency communications and 4G wireless devices. The exact frequencies affected are between 698 and 806 MHz.

If you need to replace your system, you probably will be able to keep the clip-on (lavaliere) microphones and purchase only new transmitters and receivers. A wired clip-on mike system is a good backup for when Murphy's Law enacts interference onto the wireless system.

The video department should also have at least one shotgun microphone. It may be mounted on a boom stand, just above the head of the on-camera presenter for a presentation where the talent is not walking. This can be an alternative to using a clip-on mike, and some sound techs like to use both. One mike gets recorded onto Channel 1 and the other onto Channel 2. In post, the editor can choose audio from either mike or both.

In the case of action, the shotgun mike may be held at the end of a "fishpole" boom by an audio technician. When filming outside, a windscreen should be used on both the clip-on and shotgun mikes. For better wind resistance with shotgun mikes, a wind muff is used to cover the windscreen. A wind muff is made of acoustically transparent fur (some audio technicians call it a "dead cat").

Moving onto lighting, if you are filming at an office building, you want to be careful not to trip the circuit breakers with your hot lights. Either hire an electrician to tap directly into the circuit box, or run long extension cords down hallways to divide the power. Be careful never to place a hot light near a sprinkler head; you could cause a flood if the system gets activated.

For lighting equipment that is both cool and draws minimal power, consider LED lights with diffusion filtration. Most LED systems are daylight balanced. Some systems allow you to dial in the color you need, such as 3,200 degrees Kelvin. With others, you will need to use colored gels to match indoor lighting color. Fluorescent systems are also popular because they can be easily configured as soft-lighting instruments.

Figure 14.13 Slating each shot with a clapboard helps you organize all your takes. While you don't need an actual clapboard if you are recording sound on your camera, when you film with a DSLR camera, you'll probably record audio on an external digital audio recorder. Filming and hearing that clap helps the editor keep the audio and video in sync.

Postproduction for the Enterprise

Video for the enterprise needs to be compressed before it can be transmitted over the company's network. Compression usually means compromising the bandwidth consumed by the audio and video, and managers don't want to compromise the quality of video for customer and employee viewing. They need to obtain the maximum bandwidth they can get, and sometimes they may need to negotiate with the IT team or management to fulfill that need.

The IT professionals need to conserve bandwidth, and they know that video may be compressed and still be viewable. While some IT folks may think that webcam quality is acceptable,

Figure 14.14 An HMI light with a diffuser is balanced to outdoor light and most fluorescent lighting. Sometimes a single light can complement office fluorescents.

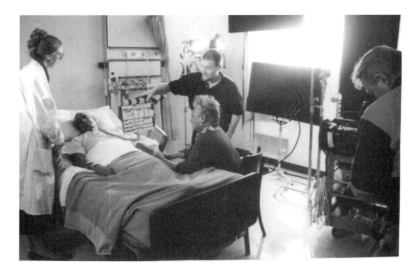

Figure 14.15 Filming a patient education video required working in tight quarters. In addition to video lights, we used window light, but we added flags to have better control.

employees expect TV-quality video. The video manager may need to lobby management for optimal resolution and frame rate or negotiate with IT to achieve a reasonable compromise.

Throughout his or her tenure at the organization, the video manager will be collaborating with colleagues in several

Figure 14.16 Many corporate studios have a ceiling light grid, and sometimes those lights create harsh shadows. We add floor-standing soft lights and reflectors to create a softer look.

Figure 14.17 A direct to edit (DTE) video card recorder enables you to record from a camera to CF cards rather than tape. You may record with QuickTime or another format to be ready to edit.

Figure 14.18 Sony's ELC Automation system consists of a suite of software, computers, operations terminals, and control panels optimized for the specific needs of a live broadcast environment.

departments, such as public relations, communications, and IT. Knowing a little about compression, the video professional can make wise decisions that minimize bandwidth and provide a realistic viewing experience for customers and employees. This knowledge will help forge a collaborative relationship with IT that could mature as technology advances.

Compression

First, never tell an IT professional that you want to push uncompressed HD through the network. One hour of uncompressed HD footage can consume as much as 500GB of storage. Using an appropriate compression scheme, video bandwidth requirements can be reduced significantly, while preserving the viewing experience. With optimal compression, few users will notice any degradation in the audio or video. Approaching compression without forethought could result in reduced quality that distracts the viewer from the content.

One procedure for appropriate compression is called "chroma subsampling." The chrominance, or color portion of the signal, receives a high degree of compression, while the luminance component is minimally compressed. Humans process luminance (the black and white component) with more precision than the chrominance. We don't notice subtle changes in the position and motion of color of images as much as we do with the picture in general. So if you compress the chroma at a higher level than the luma portion of the signal, you achieve lower-bandwidth requirements with no perceptible loss of quality.

Feature films or corporate videos shot and edited with high-end equipment usually process HD video at 4:4:4. This means that the chroma gets the same minimal compression as the luma. Broadcast television and corporate video can save bandwidth by compressing at 4:2:2, where the luma is sampled four times, while the chroma gets sampled only two times. (Chroma has two components; that's where the extra numeral "2" comes from.) Standard-definition DV recording requires much less bandwidth because it uses a 4:0:0 subsampling. The chroma does not get sampled on every scan line but on every other scan line. This is an acceptable level of subsampling and could be considered if IT has only minimal bandwidth to offer the video department.

Storage Solutions

Even with compression, you will need to use an external storage system to accommodate your files. At 10:1 compression, 50 hours of field footage consumes about 2 TB of hard drive space. Add graphics and effects renders, and you start to consume some substantial space.

One solution is to purchase a hardware-based file-sharing system such as the Xsan, developed by Apple. Designed for use by the enterprise, video departments at several corporations use this system. An enterprise-shared disk file system that encourages collaborative postproduction, it allows several computers to read and write to the same storage volume at the same time. Xsan supports large files and file systems and multiple-mounted file systems. It has a meta-data controller failover for fault tolerance, and it may be configured to support multiple operating systems.

Another storage system involves using tape. Linear tape open (LTO) is a magnetic tape storage system that uses open standards. Popular for backups in larger computer systems, each tape cartridge can store up to 1.5 TB of uncompressed data. The uncompressed data transfer rate is a speedy 140 MB/s.

Why use tape instead of a disk? When data is written to the tape, it is verified by reading back the data using the read heads that are positioned just behind the write heads. This allows the drive to write a second copy of any data that fail to verify without the help of the host system. Some large corporate video departments use this backup system.

Redundant Array of Independent Disks

Redundant array of independent disks (RAIDs) storage systems are very common in corporate video editing suites. They consist of several drives bundled together with redundancy to help find data quickly, and they serve as instant backups in case a drive fails. Several members of the production team can collaborate on projects, and RAIDS help manage data-intensive workflows.

RAID-0 (zero) is the lowest-cost RAID system, and it is nothing more than a device for storing data on two or more drives. While RAID-0 speeds up editing by writing to the drives faster, there is no security if a drive fails. RAID-1 adds redundancy. A second disk mirrors the other and has all the same data. In the event of a drive failure, the editor still has his or her work on the other drive. RAID-2 systems are not currently used because that system only checked for errors.

RAID-3 and RAID-4 systems use striped disks with dedicated parity. They consist of three or more disks to protect against loss. Two disks hold data, while the third stores parity information. RAID-5 is popular in video postproduction. The system distributes the parity information among blocks across multiple disks. Three or more disks are required, and the system will still operate if one drive does not work. That drive needs to be replaced, but work may continue. If you don't replace the failed drive before a second drive fails, you will lose data.

RAID-50 systems are found in larger corporations that require high bandwidth. Sometimes called RAID 5 + 0, they use "nested RAID levels" that consist of RAID-0 arrays configured together using RAID-5 parity distribution. RAID-0 systems are faster than RAID-5, but they lack data backup. A RAID 50 combines the best of the RAID-0 and RAID-5 attributes.

When purchasing a RAID system, consult with the provider of your video editing platform for requirements, recommendations, or suggestions. Avid platforms need four arrays to work with uncompressed HD streams, while Apple Final Cut users may use a system such as the Xserve RAID. More advanced RAID systems include fiber channel ports for data transport between the storage unit and the host computers. Some systems include spare disks that automatically activate in case of a drive failure. Others will notify the user by e-mail of a faulty drive. To learn more about RAIDs, go to http://en.wikipedia.org/wiki/RAID.

Hardware Acceleration

As you add apps and plug-ins to your system, your computer's resources may become taxed. To resolve this, manufacturers have created hardware acceleration boards that add processing power to your computer. While some manufacturers such as Avid and Grass Valley have their own proprietary hardware, other editing systems can benefit from these special I/O (input/output) boards. AJA Video Systems and Blackmagic Design are two manufacturers that provide these boards designed to work with either Adobe Premiere Pro or Sony Vegas Pro on Windows PCs, or for Final Cut Pro on Mac computers.

These boards include a variety of inputs and outputs so you can connect several devices at once. They handle format conversions, control ingest and capture, and provide multiple-monitor outputs. Rather than burden the computer with rendering effects and graphics, the boards and their accompanying software speed up the editing process with preprogrammed effects.

With Adobe Premiere® Pro CS5 and NVIDIA® Quadro® graphics solutions, editing time can be drastically reduced. At the heart of Premiere Pro CS5 is the Adobe Mercury Playback Engine, which was built using the NVIDIA® CUDA™ parallel processing architecture, so Quadro GPUs deliver real-time previewing and editing of native, high-resolution footage, including multiple layers of RED 4 K video.

High-Definition Editing Formats

High-definition video is available in several formats and recording media. Editing software offers a variety of settings, and video managers need to work together with the editors to jointly decide what works best for their individual companies. Some organizations have a large enough staff to include an engineer or a technical director who is responsible for making sure the shooters and the editors are working in formats that are compatible with one another. Even so, the video manager is wise to learn some of the technology of HD editing. For example, some camera formats such as AVCHD are ideal for acquisition but are not well suited for editing and postproduction.

Video may come to the postproduction suite as 720p (720 lines with progressive scanning), 1080i (1080 lines interlace scanning), or 1080p (progressive scanning). It may be shot on tape, such as HDV, HDCAM, or DVCPRO HD; stored on an optical disc such as Sony XDCAM; or be on a flash card. Flash card formats include the Panasonic P2, a CF (compact flash) card, or a smaller SD or SDHC card. Frequently, the camera operator will load video from flash cards to an external hard drive and provide the hard drive to the editor.

I/O connectors may be FireWire, HDMI, or SDI (serial digital interface). SDI comes as a group of three BNC connectors: Y, Cb, and Cr. Y is the luminance or the black and white element of the signal. Cb is the "color difference," which is represented as the color blue minus the luminance (B−Y). Cr is the red minus the luminance (R−Y). Color digital video is expressed as "YCbCr." Some engineers use the term "YUV," which is the analog version of YCbCr.

Bit depth or color depth describes the number of different colors that may be displayed at one time. The more colors there are, the more lifelike the reproduction. However, there are limits to what the human eye can discern. In an 8-bit color depth, 256 distinct colors are recorded and displayed. This may be the recording system of a lower-end HD camcorder. A 12-bit color depth is what mobile devices usually display: 4,096 colors. In a 24-bit color system, 16.7 million colors are displayed, sometimes referred to as "millions of colors." HDMI can support color depths as high as 48-bit, or 281.5 trillion colors, and some graphic cards go all the way to 64 bits.

HD may record at 30 frames per second (30 fps) or 24 fps. The latter frame rate is available on many camcorders, and it is used primarily when video is going to be transferred to film for movie production. Some videographers like the slightly flickering "film look," and they tone down the contrast and increase the color saturation to further achieve this look. If your camera operator has shot the video at 24 fps, most editing software can convert it to 30 fps for editing.

Electronic Filters—Softening the Skin

Sometimes HD shows too much detail, such as skin imperfections. Digital filter software can help remove some of the detail while preserving the image. Many of the same effects that the camera operator can achieve with glass filters may be obtained in the post suite with digital filter software, sometimes called "virtual filters."

Diffusion filters come in a variety of styles. Your editing software will likely come with some built-in filters as a starting point. Tiffen, one of the lens filter manufacturers, offers Dfx filter software that simulates many of the company's glass filters. Their ProMist® and Black Diffusion FX® filters can virtually take years off the face of an aging executive. Several variations of each filter give the postproduction editor options in toning down the HD reproduction of skin tones. JoesFilters.com is another company that offers digital filters for editing software. Users may adjust the white and black levels and the levels of blur and opacity.

Compositing and Effects

While the video manager prefers to produce videos that tell a story, management frequently thinks all they want is a talking head and PowerPoint graphics. Using compositing tools such as a green screen helps the video program to be more pleasing to the eye, and the messages may be more effectively transmitted. Bold graphics behind an on-camera narrator can illustrate the discussion. Particular keywords or phrases can be animated. Multiple layers of text and graphics can move in and out of attractive backgrounds.

An interview sequence can be enlivened by placing the subjects over an appropriate background. For example, one of the Google Heroes projects uses Google Earth to help track elephants in Kenya. The company posted a video on YouTube that included an interview with the founder of Save the Elephants. The camera operator shot the interview in front of a green screen, and the producer used stock footage of elephants traversing the African terrain. That stock video clip became the virtual background, as if the interviewee were filmed in Africa rather than in the studio. When working with virtual backgrounds, be careful to use lighting for your subject that matches that of the background. For example, if the light in your virtual background is casting shadows to the right, set up your studio lights to cast shadows in the same direction.

Color compositing, also known as "chroma-keying," is usually done in front of a green or blue screen or wall. Green is popular because digital video cameras are more sensitive to the color green and therefore can produce a composite with minimal video noise. Blue is sometimes used because its color is the farthest from skin tones. Blue screens are needed, rather than green, if the subject is plants or anything that is green. On-camera talent should not wear anything green when shooting in front of a green screen (or not wear blue if it is a blue screen). If your talent has green eyes, consider having a blue screen available as a backup.

Most video editing software includes tools for replacing the green background with a still image or a motion image. The editor may need to make some adjustments in the chroma and brightness levels of the subject to complete the effect. Virtual set software is available to simulate movement of the background that will match the camera dolly's movement. That way, the viewer sees the camera move as well as complementary motion in the background.

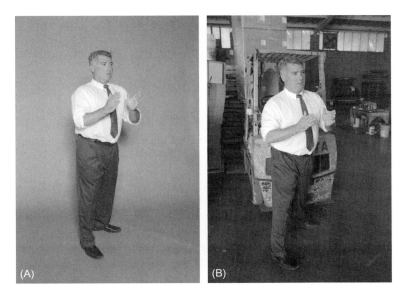

(A)   (B)

Figure 14.19 The green screen technique (also known as chroma-key) replaces the background with the background of your choice. In this case, our on-camera host is filmed in the studio against a green background. In postproduction, a shot of the forklift in a factory is inserted to make it look like the host is in the factory.

Organizations love to display charts, tables, and graphs, and you can make them come alive with special effects software. The editor can divide a chart into layers to gradually reveal different elements. Using motion and color, the editor can focus the viewer's attention and help present the material in a manner that is both pleasing to the eye and easily understood. Commercial software applications that let you produce motion graphics and layering include Adobe After Effects, Apple Shake and Motion, Boris FX, and Sony Vegas Pro.

Multiple-Camera Editing

As video production moves out of the studio and onto location, video producers need to have a way to switch among cameras to achieve the look of multiple camera angles. While systems such as the Mobile Studios portable switching system can enable the director to achieve a finished video with three camera angles, some producers choose to shoot all the footage on camcorders and perform the "switching" in post.

Avid, Canopus, Adobe Premiere Pro, Sony Vegas Pro, and Apple Final Cut Pro all offer tools for multiple camera editing. Each camera's footage is synchronized on the timeline. Generally, only one source audio is left on. The trick to synching all three cameras is to use an external time code generator or to have one camera act as the master time code, while the others synch to it physically with cables or with a wireless time code generator. However, if your cameras don't have external time code inputs, you can use the audio spike from a clapboard or the flash from a still camera to line up the three cameras at the beginning.

2 K and 4 K Editing

For video productions that will be displayed on a large screen, or just to create a higher-resolution image than HD's measly 1,080 lines, camera recording systems are available to record video with as much as 4,000 lines of resolution. The Red One camera and the Sony Cine Alta are two of the digital cinematography tools that Hollywood has embraced.

The Red Drive is an external hard drive array set to the RAID 0 configuration. The drive has FireWire 800, FireWire 400, and USB 2.0 ports, and it may be directly connected to a computer via any of those interfaces. It appears as a standard external hard drive, and files containing the footage may be used the same as with any other computer files.

Red offers compact flash drives (CF) for 2 K and 4 K resolutions, but the run times are limited with CF cards. The company also makes a RAM solid-state storage disk that provides longer run times with solid-state memory rather than a hard drive. RedCode Raw is the company's proprietary audio/video format with the file extension .R3D. QuickTime may be used to open the files, or the R3D files may be processed by software that natively supports the RedCode codec.

Whether you are producing 4 K or just want that good old trusty 1,080 or 720 HD, collaboration is the key to organizational media production and editing. Collaboration takes place when negotiating bandwidth with the IT department. It involves sharing image and sound files with marketing or working as part of the production crew. Shooters and editors in the enterprise need to share files and resources, and they need to make sure their partners have ready access to their assets. File storage systems are one of the collaborative tools for corporate video producers.

The video manager needs to stay current with camera and editing technology. Developments in image processing take place at breakneck speed. The video hardware and software manufacturers compete with one another for your business. Similar to the posture your corporation takes when seeking a larger share of their customer market base, video manufacturers engage in research and development to provide you with products that are faster, cheaper, and smaller. Unlike your corporation that may lose market share to a competitor, when video manufacturers compete, *you* win.

CORPORATE VIDEO TRAINING

Introduction

While video production budgets for sales support seem to be easier to justify than those for training, video has proven itself through the years to be a cost-effective and motivating medium for employee education. Rather than hiring a consultant to speak to staff in a classroom, that same consultant's message can be delivered to each employee's desktop display or mobile device in a consistent manner and as frequently as needed. On-the-job training, whether it is learning industrial techniques, developing supervisory skills, or showing a customer how to use software, gets a boost from motion, color, and sound. Learners may view the materials at their own pace, and interactivity can be built into the video programs so the viewers get regular feedback and management has an evaluation mechanism.

Cost Justification for Training Video

A thousand-dollar consultant may be able to speak to a group of only 50 employees at a time. That translates to $20 per employee. But what if you film the consultant and post it to a server that makes it accessible to the whole enterprise of 5,000 employees? Add about $1,000 for the filming, and that $2,000 investment now costs only $2.50 per employee. You have just saved the company $87,000 with a single video production. Do one of these a month, and in a year you have saved your corporation over a million dollars—enough for an annual video department budget!

This is a simplification of a more involved process of developing instructional programs and budgets. However, it demonstrates that the dollars spent on training video production can represent a significant payback for the enterprise—possibly even a quick return on investment (ROI). Even if video productions don't generate revenue, they save costs in employee training and development. For example, video can improve the efficiency of supervisors who may be performing one-on-one training. Rather than taking a new worker out of the field each time one comes on board, the video manager can arrange for the supervisor to produce a video demonstrating a procedure. Each new employee can view that one-time presentation, even repeatedly, and the supervisor can focus on his or her core functions.

Another way that video saves staff hours is that each employee can view individual chapters or segments of a video that are specific to his or her needs. In essence, the employee may compress time by viewing only the material that is relevant to fulfilling the objectives. An employee won't have to sit through an hour-long lecture if he or she needs only a nugget of information from it. With an indexed video, the viewer jumps to the portions that are relevant to him or her. Videos could be produced in a modular form so the viewer could easily find the segments that are organized by chapter or time code number. The only other way to get this individualized instruction would be if the employee and instructor could meet one-to-one.

In some cases video can compress time when the scriptwriter creates a video that is shorter than a classroom lecture. A professional instructional designer can review a lecture, extract the most relevant material, and condense it to a shorter video production. In *Training with Video*, author Steve Cartwright reported, "At the Pima County Sheriff's Department in Tucson, AZ, where video is used as a training delivery method, what once took an hour of instruction is now delivered in a 20-minute tape." Cartwright adds, "Not only does the use of video in training save student time, it also saves instructor time. No longer tied up in the classroom, instructors can devote more time to program development. This translates to more information being delivered to the student."

Another corporate cost saver is that employees sometimes view training videos from home after scheduled work hours or between assignments. When they feel motivated to learn, they will learn more. This individualized education is an opportunity for them to get training at their own time and pace, frequently without the distractions of coworkers. Some companies, especially those with union staffs, may prohibit this kind of off-the-clock learning, but it is an option that is increasingly common, especially with firms that allow employees to telecommute. It also adds to the efficiency of companies with staffs on the job 24/7.

Video as a Consistent and Repeatable Training Medium

Those swing shift and graveyard shift workers can receive the same information as their colleagues working during the day. Video creates a consistent message that can be designed to be engaging and evaluated to be accurate. Management need not worry that an instructor might forget something or that his or her delivery may be less than ideal on a particular day. Videos can be scripted and produced with the scrutiny necessary to make certain that each viewer gets the message as originally intended.

Consistency is important to management, especially when the company's reputation is on the line. A video message can be designed to use repetition and other memory devices to train employees to represent their companies with the terminology and philosophy that the firm so carefully crafts.

With a video production and distribution system in place, the company CEO can speak with all of the employees worldwide. Some firms set up a system for live transmission of executive messages, either by satellite or Internet protocol. At some companies, the CEO takes along a Flip camera on trips and quickly uploads the video to YouTube. This is the case with Cisco Systems' John Chambers speaking from outside the Financial Analyst Conference in December 2009. Executive messages to the staff, introductions of new products, and industry news are more justifications for development of a video production budget for employee training.

The organization's philosophy and attitudes are best delivered to employees directly by an executive or a manager rather than left to interpretation by an instructor. The only ways for executives at major corporations to speak with large numbers of employees are through personal visits, webcasts, or video messages.

Video as an Engaging and Exciting Medium

The instructor at the whiteboard or even with PowerPoint slides can get bogged down with technical formulas and financial analyses. At this point, employees, especially new hires, become confused and frustrated, if not overwhelmed. However, this detail can be delivered with carefully designed graphics and animation as part of a video production. The video manager or producer could bring together an instructional developer and a graphic designer to create eye-catching imagery that is not only attractive but conveys the concepts. As part of the scriptwriting process, the video producer and her team collaborate with the content specialist, the instructional developer, and a graphic designer to create visual representations of the material.

Employees are treated to "eye candy" when they view television news and movies, and they expect that same level of stimulation in corporate videos. While informational video producers need not indulge the sweet teeth of their viewers, they can excite the senses with visual appeal and at the same time nourish their minds with substantial data. According to Cartwright, "Color and visuals can accelerate learning by 78 percent and improve and increase comprehension by 70 percent." Furthermore, Cartwright writes, "They can increase recognition and perception and reduce errors. Color and visuals affect motivation and participation."

Along with the visual appeal of video is the opportunity for emotional connection. For a safety video that my company produced for a Kaiser Permanente hospital, we started a scene with a warehouse worker climbing shelves to get a box off a top shelf. He falls, injures his back, and the boxes fall on top of him. Of course, we used directing tricks to simulate the fall, and the boxes were empty. However, the workers viewing the video got the message right away. They empathized with the injured employee. The scene affected the viewer not only on a cognitive level but on an emotional level as well. Who wants to suffer an injury on the job? The next scene shows a different worker getting an appropriate ladder to retrieve the box, but it is probably not even necessary to show the correct way or have the voice-over narrator state the appropriate procedure. The viewers get it; television works in this case as a dramatic medium.

Supervisor training also can benefit from a dramatic reenactment of a conversation between a supervisor and an employee. A common management concern is that when technicians are promoted to supervisors, they have a hard time motivating or disciplining their former colleagues. In this case, the video department can produce a simple video demonstrating the appropriate conversation between the supervisor and employee.

For example, Joe has been late completing assignments, and his supervisor, Samantha, needs to see improvement or she may have to fire him. The video could use professional actors, or the producer could ask a supervisor to simply play herself and hire one actor to play the role of Joe. Perhaps the producer could cast both roles to be played by the employees themselves. The producer would need to audition the nonprofessional

Figures 15.1, 15.2, and 15.3 When directing a falling sequence for a safety video, we edited together three different shots to give the illusion that our actor had actually fallen. In the second shot, our crew merely threw empty boxes down. In the final shot, we positioned the actor on the floor and asked him to jerk his body. The result was a flow of action that leads the viewer to believe the employee had fallen because he used a chair instead of a ladder.

talent to make sure they can perform these roles. In this case, since the video scene is short and the roles are familiar to them, casting an employee, at least for the role of supervisor, is a likely possibility.

Role modeling, safety demonstrations, documentation of processes—all of these are examples of simple but effective ways that video can facilitate employee training in the enterprise. The vicarious experience for the viewer and the realism of video are unmatched by any other medium. Dramatizations, when professionally produced, can have a lasting impact on the viewer and can help the employee to learn skills and retain important information.

Call Center Training

In addition to dramatizing an interaction between supervisor and employee, video can teach basic skills for employees in a variety of positions in the company. Several years ago, my company produced call center training videos for Clorox. In one, we used employees, who played themselves, to stage mock phone conversations between consumers and call center employees. The objective of this video was for the call center personnel to properly assist callers who may be at risk of injuring themselves by inappropriately using Clorox bleach products.

We wrote a script, and during filming, we displayed it on the employee's monitor as she pretended to be speaking to the caller. We used the refrigerator in the employee break room as our simulated home kitchen background, as another employee played the role of the customer calling the center. The caller is anxious because after several hours of using bleach without gloves, her hands have turned red. Had we used professional actors, we might not have had as much giggling as we did on the set, but we shot enough takes to finish the scenes. The training manager served as our on-camera host; he set up each scene and appeared after them to explain proper procedures. The result was that new employees in the call center have a consistently accurate method of learning the procedure, and existing employees can refer to the short video whenever they want.

Another call center video we produced was on the operation of the Brita water faucet filter. (Clorox bought the Brita company because they wanted to compete with the Pur faucet filter.) Since few households use a faucet filter, and the customers have to install the filter themselves, Clorox anticipated a large volume of calls after the initial marketing campaign. Together with the content expert, we wrote a script, filmed the procedure at the Clorox lab, and recorded a voice-over narration. We incorporated simple 2D graphics to demonstrate the flow of water through the filter. The video showed the installation, operation, and filter replacement procedures. Call center staff viewed the video before receiving any calls, and they had to try out the faucet filters themselves. The instructions were accurate and consistent, and the video became the standard visual representation of the procedure for installing and replacing the faucet filter.

In addition to basic skills such as call center protocol, the consistency of video is a boon to learning telephone sales techniques and clerical procedures. Interactive video takes the tedium out of teaching software operations over and over to new employees. The ability to teach step-by-step procedures helps training in equipment operation techniques, work flow procedures, and other skills.

Safety Training

Rather than a planned program with forethought and instructional design, safety training can be a knee-jerk reaction at some companies. An accident occurs, and suddenly the safety team jumps into action. Teams frequently are composed of middle managers gathered together from several different departments. A copywriter is employed to write a manual, and the video department is called to produce a video. This is an opportunity for the video group to demonstrate not only their high production values but also the effectiveness of the video in reducing accidents. Make sure you have a means to measure the accident rate, or whatever the problem is, prior to the video. For example, you could analyze data that indicate there was an average of one incident per month during the past 12 months. Then compare the results after employees have viewed the finished production. This data on accident reduction could be translated into dollars that could help you budget the expansion of your video department.

When I was the staff media specialist at Mills Memorial Hospital in California, I was asked to produce a safety video to mitigate three problems: employees were not following correct procedures for handling electrical equipment, the responses to a fire or fire drill were not consistent from floor to floor, and there had been little training to coordinate a response to a natural disaster such as an earthquake. The disaster I encountered when I started research for the script was that I could not find a content expert within the organization. The director of the security department had been given the task of training employees in safety procedures, but the hospital had not put together a concise training program for employee safety.

Fortunately, the county had a disaster plan that included procedures for hospitals to follow. The city's fire department helped me by providing a procedure manual for hospital fire prevention and what to do in case of a fire. And some of the equipment manufacturers had electrical safety precautions written as part of the user manuals.

After I wrote a treatment, I submitted it for approval to both the security manager and my manager. Even though they quickly signed off on the script, I wanted to make sure no one would request changes after the video was completed. I auditioned on-camera hosts on video and showed the talent of my choice to my manager for approval. We wanted just the right look to represent our hospital. I offered to show dailies of each day's raw footage to my manager, but he didn't have time to view them.

The video starts with on-location scenes as the narrator, in voice-over, asks three questions that represent the three areas covered in the video: "The fire alarm bell is going off. Do you know what to do? You have to plug in this piece of equipment, but the plug is loose. Now what do you do? The building is shaking, and it feels like an earthquake. How do you protect your patients and yourself?" Then each of the three objectives is addressed with a combination of documentary footage and on-camera presentations. In some cases, the host walks into the scene to explain the procedures that the employees should follow. Next, the viewer sees those procedures enacted (by nonprofessional actors). The video concludes with a review of the three problems and each associated solution. The video's overall design was an attention-getting introduction that quickly stated each of the three problems; the body of the video divided into three segments, each with a similar problem-solution format; and the conclusion with a recap showing shots from the three scenes. We applied the adult learning theory that people remember information in groups of three. We used the technique of repetition: We told them what they were about to see, we showed it to them, and then we repeated it at the end. Since safety is such an important topic, this technique of repetition helps to ensure that the employees learn these vital procedures.

Product Training for Retail Customers

Point of purchase (POP) videos are a sure hit with customers in retail fashion stores. Data projectors enable the stores to enlarge the image for maximum impact and draw in even more customers. Some stores on fashionable streets, such as Rodeo Drive in Beverly Hills, run large-image projections all night long for passersby to drink in the excitement. While designed as sales pieces, POP videos also provide training on new product arrivals for retail clerks and store managers.

The latest television commercials are common content for POP displays, since they grab the attention of shoppers by showing images that are familiar. Stores that don't produce TV commercials can still benefit from product videos shot by the company's in-house video unit or by a video production contractor. Since customers usually are in the stores already, these videos can be considered customer-training videos. Shoppers get to see how certain merchandise is paired with accessories. They learn the latest fashion styles and see how an interior designer arranges household items.

Fast-moving imagery and fun scenarios serve as eye candy for the casual observer with a short attention span. In malls, retail stores with video displays have the advantage of motion and rapidly changing images, rather than static window displays. However, for the customer in a store, some companies use a smaller interactive display. This is a more intimate way to educate the customer. They can see how different colors of paint or fabric might look together in a room, or women can see how a new brand of makeup or eyeliner should be applied.

Steve Madden retail locations feature multiple video displays in small stores throughout the country. The company's signature platform shoe helped them partner with such rock musicians as Jesse James to perform in their commercials and at a store opening. The company produced a video of the excitement surrounding a performance and displays clips in their stores. Not only are customers drawn into the stores, but they learn about the new shoe styles as well as other apparel the company sells.

New Employee Orientation

Fortunately, few companies today force new hires to sit through a boring video about employee benefits or hear the CEO drone on about the history of the company. Most employee orientation videos today are designed to give the newcomer a taste of the corporate culture in an engaging and pleasant manner. Google produced *Life at Google*, a series of short videos designed to show the new employees some spectacular benefits at the Googleplex. A variety of staff are shown in a fast-paced montage welcoming the new employee, and they present a glimpse of the corporate culture the new hire will be joining. In an orientation video I produced for World Savings, we incorporated news headlines and a recent video clip of the CEO speaking before Congress about the controversy surrounding the banking industry.

Employee orientation videos set the stage for the new hire to feel welcomed by his new employer. The objective is to help the employee to find his or her place within the enterprise and to maintain the high level of enthusiasm they had during the hiring process. Employees usually want to get to work soon, so a short video with few details works best.

At Mills Hospital, I produced an orientation video that was designed to give the viewer a virtual tour of the facility and see smiles on the faces of their upcoming coworkers. We hired a scriptwriter who had experience writing videos for new employee orientation, and we used a voice-over narrator who had an upbeat tone. We highlighted some of the unique departments and services that the employees might not get a chance to see once they are on the job. For example, the hospital had a program to reduce patient stress with visits from "cuddly pets." An occupational therapy department housed an automobile, indoors, for wheelchair patients to practice getting in and out of a car. And the food service department hosted a monthly barbecue for employees outside the cafeteria.

Orientation videos are sometimes the employee's first look at the video production style of the enterprise, and it is an opportunity for the video department to be creative in its approach. The video manager can initiate the idea of producing a new employee orientation video. Welcoming the new hire can be the start of a new friendship between human resources and the video unit.

Media Training

We have already discussed ways video can save the enterprise money by avoiding accidents or reducing the amount of time supervisors have to spend on training. However, video can also be a revenue generator. One such money tree for certain types of organizations is "media training." Media training is a process where the video producer, together with a former news reporter, trains executives to speak with news media. At Pacific Gas and Electric (a San Francisco utility company), the video department charged other departments for this media training. The department, at the time, had former news reporters on their staff. These professionals applied their skills to training the PG&E executives and others who might be corralled into a TV interview during times of controversy. This class proved very popular, and the fees the class generated helped finance the in-house video studio.

The need for media training arose from the popularity of ambush interviews similar to the style of CBS's *60 Minutes*. When a controversy surrounded PG&E or there was an accident, local reporters would sometimes catch a PG&E exec unaware. The media training would prepare the execs to remain calm under the pressure of lights, cameras, and an inquisitive, if not aggressive, reporter. Your company need not be in the midst of a controversy; some firms hire media trainers because this type of training helps people represent their companies clearly and unemotionally.

The training is done one-to-one or with a small group of employees who might be asked to represent the company. The process involves filming the employee responding to questions on camera from a mock reporter and playing back the video clips. The camera operator usually has a bright, camera-mounted light, and the trainer plays the role of the inquisitive reporter. He or she pokes a microphone into the employee's face, and sometimes the camera operator is instructed to get a little too close for comfort. The questions are styled to be confrontational and to elicit a charged reaction from the employee. The trainer explains that reporters compete with one another to get their film on the evening news, so a spirited reaction by a representative of a newsworthy company is hot stuff.

During the playback, the trainer starts out by noting the correct responses from the employee in an effort to be encouraging. Frequently, the employees themselves recognize their own lack of control under the pressure of the reporter and the camera. Through a series of role-playing and guidance, the trainer gets a little harder on the employee, both during reporter role-playing and during video playback. The student gradually learns how to appear on camera and how to present the company position in an unruffled fashion.

Media training can be expanded to showing the on-camera employee how to use an earpiece intercom, how to present material in sound bites, and how to focus his or her attention toward the camera lens. Most media training is often completed in a single day, but in some cases the employees may take home DVDs or video files for further review. They may practice their presentations themselves and return the following day. Further training includes techniques to resist inappropriate questions from the reporter, work on one's body language, and present themselves intelligently on a longer talk show segment.

Presentation and Speech Training

Supervisory and marketing employees frequently need to give presentations to customers, associations, and community groups. Some people characterize speaking in front of an audience as more frightening than death. However, consultants with specific training are available to help corporate employees create and deliver presentations with ease. These trainers are aware that the employees in their classes are anxious each time they get up in front of the class to make a presentation, so they know how to handle their students with consideration.

Many organizations incorporate video feedback into these presentation classes, and when handled thoughtfully, video playback can be a valuable tool in helping to bring out the best of these new presenters. Usually an entry-level videographer is assigned to film the presenters in these classes, and he or she needs to be sensitive to the vulnerability of the students in the class. The recording systems include playback to a large display and storage onto a DVD or flash drive that the students may take home with them.

The instructors usually start with easy, short speeches, where the students can simply talk about themselves. During playback, when the students are most vulnerable to criticism, the instructor points out the strengths of the presenters and encourages the other students to do the same. With the successive speeches, during playback, the instructor will gradually point to the areas that need improvement.

A class in presentation training usually takes two or three days. Sometimes students are asked to play their video clips at home or even to record themselves on their own using a camcorder or webcam. The videographer during the classes is usually busy making sure each student's clips go into his or her folder and are readily playable. The benefit to the organization is that salespeople can be trained to deliver motivating presentations, supervisors learn how to inspire their employees via speeches, and managers learn how to represent their corporations.

In-House Video Repurposed for External Distribution

The enterprising video producer could make his or her department self-supporting by producing a training video that is generic enough that it could be used not only for in-house training but also for national or worldwide distribution. Such was the case with one of my company's clients, Spectrum Schools, which operates a number of schools in northern California for kids with special needs.

The state of California announced that private schools throughout the state would need to train their staffs in safety techniques to prevent the spread of HIV, hepatitis, and other diseases distributed by contact with blood. The school administration needed to train all the teachers and staff in their ten schools, and they decided video would be an appropriate and cost-effective method. However, they also knew that to do it right, the video budget would necessitate withholding their funds from important teaching programs. So they decided to produce a video that would meet their needs and would be standardized for other schools so they could sell copies to them. Since the new regulations would be in place before long, we needed to produce the video, and the associated print materials, in short order.

We partnered with a graphic designer and a printing facility to produce materials that would correlate with the graphics in the video. The client provided an instructional designer who helped us develop the script content so it would fulfill the learning objectives for our client's schools as well as schools that would purchase the video.

We wrote a script based on demonstration frameworks, and we hired, as the on-camera hostess, a local actress who had appeared in televised health programs. We arranged for child actors through a talent agency, and we filmed the program at two schools, after hours. As we proceeded through the postproduction process, the instructional designer was supervising the printing of materials. The company's marketing person was developing contact lists of schools that needed to provide training to fulfill the state's regulations. The company had a strategy that included a production and marketing schedule, and they had in place duplication and distribution for the video. To speed up the production completion, the client offered us a bonus for early delivery of the edited master. My editor and I worked on Super Bowl Sunday to earn our bonus! The video was the first to get into distribution, and the sales from it helped Spectrum Schools expand their educational programs.

The key to producing a video that can be marketed to other companies is to keep it generic, develop a marketing strategy, and choose a subject for which a video is not already available. A level of confidentiality needs to be maintained during the production phase, and it would be prudent for the company to have in-house staff and outside contractors sign nondisclosure agreements. The video could be sold outright to a publisher that would get an exclusive contract, or it could be distributed via wholesalers. Choosing the exclusive publisher route relieves the producer from the costs for marketing and DVD replication. The downside is that an exclusive contract may prohibit your company from its own marketing efforts, and sales could be limited. However, the costs associated with replication and marketing to wholesalers could exceed the production budget. The decisions and resources required to produce a video for external distribution may be more than your company wishes to take on. However, the income derived from sales of training videos could help your department develop a budget that does not rely on the vicissitudes of your company's financial position.

When Video Is Not Effective

With video having so many success stories, it is easy to see why some managers think they can solve nearly any problem by producing a video. But video is not the panacea for all problems. If not used wisely, it could backfire and misrepresent reality, as James G. March discusses in his book *The Ambiguities of Experience*. March says that while compelling storytelling is an effective medium for corporate training, sometimes a story can distort reality. The truth of experience is usually more complicated than what we can distill into a short story. March writes, "The more accurately reality is reflected, and the more comprehensible the story, the less realistic it is." March cautions that in the process of writing a short script, we may fall into the trap of simplifying and even adding our own points of view. While corporate training emphasizes experiential learning, experience is complicated. March adds, "Experience may possibly be the best teacher, but it is not a particularly good teacher."

When used to simplify complicated data rather than present a clear understanding of the information, graphics and animation can slant toward a particular point of view. In a 2010 article in the *Harvard Business Review*, Neal Roese, a professor of marketing at Northwestern University's Kellogg School of Management, and Kathleen Vohs, an associate professor at the University of Minnesota's Carlson School of Management, write, "Our research suggests that bias is becoming stronger, thanks largely to an abundance of visual information, including recreations and simulations." They add, "Complicated animated visualization is appealing because it can help make sense of highly complex information, but it's also, quite literally a point of view. The information can be conveyed with certain emphases, shown from certain angles, slowed down or enlarged. Animations can whitewash the guesswork and assumptions that go into interpreting reconstructions. By creating a picture of one possibility, they make others seem less likely, even if they are not." The video producer, when working with a trainer or content specialist, needs to keep the program objectives and the audience in mind. Roese and Vohs caution, "A manager with tools to animate financial data sets, such as sales forecasts, can easily—on the basis of the story the visualization tells—misidentify trends, place the blame where it doesn't belong, or become overconfident about an action plan."

In employee training, it is best to keep the data to a minimum. For example, new employees need to learn about the company benefits, but video may not be the best way to explain them in detail. The information probably is full of data, and it may change over time. Similarly, a video showing employees how to fill in forms again may be too detailed. An interactive computer program or one-to-one peer instruction may be better ways to learn form completion.

Video producers snicker when they use the term "talking head" in a pejorative sense. When someone speaks on camera and the viewer loses interest, the presenter can appear to be nothing more than a talking head. Certainly, recording an instructor or consultant teaching a class is appropriate, but these productions become more interesting with the addition of slides and other visuals. A video of the CEO or a manager speaking to employees works best when it is short and when the on-camera presenter is engaging.

Instructional Design

Videos are most effective when they are short, engaging, and self-paced. Rather than a linear program, such as those on old videotapes, DVDs or file-based programs with several chapter points allow for individualized instruction. Employees at different learning levels may choose what they want to learn, and can rewatch segments if they want.

Some companies employ an instructional designer who applies adult learning theory to developing training programs for employees. The designer assesses the level of understanding of the audience for a video, takes into consideration the background and interest of the viewer, writes the learning objectives, assists with scriptwriting, and develops an evaluation mechanism to measure the effectiveness of the video. However, many organizations do not employ an instructional designer, and the video producer needs to take on these tasks when planning video programs.

Learning about instructional design, developing programs that motivate adult learners, creating self-paced and interactive videos, and helping the enterprise with general employee training are yet more tasks for the video producer or video manager. Measuring the outcomes and reporting on the success of the training videos enable the video department to grow and prosper.

MARKETING AND SOCIAL MEDIA

Introduction

Video has been an essential tool for corporate marketing from the start. From TV commercials to sales support clips, video helps to show products and demonstrate the importance of services. With the advent of streaming video and the explosion of social media, corporate video use has increased dramatically. A Forrester Research study showed a 378-percent increase in corporate website video use from 2008 to 2009.

Peruse the websites of major corporations, and you'll probably find a video link either on the home page or at most a click or two away. General Electric has a 1:56-minute video on smart grid technology that includes customer testimonials from both consumers and industrial clients. German electronics giant Siemens has five videos that document new gas turbine technology that the company says provides higher efficiency for a greener future. Home Depot has a 22-second *Quick Project Tips* video on how to use a potato to remove a broken lightbulb from a socket. Users may click to share this video via e-mail, instant messaging, Facebook, and Twitter—mediums of communication that didn't even exist a few years ago.

Burson-Marsteller, a public relations firm, conducted a study of the international Fortune 100 companies' use of social media in early 2010. Twitter led the pack with 65 percent of the corporations using its social network platform, and most of the companies had four or more Twitter accounts. The study concluded that corporations are becoming more comfortable communicating using social media. A third of the companies reported that they responded to user comments by retweeting or posting the comments on their companies' blogs. The report said that rather than simply broadcasting their messages, corporations use social media to engage and interact with customers and shareholders.

According to eMarketer senior analyst Jeffrey Grau, "Retailers are making the case that videos boost their sales conversion rate, a measure of the increase in the percentage of shoppers who make a purchase after viewing a product video. Retailers also claim videos reduce shopping cart abandonment rates and diminish product return rates."

Some corporations utilize innovative engagement tools for their website videos such as user-clickable overlays that lead to shopping cart purchases. User-generated content (UGC) websites let enthusiastic buyers tout products' benefits with their homemade video testimonials. And nearly every major corporation is using YouTube to distribute their commercials and other video content.

YouTube for the Enterprise

Have you visited YouTube lately? It's more than just human skateboards and iPhones in blenders. Corporations have embraced this home-brewed social network and are gaining customers without paying for airtime. Some use the platform to publicize their social responsibility programs. Go through the list of the largest worldwide corporations, and nearly every one has a YouTube page.

AT&T shows their TV commercials, but they also post videos of their employment diversity programs. Wal-Mart also shows commercials, and they have clips about organic produce and wind harvesting. BP ran a series of videos explaining their progress in containing the Gulf oil spill. Many of these companies have links to their YouTube clips right from their home pages.

On the Ford Motor Company YouTube page, you can watch their commercials and some cute videos, such as the one comparing a Fiesta to a Lamborghini, and a silly series about a zombie. However, you can also see their own Scott Monty, who claims to be the "Head of Social Media" at Ford. He says on-camera, "The social media strategy at Ford is about humanizing the company by connecting our employees to our constituents and with each other when possible and providing value along the way."

Ford's Monty knows about the captions tool because you have the option of turning on captions when you watch his video. YouTube employs voice recognition, technology from Google Voice, to create captions for the hearing impaired and to display text translations. As of this writing, the voice recognition display included some humorous inaccuracies, but their heart is in the right place. Captions are text that Google searches for when users enter keywords. Video producers can enter the script of the text as part of the metadata with a YouTube video, and potential customers who perform a keyword search could find the video.

Two billion hits a day—that's YouTube's statistic as of this writing. Major corporations that once relished the exposure that broadcast television brought them are now moving their sights to YouTube's vast audience. YouTube and other social media sites facilitate "narrow-casting," where companies can target specific markets. Users with particular interests gravitate to those YouTube's categories that pique their curiosity.

Look at the growing number of do-it-yourselfers. Users log 35 million searches a month on YouTube just for "how-to" videos. Most companies can find some area of interest to the do-it-your-selfer, whether it is how to remove a broken lightbulb or how to invest your money wisely. How-to videos are the content that consumers crave, and they are a portal to the enterprise website with new brands to promote, the locations of the nearest stores, or community programs the company has adopted.

Some companies develop a community of customers and supporters by asking visitors to subscribe to their YouTube channels. This offers even more exposure to the company's brand because each of the subscribers gets e-mails every time you post a new video. BASF Agriculture Products produced a 4:00-minute animation titled *Hungry Planet* (http://www.youtube.com/watch?v=joUggaD6Mr0) that discusses how farmers can preserve the land and get the most out of every acre. This is one of 27 videos that include talk show segments with farmer phone-ins, commercial spots for herbicides, and grower testimonials about the company's fungicides.

Liberty Mutual Insurance features their "Responsible Sports" YouTube channel, where they feature short clips from coaches. "Responsible Sports" is Liberty Mutual's program dedicated to supporting volunteer coaches and parents. Each video is branded with Liberty Mutual's logo on the screen, and viewers see the coaches wearing shirts festooned with the company's brand.

Hewlett-Packard posts video instructions for setting up printers. A colleague once told me he was having trouble installing a new printer and could not find the answer in the manufacturer's help pages. He went to YouTube and found a video that HP had produced that walked him through the steps. It included screen shots from the driver, as well as live film of the printer's display.

Recreational Equipment Incorporated posts commercials to YouTube (http://www.youtube.com/reifindout), but they also have a catalog of instructional videos they call "Expert Advice." You can watch "Ed" at the Seattle store demonstrating how to use a GPS, together with a map and a compass. Shot with relatively low production values, Ed is framed in a static, medium close-up, and the video uses dissolves to cover jump cuts. Nonetheless, the 4:52-minute video is a classic instructional video with bulleted text and handheld cut-ins to the GPS unit in the field. Ed teaches classes at the store, and he explains the GPS operations well enough on camera to help hikers avoid getting lost.

Some companies track their YouTube hits by directing viewers to one of their own websites' URLs. They can entice potential followers by offering a coupon or contest. Other corporations conduct their own film festivals by asking users to submit their videos, be they ideas for a commercial or new ways to use a particular product. The competition campaign develops excitement and customer loyalty, and the company gets videos produced by their customers that they might use for themselves. Whoa! Is that going to put the corporate video producer out of work?

Engagement Objects on Websites

That's where the creative corporate producer can use his or her knowledge about the medium to deliver video experiences that wow users and keep them at the site. For example, Nike uses social media with a customer-oriented site nikebiz.com where shoppers can customize their own shoe designs.

The *NIKEiD Builder* video is a 1:36-minute film that demonstrates how to use the NIKEiD website at nikeid.com to select materials, choose colors, and design your own custom shoe. The software lets you see the design from several angles, and you can see creations of other users. Design Search offers inspiration from other Nike users. You tag your design, select your size, add it to your shopping cart, and wait for its delivery. The video has screen shots from the software accompanied by voice-over narration.

In an upbeat 2:00-minute video, Nike unveils its London NIKEiD Studio at the NikeTown Store in central London. At the store, customers can create custom designs for the colors and styles of their shoes, which are then produced and shipped.

The champagne pours at this grand opening spectacle with the glitz and glamour of a Hollywood premiere. The video features celebrities like Dustin Hoffman, a celebrity DJ, quick shots showing the user-customizing process, and interviews with guests, who explain the color palettes they used and the names they gave to their designs.

In a 2:49-minute video titled *Nike + Human Race*, documentary-style footage shows the 25-city running event that spans multiple continents. Viewers see a few seconds of each city, with fast-action scenery paired with runners making their ways through the city streets. The site includes several commercials highlighting Nike products that are featured in sporting events around the world.

Not to be outdone by their competition, Zappos, the online shoe dealer, offers clickable overlays on their videos. In a partnership with Overlay.TV, users click on a product, which takes them to its landing page. There they can find additional information on the shoe, see video testimonials, record and upload their own videos, and make a purchase.

Overlay.TV provides "clickable hotspots" within videos, where customers can click and shop directly from the video screen. The company provides the infrastructure for customers to upload video testimonials and product reviews from their webcams. Users may post the video link on their Facebook, Twitter, and other social media pages. Overlay.TV also offers online video chat between a company's call center and the customer. And the service includes detailed analytics to understand customer shopping habits.

Top Corporations' Video Sites

Major corporations dedicate major bucks to understanding buying trends and developing effective and innovative marketing techniques. It is no wonder that so many of them turn to video to engage their website visitors and to develop communities of customers.

Retail grocery chain Wegmans devotes a website (http://videos.wegmans.com/) to Wegman's Videos with a catalog of films that includes recipes, how-to's, organic foods, and wellness. Visitors use a player on Wegman's website to watch the company's jeans-clad nutritionist speaking from a grocery store or kitchen. You can learn about such "super foods" as quinoa and view videos titled *Brain Food for Kids* and *Half Plate Healthy*. The site lets you share videos with your friends on any of the 60 sharing and bookmarking sites the company offers links to.

Colgate features its chairman and CEO Ian Cook in a 1:45-minute video as part of its online annual report (http://www.colgate.com/app/Colgate/US/Corp/Annual-Reports/2009/Dear-Colgate-Shareholder.cvsp). Shot in a studio with a green screen, viewers see B-roll of products and happy customers and employees, as well as graphics of the key financial reports.

JP Morgan Chase has links to its videos right at the prime spot of its website: the right sidebar. One is a 2:55-minute video about the company's donation of homes to families of wounded military veterans (http://www.jpmorganchase.com/corporate/Home/home.htm). Shot at a benefit concert and featuring presentations from executives and testimonials from vets and their wives, the video plays from the company's website and includes closed captions.

Some corporate websites link to their videos through their home page "media center tab," such as with global home products giant Unilever. In five video segments, each running 2 to 4 minutes, their CEO discusses financial highlights of the past year and the company's commitment to sustainability (http://www.unilever.com/mediacentre/multimedia/?WT.GNAV=Media_centre).

IBM uses YouTube-embedded videos that play from the company's website. Their "Smarter Planet" page (http://www.ibm.com/smarterplanet/us/en/index.html?ca=v_smarterplanet) has five videos from what they call "IBMers," who discuss smarter analytics, smarter predictions, smarter insights, smarter context, and smarter systems." The videos open with multilayered montages as we hear poignant sound bites from the interviewees. Then we see several IBM staffers who are technology specialists. In one shot, the camera shows the production set—a loft-type room with huge windows, soft lights, C-stands, a boom mike, and the usual array of grip equipment. Users may click through to the website annotation from the YouTube player.

General Motors uses both YouTube and a Flash player on its own site to display a catalog of videos that include customer testimonials, videos about fuel cell assembly, and a fun film about the 50th anniversary of the Corvette. The Chevy Cruze engine video features a company engineer speaking in the studio with the engine on a pedestal at his side. The video incorporates 3D animation showing the engine construction, animated text, graphics, and futuristic music.

Walgreens has several customer education videos on its site (http://healthcorner.walgreens.com/). The videos are branded "Health Corner TV®" and include videos on exercise, cooking, and medications. In *Medications that Interfere*, the company uses a TV news framework where a physician on a set speaks to a pharmacist in the field. Using side-by-side screens, the two appear to be in a satellite-linked conversation with each other. The videos open in a window on Walgreen's site, and users have an option of playing the video or viewing the transcript. In *Start Walking*, Donny Osmond, who says he is a grandfather now, talks in an interview format about establishing your own walking program.

This video has no reference to Walgreens, but the sidebar on the right lets you click and "shop now" for blood pressure products.

High blood pressure is not a worry once you replace employees with robots. *Living with Robots* is the title of an engaging 8-minute film on Honda Motor Company's website (http://dreams.honda.com/videos/living-with-robots/). Asimo, Honda's robot, is gradually revealed with cinematic imagery and science fiction music. Produced as a minidocumentary, the film features interviews with Honda researchers and other scientists about robotics research. The film shows how the company researched human walking to develop products to aid individuals with limited mobility. This film has high production values with artistic lighting, multilayering, and film-look processing. After viewing the video, the website lets you leave your text comments, or you can share the video via Facebook, Twitter, Digg, and Delicious. Click the "more options" button, and you can post the video to such networking sites as Blogmarks, Fark, LinkedIn, MacBlips, MySpace, Reddit, StumbleUpon, and Technorati. The site has an "embed/copy" button that reveals the embed code and the link.

Facebook, Twitter, and Other Sharing Sites

Corporate web developers can add such a list of social networking site icons to their own companies' websites. When visitors to a site like a particular video, they can share it on Facebook and other sharing sites. They can also bookmark the page and share their bookmarks using bookmark-sharing sites. While Facebook is a popular portal for sharing links, a company's community of supporters can now post the link to any of the growing number of networking sites.

Addthis.com is a bookmarking tool that companies and individuals can add to their websites. When users click the Share button, a window pops up with an array of social networking sites icons, including Facebook and Twitter. According to the company, "AddThis helps website publishers and bloggers spread their content across the web by making it easy for visitors to bookmark and share content to their favorite social destinations." There is no charge to use AddThis, and it "offers sophisticated analytics to help users understand how and where their content is being shared." You'll find the AddThis share window on the "Mission" page at General Motors' website (http://www.gmreinvention.com/index.php). Here, visitors are treated to film clips of their favorite cars in action, as well as videos that discuss fuel efficiency and reducing carbon footprints. After viewing the videos, users can click the AddThis

Figure 16.1 AddThis is a website that lets you add links to a slew of social media bookmarking sites. Visitors who like your website or videos can bookmark them and let their friends know about their bookmarks. This is another technique to help videos and web pages go viral.

Share button and go to the window that lists Facebook, Twitter, and a slew of other sharing sites.

Facebook isn't just for teenagers looking for friends. In Burson-Marsteller's study of the international Fortune 100 companies' use of social media in early 2010, they found that Facebook surpassed YouTube in corporate use. Several major corporations use Facebook to develop a community of supporters who "like" them. A few use the site's video player to distribute their clips, and some companies have more than one Facebook account.

AT&T has at least three accounts. One is an AT&T page that looks like an advertisement with offers for wireless calling plans. Another Facebook page is the AT&T "Share" site with a quarter-million fans and video clips. One page features a series of 2:40-minute episodes of a show called *Dial Star*. Produced by NBC Universal, the clips are light stories with high production values, each one featuring young people texting one another using AT&T data plans.

At AT&T's Twitter page, each tweet includes a link to either an AT&T page or to a news item about AT&T. One Twitter link goes to a Fast Company report about AT&T's use of Cisco's

Telepresence system for videoconferencing. The report cites an AT&T-funded study that reports that by 2020 videoconferencing can save a $1 billion in travel expenses and $19 billion in reduced CO_2 emissions. The report adds that AT&T has a vested interest in videoconferencing.

According to an Associated Press report in June 2010, Twitter use in Japan had exceeded that in the United States, with 16.3 percent of Japanese Internet users who tweet, compared with Americans at 9.8 percent. A Japanese retail clothing chain, Uniqlo, uses Twitter to encourage sharing among their followers. This marketing technique aims to convert tweeters to shoppers by offering freebies. Tokyu Hands, a large department store in Japan, is another heavy user of social media. They use Twitter to respond to questions from their followers, and they encourage folks to retweet their posts. Their website offers several YouTube-embedded videos, including one that measures the weight of their featured folding umbrella against the weight of an iPhone.

Wal-Mart is among a large number of retailers that use Twitter to post daily specials. Wal-Mart has six Twitter accounts. In addition to the "Wal-Mart Specials" page, visitors may read tweets from the "Wal-Mart Can," where some tweets link to the Wal-Mart Community Action Network on YouTube. In the video, a Chicago resident exclaims, "We all are praying for this Wal-Mart!" (http://www.youtube.com/user/WalmartCommunity#p/u/0/-wB1rjaUtRM). The 1:40-minute video includes interviews and B-roll about how a neighborhood with few jobs and without access to fresh groceries could benefit from a Wal-Mart.

Customers who appreciate your company's products may post a video response on YouTube or on one of several user-generated content sites that encourage visitors to be on-camera reviewers. ExpoTV.com offers rewards to users who upload video product reviews. The site gives points for uploading videos, and points may be redeemed for products or gift cards. Some customers record their reviews via their webcams. For example, you can watch a female homemaker spend about three minutes giving her opinion of Cheer laundry detergent as she shows the box to the camera. The video includes this manufacturer's disclaimer: "Cheer does not represent the accuracy of any statements or product claims made in this community, nor does it endorse any opinions expressed within these videos." The video producer should consult with the company's legal department before linking to any user-generated videos to avoid any liability for misrepresentation.

Several sites have sprung up to integrate video sharing with Twitter. Extending the microblogging concept to video, "microvideos" are very short videos that you can link to your Twitter tweets. With the video-sharing site "12seconds," your video posts can't exceed that short time frame. You upload the video from your hard drive, webcam, or mobile phone and then send links to customers and supporters. TWiddeo is another video-sharing service that you log on to via your Twitter account. While there are no time constraints, videos may not exceed 100 MB in size. Vidly supports 720p HD video with a 1 GB upload maximum, while Twitvid lets your videos be up to 2 GB in size. Twitvid also has an analytics tool to report such statistics as when users are viewing your videos, from what country, and which sites referred them to you.

Dailymotion, Vimeo, MetaCafe, and Veoh

But wait, there's more! The list of video-sharing sites increases almost daily. Dailymotion is a video-sharing site with headquarters in Paris that includes brief commercials that precede many of the user-generated clips. One of its video content providers is Autoline Detroit (http://www.dailymotion.com/AutolineDetroit), which provides daily automotive industry news and analysis in 5- to 7-minute videos. Com.puter.tv (http://www.dailymotion.com/ComputerTV) posts several videos of tech toys, usually sponsored by a computer dealer such as TigerDirect or CompUSA. The 4-minute videos show the features of cameras and computer gadgets, but don't expect to see an unbiased review from this sponsored site.

Vimeo claims to be the first video-sharing site to offer HD video uploading and playback. While YouTube later offered HD, Vimeo differentiates itself from YouTube because they accept only user-created content—no mashups of TV shows. In addition to the free service, Vimeo Plus is a $60 per year service that allows uploads of up to 5 GB of videos per week and two-pass video reencoding.

CU Companies, a consortium of credit unions, uses Vimeo to distribute instructional videos about mortgages, auto loans, and business loans (http://www.vimeo.com/10556104). Another corporate Vimeo user is The Earth Institute, a nonprofit established by Columbia University to using existing technology to promote sustainability. Their Vimeo videos include *Surveying the Sea of Marmara to Understand Faults and Earthquakes in Turkey* and an address by Mexican President Felipe Calderón.

Zacuto USA, a video accessory manufacturer, showcases its products via Vimeo videos. In a video about its DSLR optical viewfinder, the company uses a news story framework with two staffers showing the setup and operation of the device.

Black Diamond Equipment, a manufacturer of climbing and skiing equipment, uses Vimeo to post adventure videos, some about 10 minutes long, that show the company's equipment in extreme conditions. Their *Alaska Expedition 2010* demonstrates the testing procedure to become a certified rock guide. WebTV Italy is another company that uses the Vimeo platform as their video travel guide. Their educational videos include the 1:53-minute *500 Churches of Rome* and the 2:53-minute *The Pantheon HD*.

Metacafe is a video-sharing site that specializes in short-form entertainment and how-to videos. The site says the average video length is 90 seconds, and Klondike displays minute-plus versions of their "What Would You Do" commercials. Metacafe uses a VideoRank™ system that they say "identifies and exposes the most popular videos by automatically gauging every interaction each viewer has with a video." Eastern Shore Chiropractic has a 1:28-minute ad that encourages viewers to send for their guide on choosing a chiropractor. SOFY is a feminine hygiene product that is promoted with a group of young women on an adventurous road trip. Metacafe plays sponsored videos of movie trailers between user selections, but there is a "continue to video" button to skip through those commercials.

Veoh was one of the first video-sharing sites. In addition to showing videos, it enables users to use social features such as video, voice, and text chat, which allows users to view online content while having the ability to see and chat with one another. Vogue magazine's Vogue.TV uses Veoh to promote new products such as Fashionistas (http://www.veoh.com/browse/videos/category/news/watch/v18031218eNfey2d8), showing the Kurt Geiger designer shoe collection. The 2:54-minute video shows a photo shoot with leggy models, a fluffy dog, and an upbeat soundtrack. Similar to Metacafe, some videos are preceded by a brief commercial. Veoh has local business videos such as the JMK BMW dealership with a 4:11-minute video (http://www.veoh.com/browse/videos/category/autos_and_vehicles#watch%3Dv16608914Rp9J9xA9) that describes the staff's passion for BMWs.

These are among the many video-sharing sites that enable companies to expand their distribution networks. When customers have more avenues to view videos, the odds increase that your company and its products will have added exposure. Developing a community of supporters who like your business helps the videos to go viral.

While corporations still produce product videos to support their sales staffs, social media has been a boon to big business.

With the vast numbers of YouTube and Facebook users, and the ability for corporations to narrowcast their messages via the Internet, social media is a natural marketing tool. The corporate commitment to using video on social media networks is demonstrated by the large numbers of them using YouTube to connect with the public and the high production values of some of these microvideos.

CORPORATE EVENTS: FILMING CONFERENCES AND MEETINGS

Introduction

A frequent function of the corporate video producer is recording conferences and meetings. These recordings can be played back for employees at remote locations, and some events, such as a shareholders' annual meeting, are even streamed live over the Internet. This chapter includes information on shooting in an auditorium, iMag projection, and working with PowerPoint slides.

Meetings, Bloody Meetings is the title of a training video starring John Cleese of Monty Python. The title alone suggests that corporations have more than enough meetings and that they have become increasingly distasteful. Meetings can range in scope from a trainer conducting a class of 20 employees to an annual corporate meeting in an amphitheater with 20,000 shareholders.

Videotaping conferences and meetings is a different kind of production than the scripted training and marketing videos the corporate producer is more accustomed to providing. There is little planning, probably no editing, and the video producer has little control over the way the event proceeds. However, recordings of these corporate events are vital for the company that wishes to have efficient ways to train more employees and reach more of the public.

Your involvement and presence at these events boosts your visibility in the organization. While you may be relegated to sitting in the back of the room or in an anteroom, directing the shoot (rather than sitting at the banquet table with the invited guests), your ability to help the organization preserve and distribute its message increases your value to the company. This, of course, can lead to future work.

Whether the organization brings in a consultant to present ideas to a small gathering of managers or the company has rented a large venue to roll out a new product, or any event in between, a video of the proceedings lets the corporation share the words and images with others on their staff.

Videos of meetings can be simple documentations with a single camera, or they can be multicam events streamed live over the Internet. Some meetings will benefit from live switching that enables such embellishments as titles and PowerPoint slides. Some meeting videos may include interviews with participants, segments shot from breakout sessions, inserted video clips, and high-energy roll-in video montages.

Plan on capturing some B-roll before or after the event. It could be simply the signage for the event, or it could include shots of participants arriving and mingling. This can serve as a roll-in opening with music for your final, edited version of the meeting video. Consider interviewing participants in the hallways, especially after the event. Spontaneous accolades can add emotion to an otherwise mundane video, and they can be used in a roll-in for the next year's event. Sound bites and short clips from these testimonials can also be used as promos for the web.

Early on, you'll need to decide how many cameras you wish to film the event with. Two cameras enable you to capture audience responses and interaction. The audience footage gives you some cutaway shots to use in editing, too. Three cameras allow for one camera to shoot a wide shot, one to capture close-ups, and one to get audience reactions.

You can shoot the event either with live switching or with "isos," where each camera is recording to its own isolated flash drive or VTR. Then you combine all camera recordings together in the editing room to build the final track. Live switching eliminates most of the postproduction time but requires a more elaborate on-site production. You will need to safely and securely run cables between cameras and the switcher, and you will need to provide an intercom system for the camera operators and the director who will call the shots during the shoot.

Shooting in an Auditorium

As with any location at which you have never shot before, you should scout out the auditorium well in advance. Decide the best places to situate cameras so you can get a good line-of-sight without blocking the view of any audience member. If you are shooting multicam, do all you can to avoid seeing a camera in any shot. You can sometimes straddle the chairs by removing the spreader from your tripod. In some cases you may need to construct a platform over some seats, covered in black, for your camera.

Think through where cables will run. Gaffer-tape any cables that are in an aisle or hallway. Consider running cables over door frames. You can screw brackets above the frames to hold the cables. Keep power cables away from audio and video cables. Make sure your equipment and cases are not going to get in the way of any audience members.

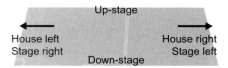

Figure 17.1 "Stage left/right" directions are from the talent's perspective. "House right/left" are from the audience's perspective.

Think through the process of bringing in equipment, including vehicle unloading and parking, as well as the path and method of moving equipment in and out. Be sure to be completely set up before the house opens and the audience arrives. Make sure your monitors and desk lamps are not visible to participants and that any crew members talking over headsets are quiet enough so they are not heard by audience members.

In some cases you can be on the intercom headset with the stage director. It is a good idea to learn a little of the terminology that actors and stage personnel use. The event coordinator or stage manager may tell you that the CEO is entering from "stage right" and walking "downstage." This is the opposite from your perspective. Figure 17.1 shows the stage directions.

Depending on the size of the auditorium, you may want to shoot from a position closer to the stage rather than from the back. In some cases there is a center aisle, parallel to the stage that you may shoot from. If the auditorium is large and your camera is equipped with only 14X zoom, you may not get a tight enough shot. If you need to shoot from the rear of a large auditorium, consider renting a camera with a 24X lens or longer.

iMag Projection

iMag is short for image magnification, and it refers to projecting the image of the people on stage onto a large screen or two. You've probably seen iMag projections at concerts and conventions. Large auditoriums and conference halls use them to project the performers onto a large screen, and corporate videographers frequently are called upon to magnify the speakers at the podium.

Since the image is magnified, any of your slight camera movements are also magnified. You'll need a stable tripod and high-quality fluid head, together with remote zoom and focus controls on the tripod handles. If you will be shooting on a platform such as a riser, you may need to slip in wedges or blocks at a corner or two to add to its stability. Furniture stores and hardware stores sell small plastic wedges for tables, and you can double them up if needed. Make sure participants don't decide to sit on your riser; their fidgeting could ruin your shot. And don't ruin your own shot; get yourself a chair or a padded barstool, so you can sit rather than having to stand and shift from leg to leg.

Connect the video output from the camera to the video input on the video projector. If your camera and the projector have component or SDI (serial digital interface) connectors, you can project a high-resolution image. Frequently, the event coordinator will want to project graphics, or the presenters will want to show PowerPoint slides. That's when you'll need a switcher and a technician to switch between the iMag image and the graphics. Be certain to record the audio and video onto either a camcorder or a hard drive so the event coordinator has a recording of the event.

Lighting Considerations

While nearly any video camera can shoot in a conference room under fluorescent lights, auditoriums present their own lighting challenges. The auditorium probably has spotlights and a dark background behind the stage. The subject is lit with a bright light, and the dark background can make it difficult to obtain correct exposure.

You'll need to set the camera to manual iris control or, if you are using a consumer-grade camcorder, engage the spotlight compensation function. That may be found in the "program AE" feature of the camcorder. With a camcorder set to automatic, you'll run the risk of the subject becoming overexposed; faces could look pasty white as the autoexposure system reads the dark background and opens the iris to brighten it.

If possible, ask the auditorium technician to install diffusion gels in their spotlights. This is a routine task, since technicians frequently put in color gels to add color to the set. Offer to supply the diffusion gel yourself; they may be purchased at theatrical or photo supply stores. Alternately, you can set up one of your portable soft lights, such as one with a built-in diffuser or reflector. While you probably will need to place it on the stage, when you compose your shot, you can get in close enough to avoid showing that light with its stand.

The auditorium probably has backlights that can be aimed at the heads of your subjects. A backlight helps separate the subjects from the background, especially if they have dark hair. You don't want a video image of a face floating in a black background, do you? Some auditoriums have side lights. Those can help eliminate shadows on faces and give you a more flattering image than just front and back lights. The event you are filming may employ a technician with a follow-spot from the rear of the auditorium. Just make sure it is not so bright that it blows out your video image.

Measure the illumination from all the lights well before the event, using either a light meter or the zebra stripes in the camera. If necessary, ask the technician to darken the spotlight with either neutral density filter or a rheostat. The latter may produce a more orange light, but it is better than overexposure.

Mikes at Meetings

The meeting organizer and the presenters should know in advance that they may be asked to wear one or two mikes. There may be times when you want the on-camera presenter to wear your wireless lavaliere mike, maybe in addition to the amplified mike he or she is already wearing. Ideally there will be one microphone per presenter, and it will feed the auditorium sound system as well as your recorder.

The clip-on wireless mike (also known as a lavaliere) has a belt pack that clips onto the back of a belt or waistband. The mike clips onto a collar, a lapel, or a necktie. If the presenter wears clothing that does not accommodate this, it could present a problem or embarrassment. Keep in mind that even the most seasoned speaker feels nervous before speaking to a group. The last thing they need is an AV tech wanting them to wear a microphone they were not anticipating.

If you ever worked in television or films, you know that actors were used to wearing mikes, and they assumed a technician would want to attach a microphone to their clothing. In many professional studios, it is standard practice to let the sound person physically attach the microphone, which frequently includes reaching around to the talent's backside or sometimes even running the microphone inside the talent's clothing.

In the corporate world, where on-camera presenters have no TV experience, you need to be much less intrusive. Hopefully you have sent a message far in advance to the presenter, but when you need to approach him or her, do so in a relaxed and supportive way. They are already anxious about their upcoming speech, so a careful approach is important.

Some sound techs will demonstrate on themselves where to clip on the mike. They might attach the mike element to a collar or a necktie. They may show the belt pack and how it clips onto the rear of one's belt or waistband. They may also show how to hide the mike cable within clothing, and if they use some gaffer's tape to secure it against the inside cloth, they should explain that this is a special grade of tape that does not damage fine clothing.

Tying into the Sound System

If the presenter is already wearing a microphone connected to the house sound system, it is a good idea to have him or her wear your mike as well. This ensures that you will get clear audio without needing to rely on the output from a mixing board or on the expertise of the person running it. If the presenter chooses not to wear your wireless lav, it is a good idea to have it ready to go as a backup if the sound system feed suddenly gets noisy.

Auditorium sound systems vary from the old amplifier cemented into a wall backstage to a multi-input mixing board positioned in a booth or at the rear of the auditorium with plenty of accessible outputs. Most likely, the mixing board could be in a projection booth in the rear or in an equipment rack at one of the wings to the side of the stage. In advance of the event, schedule a time to go to the auditorium to perform a sound test. Bring your audio kit and headphones and maybe even your own portable mike mixer. Make sure the technician plugs in at least one microphone and knows how to operate the mixing board.

On the day of the shoot, be prepared for a different technician than the one you tested the system with, and don't be surprised if the sound board feed no longer works. This is Murphy's Law. Bring with you one or more of your own wireless lav mikes and your own portable mixer. Be prepared to get a recording whether or not you tap into the mixing board. An audio kit should consist of the following:
• Direct box with XLR and 1/4-inch connectors
• XLR to XLR cable
• 1/4-inch to RCA adapters
• 1/4-inch stereo "Y" adapter (with two female ends for two sets of headphones)
• A small mike/line mixer

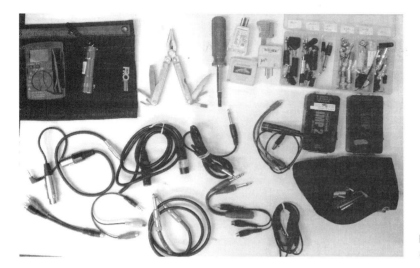

Figure 17.2 Adapters and accessories for your audio kit.

- Headphones with adapters to go from 1/4 inch to 1/8 inch
- Gaffer's tape (to tape down cables so guests don't trip)

If a technician will be available to turn on the equipment and perform the sound test, ask him or her to plug a microphone into the system and to count to 20 into the mike as you test sound levels and quality through your little mixer. The technician will probably give you a "mike out," a "main out," an "auxiliary out," or a "tape out" connection on the board for you to plug into. Their output signal can be either mike level or line level; that's why it's a good idea to bring a direct box and your own small mike/line mixer so you can switch between the different levels. If none of those outputs works, and if the technician hears audio through the headphone jack on the mixer, you can plug into that connector. Use a 1/4-inch stereo "Y" adapter so he can still use his headphones. Make sure that the technician will not change the headphone volume setting while you are recording. A little gaffer tape over that slider or knob will help ensure that your levels don't vary.

Place a microphone near your camera for applause, and consider placing another microphone at the stage to get stage "ambiance." You will need at least one of these mikes during applause, since some sound technicians turn down (or abruptly turn off) the audio when there is applause.

Recording questions or comments from the audience can be a challenge, but you have options. In a smaller auditorium, consider hiring several assistants with handheld wireless mikes who can bring a mike to the questioner. The assistant would either hold the mike or hand it to the participant. Alternately, the assistants could be equipped with wireless or wired shotgun mikes. In advance, ask them to sit or crouch to be unobtrusive. Ask the assistants to wear black so they don't draw attention to themselves on camera.

Another technique is placing two or more microphones on stands at the foot of the aisles. The guests then walk to one of the microphones to ask their questions. One of the largest venues where this takes place is at the Berkshire Hathaway annual meeting of billionaire Warren Buffett fame. These shareholder meetings take place at the 20,000-seat Qwest Center in Omaha, Nebraska. About a dozen mikes are placed in the balconies and on the main floor, and each is illuminated with a spotlight.

Feeding the Audio and Video to a Remote Site

Warren Buffett's Berkshire Hathaway meetings are so popular that the company sends remote feeds to adjacent rooms at the Qwest Center and to nearby hotels. The company uses closed-circuit AV cables within the building and microwave transmitters to beam the signal to the hotels.

If your meeting will have fewer attendees than Berkshire's, you may need to simply run long audio and video cables from one room to the other. If you are running a video cable longer than 50 feet, rent or purchase a video amplifier or a video distribution amplifier to boost the signal. Audio sent through XLR cables as long as 400 feet usually does not need to be amplified.

Microwave transmitter-receiver systems may also be rented. They are not the large dishes you see on TV trucks but are smaller systems not much larger than a camera. Mount them on tripods and send the signal via line-of-sight from the transmitter to the receiver. You'll need to secure the tripods with sandbags or some other stabilizing device to prevent them from accidentally getting misaligned during the transmission.

Live Streaming of Meetings

Here is an opportunity for the video producer and the company's IT department to join forces to bring the immediacy of an important meeting or conference to the staff or shareholders who are not able to travel to attend. While you will probably upload it to a server for later viewing, nothing can match the excitement of watching an event live.

One consideration is that this is live TV. There are no second takes. Any sarcastic comments or misstatements cannot be removed. Also, make sure that you have a graphic with audio displayed just before the scheduled start time and for a little while after. That way, if the event starts late, viewers won't be seeing a live camera focusing and framing, nor will they hear the presenters at the podium making nervous remarks that they don't think are being transmitted.

The facility hosting the event will need to have a fast broadband upload speed. Don't confuse this with the download speeds, which usually are faster. Ideally, the facility will have a T1 connection or equivalent. Some content distribution networks (CDNs) can work with an upload speed as slow as 300 kbps, and some live streaming service providers indicate they can work with upload speeds as slow as 128 kbps. Some service providers use a wireless upload card linked to a 3G or 4G network on Sprint, Verizon, ATT, or other network. If you work with one of these companies, choose one that can provide redundancy by using more than one network to avoid the "Can you hear me now?" syndrome.

It is best if the event room has an Ethernet connection, but if it doesn't, you can send audio and video via cables or microwave to a different room that has the network connection. If your company does not have an IT department, you can hire an outside firm to provide the live streaming service for you. You can outsource the entire service, including camera and operator, or you can use the vendor just for the live streaming portion.

If you plan to upload the event yourself, plan on bringing your laptop or desktop computer with you. You'll need to have encoding software and a board capable of fast streaming installed on your computer. The software vendor gives you an IP address to upload the stream, and they provide a website for viewers to log onto.

If you don't want to install software on your computer and bring it on site, you can purchase a dedicated webcasting appliance such as one from Digital Rapids, ViewCast, or Newtek. Appliances are a turnkey system with hardware and software designed for live streaming. Appliances such as these are usually rack-mounted, but some are configured like a small computer tower. The appliances have a built-in CPU, a streaming encoder board, and software. You plug your camera into the appliance input, and the output goes to the facility's Ethernet network. Once logged onto the Internet, you then send the audio and video to a streaming website server or service. Bring the appliance on location with you instead of a computer, and you are ready to stream. Some of the appliance manufacturers also offer software and a special video board designed specifically for live streaming.

In addition to the hardware and software, you'll need a distribution server such as Adobe Flash Media Server, Windows Media Services, or Apple's Darwin Streaming Server. You'll also need an Internet upload speed fast enough to serve all your viewers. If you have a small number of viewers, your own distribution server may be adequate.

Alternately, you can use a content delivery network (CDN). A CDN lets you distribute to a larger number of viewers and can be useful when your upload speed is limited. It also eliminates the need to invest in your own distribution server. A CDN will multicast your video, since they have the bandwidth and control of the network architecture that a videographer rarely has. Many of the appliance manufacturers can refer you to a CDN, but popular CDNs include Highwinds, Akamai, and Limelight.

Conference Highlight Videos

If your organization is having a company-wide conference or a multiday event, consider offering to produce a short, edited video to play at the dinner or final session. Projected on a large screen with dynamic graphics and snappy music (legal, of course), it could be an exciting finale to a morale-boosting meeting.

You will need to have the time and resources to perform production planning, shoot plenty of B-roll, edit it on location, and project it in a large hall. The video should be short, and it need not have a script or narrator. The soundtrack could be music with a few live sound clips included when appropriate. Attendees will be entertained and energized, and it could have a very positive impact on your position in the firm.

Here is your chance to be creative. Discuss this production idea well ahead of time with your supervisor/client and the meeting planners. Plan to show the video near the end of the meeting, hopefully at a banquet where spirits are high. Incorporate graphics and titles from the conference, and perhaps think of a concept or message that your video will deliver. Consider making it as short as a minute but not much longer than five minutes. The meeting planners have plenty of other items on their agenda during this final session. The downside of offering to produce this quick turnaround video is that you probably will be working on it late into the night in your hotel room, and if your client/

supervisor has editorial control, it could take much more time to complete.

While recording meetings and conferences may not always offer the video producer much control over the production, and they sometimes don't let the producer flex his creative muscles, they are an opportunity for more visibility in the organization. Whether it is a small class for employee training or a convention-size shareholders' meeting, the corporate video producer's ability to get a crew together and take responsibility to record just about any size conference or meeting can help establish video production as a solid contributor to the corporation.

A Guide to Videotaping Meetings

Give this one-page guide to clients who want you to record meetings in conference rooms and hotels. These are ways that the video producer, the client, and the facility can work together to make sure the audio and video are topnotch and that the videographer remains as unobtrusive as possible.

Recording Clear Audio

Audio is our first name, and we want to make sure the viewers of your video can clearly hear the presenters. We have a bag of tricks to accommodate almost any location. We may attach one of our wireless mikes to your podium mike, or we might tie into the room's PA system. We will want to know how many mikes you plan to have at the meeting. While we don't usually provide a PA system, if you wish, we can subcontract for that service.

Wireless Microphones

Wireless mikes let the presenters move around while they speak. We can tap into the facility's wireless mike signal, or we can tie together our wireless mikes with the facility PA system. Usually the wireless mike is a clip-on mike. The presenter will need to have a collar to attach the mike and a belt or waistband to clip on the little transmitter.

Questions and Answers

Audience questions are difficult for mikes to pick up. One way to handle them is to set up a mike or two on stands in the audience. Another is to have assistants hand one or more handheld wireless mikes to the questioners. While we can aim a directional mike at the audience, it sometimes doesn't pick up quieter speakers or those farther away from the mike. If the audience will not be miked, please ask the presenters to repeat the questions within their answers.

Camera Placement

When planning the room setup, please choose a location where the camera can be placed. We usually like to position it in the rear of the room, directly opposite from the presenters. If slides will be projected on a screen, we like to be opposite the screen so we can get a straight angle on it.

(Continued)

A Guide to Videotaping Meetings (Continued)

If the facility provides a riser platform for the camera and camera operator, please request one; it helps avoid heads in the way. Similarly, use a raised stage so audience members and the camera can see the presenters. We usually plug into electricity. We will run an extension cord to the nearest outlet and will tape it down to the floor to avoid people tripping on it. Please make sure the facility will provide electricity.

Multiple Cameras

While we record most meetings with a single camera, we can set up two or three cameras. One way to accomplish this is with live-switching between the cameras so the final video is ready at the end of the meeting. This requires additional time to set up, running extra cables between the cameras, and additional equipment and personnel. Another multicam technique uses simultaneous camcorders with the tapes edited at a later time in our studio. We will be happy to explain the pros and cons of each technique and can provide you a quote for either of these options.

Lighting

Our digital cameras work well in low light, and in most cases we don't need auxiliary lighting. However, if the facility has spotlights, please order them and make sure they are properly aimed. Good lighting can make for a more pleasant video image.

If there are windows in the room that cannot be covered, please try to avoid placing the presenters in with a window behind them. If that can't be avoided, let us know, and we will bring a bright spotlight.

PowerPoint Slides and Other Projected Images

We can take your PowerPoint data disk and combine it with the video of the meeting. Alternately, we can shoot your meeting with two cameras: one aimed at the screen and the other at the presenter. We can also shoot a PowerPoint presentation with a single camera. We pan the camera between the presenter and the images on the screen. Since lights are usually turned down, we can bring a spotlight and aim it at the presenter. This works best if the presenter stands a distance from the screen. Call us ahead of time, and we can help with designing the room setup to accommodate this.

Logistics

Please ask the facility contact person how the videographer can best move equipment in and out. Will the security department need to be contacted? Will there be any locked doors? Is there a loading zone? Are there any restrictions bringing equipment in the lobby or in passenger elevators? If you can arrange for the videographer to have a standard parking space, that will help avoid delays. Also, if he needs to get something from the car, it will be quick. If there are special driving directions, please provide them to us. We are happy to speak directly with the facility contact person or his or her audiovisual technicians.

NONPROFIT ORGANIZATIONS

Introduction

Producing for nonprofits can be gratifying for those who enjoy documentary formats and storytelling from the heart. Such videos may provide the education and training to affect significant social change and even save lives. Nonprofits range from tiny community organizations with a small storefront office to huge associations like the Red Cross and the American Cancer Society, with divisions across the country if not the world. Much of the work of nonprofits involves fund-raising, now frequently referred to as "development." The video producer in the nonprofit sector frequently works together with the organization to apply for grant money to produce a video. Sometimes he or she does all the legwork to get the grant.

Most community nonprofits wage an uphill battle every year to raise enough funds to provide services to their communities and to maintain their administrative staffs. Nonprofit organizations frequently form alliances with corporations by asking some of their officers to serve on the boards of the nonprofits. Not only do the corporate leaders understand finances well enough to help manage the nonprofits, but they often have colleagues who regularly make charitable donations.

The enterprising video producer can make some good contacts in both the for-profit as well as nonprofit communities by providing video services to a prominent nonprofit organization. While the nonprofits will welcome your offer of pro bono services, they often do have budgets, at least to produce materials that can be used for fund-raising.

Multiple Constituencies: The Politics of Nonprofits

In addition to the CEO and the board of directors, nonprofit organizations have additional powerful constituencies who may call the shots more than the CEO or board chair. They include donors, especially the top ones; volunteers, including the volunteer coordinator; the spouse of a local corporate CEO; the leaders of the community that the nonprofit serves; and other local community organizations. In a for-profit company, the chain of command is clear: the corporation exists for the stockholders to earn a profit. In a nonprofit, you may get requests for service from different constituencies; knowing who comes first could be a challenge.

In my own experience, when I worked in the training department for a nonprofit health care organization, the development department would frequently call me to videotape or photograph fund-raising events. The budgets and the priorities for this department were higher than those of the other departments for whom I provided training videos. It didn't matter that I worked for the training department; my camera and I were fair game for anyone.

One day I got a call from the PR director to photograph a donor giving a check to the organization. I told her that we had a video shoot scheduled with the physical therapy department at that same time. The physical therapy staff had already been lined up to participate in the filming, and we had spent several weeks preparing for this shoot. The PR director would not accept my "no" answer and called a vice president, who called my department manager. Without hesitation, my manager told me to cancel the training video shoot and photograph the high-profile supporter presenting the check to the president of the organization. While training videos are a cost-effective way to better develop the skills of employees, in the nonprofit world training may take a backseat to an opportunity to "show me the money."

Case Studies: Nonprofits

The following are examples of videos for non-profit organizations produced with my company, Audio Visual Consultants.

Saving Lives with Video

For the video professional who wants to produce programs for health, a corporate application is available. After leaving PBS-affiliate WGBH in Boston, Steve Gilford headed out on his own. As an independent producer with a reel that included an award-winning video on health, Gilford approached a major publisher with an idea: What if he could produce a video to help people quit smoking within three weeks? The audience would be the millions of smokers who want to quit but can't. A celebrity would host the video, and the program would carry the imprimatur of the American Cancer Society.

The mass-market video was titled *21 Days to Quit Smoking*, and it was divided into chapters, each about three minutes in length. Comedian Robert Klein introduced each segment and instructed viewers on their tasks for that single day. Rather than overwhelm the anxious smokers, the video moved them along in baby steps. The viewer would stop the tape and wait until the following day for the next action step.

A smoker himself, Gilford knew how easily smokers could get discouraged when they backslide. So he developed a script that would encourage and motivate viewers by creating several successive benchmarks that were easily achievable. Gilford said that he rationalized his own smoking to the point of sneaking a cigarette in the bathroom of the American Cancer Society offices. He added that prior to mailing the script to his content specialist at the American Cancer Society, he had to flick cigarette ashes off some of the pages.

Shot in a studio and on location, the video relied on ACS-provided script consultation and visual materials. The society later followed up the successful video with a book based on the same three-week process. Gilford noted that many years after the video's release, he heard from a woman whose father quit smoking as a result of the video. She stated that he probably would not have been alive had the video not helped him to quit. In addition to earning royalties on sales of both the video and the book, Gilford benefited much more than financially: he quit smoking himself.

The American Cancer Society

For several years, my own company produced quarterly videotaped reports presented by the president of the California division of ACS. Usually about seven minutes in length, each video would show the president speaking to her staff and volunteers, with photos and text graphics illustrating key points. On some of the videos, she would interview one of her vice presidents or department heads. These were simple, low-budget videos that would be cost-effective because they eliminated a lot of staff travel. This is an easy way to justify a video budget, especially for nonprofits. Travel costs can quickly overwhelm a typical video budget.

We also videotaped the annual meetings so if any staff members were unable to attend, they could see the presentations from the speakers. For example, the chairman of the board, who is a cancer survivor herself, told her story and framed it in the context of achieving the ACS goal of reducing cancer deaths by 50 percent within the next 15 years. One of the vice presidents spoke and showed slides of a trip to China—the society's mission to bring smoking cessation programs to a country that loses nearly 2 million citizens to cancer annually.

Documentary-style interviews we produced became a popular video for recruiting volunteers. We filmed three people—all cancer survivors—of different ethnicities, who told their stories. Since this was designed for the on-camera presenters to speak directly to the audience, they looked at the camera when they spoke. Then we transcribed the presentations and edited them down to about one minute each. The common theme was that the process of volunteering gave each of them another purpose in their lives: helping their fellow cancer survivors.

Shooting CEOs for the YMCA

Rather than just asking donors for checks, many nonprofits hold awards banquets where they honor volunteers and board members who have served the organizations. A consortium of YMCAs in our community held such a banquet and hired my company to produce several short interviews to be shown there. At this particular banquet, a board member with a long tenure was retiring, and the YMCA's development department asked that we interview a number of their other board members to offer their kind words on camera. These board members were local corporate CEOs and other established community leaders.

While a couple of the shoots were at the YMCA office, we conducted the majority of the interviews at each board member's office. While we wanted to create the most flattering setting using soft lighting and interesting backgrounds, our crew knew that we needed to produce these interviews with minimal impact on the interviewees and their staffs. Since we would be asking them to leave their offices as we set up the equipment, we agreed that each of the setups would take no more than an hour.

We scouted the locations in advance to determine the best settings. We sought interesting backgrounds and quiet rooms. The crew ran long extension cords down hallways rather than tap into the circuit boxes. With prior permission we moved plants, paintings, and furniture to create the sets. In my role of producer-director, I briefed the guests in advance about what we wanted them to say on-camera and the time lengths they had. The structure of the video was that each of the five board members would speak for one to two minutes. The on-screen comments would be projected onto a large screen between dinner courses.

California Department of Public Health

Rather than incur the travel fees to send a team of consultants to public health offices in nine cities in California, my company videotaped the one- or two-day seminars and sent DVD copies to the remote offices. This was an easy budget decision, considering that the training team's travel expenses far exceeded the video production costs. We simply videotaped the seminars, inserted the PowerPoint slides (adding a few zooms and pans), and duplicated DVDs.

The videos were relatively low budget: a single camera in the rear of the room, tie-in to the sound system, and inserting the slides during postproduction. The organization considered online distribution, but at that time the cost of contracting with a CDN (content distribution network) exceeded the cost of duplicating and shipping DVDs. Many nonprofits want to include an evaluation mechanism to justify the cost of training and video production. In this case, the client developed a pretest and a posttest that were given to the participants who viewed the DVDs.

The production logistics included obtaining access to a secured public health lab (no small task in the wake of 9/11), obtaining permissions from the speakers, obtaining a clean audio feed from the sound board, and organizing the material into DVDs that followed the seminar syllabus.

The American Indian Cancer Control Project

This Berkeley California nonprofit organization contracted with my company to produce two community education videos over a two-year period. The first video was on smoking cessation for American Indians, and the other was developed to encourage Indians to get a Pap test, despite the culture's practice of favoring the health care traditions of their ancestors.

Our white-owned company with an all-white crew was surprised to be chosen by this organization. The organization had experience producing text-based training programs, and they followed many training development standards, such as determining behavioral objectives, directing the message to their select audience, and creating a measurement tool to confirm if objectives were achieved. But their experience with video had been limited to producing poor results with a consumer camcorder.

With their preproduction help, we wrote a script that had as its centerpiece a group discussion called a "talking circle." The circle consisted of a group of American Indians, some who have quit smoking cigarettes, some who want to quit, and some who have lost loved ones to lung cancer. They passed a ceremonial feather, and each participant waited to hold the feather before he or she spoke—a tradition of their culture.

The video started with an elder healer reciting a traditional prayer while burning sage. The voice-over narration juxtaposed the prayer as the narrator spoke about the use of smoke in religious rituals. Indian art and spiritual music accompanied the narrative and on-camera demonstration. Suddenly, a noise and a flash of light revealed a package of American Spirit cigarettes. The music abruptly stopped, and the healer's voice was drowned out by a wailing sound as more images of the cigarettes appeared along with Native American people smoking.

The scene then changed to an exterior desert scene that resembled an Indian reservation. (This was shot at the University of California Botanical Garden in Berkeley.) An American Indian woman walked alone in the setting. The soundtrack consisted of her thoughts as a voice-over talking to herself about the close relatives she had lost to lung cancer brought on by smoking. She expressed her sorrow and wondered what she could do to prevent more deaths of her people from smoking-related cancers. In the next scene, the same woman was in the talking circle. The live sound dipped as a voice-over narrator explained the tradition of talking circles and how they may be applied to modern-day life. Other members of the circle shared their stories. Text graphics and narration related the stories to phases of the smoking cessation program.

Starr King School of the Ministry

We produced a documentary-style video to acquaint viewers with the curriculum at this school for Unitarian ministers. Interviews with faculty, students, and graduates combined with voice-over narration presented the complex issues and questions that are part of daily life at this school. My company's location served as the production facility, and we brought in an Oscar-nominated documentary director, Mark Kitchell, to write and direct the film. Kitchell had experience with documentary production, and he was also familiar with the school and had conducted research about the faith.

We scheduled the two-week production around the visit of school alumnus Robert Fulghum, author of *All I Really Need to Know I Learned in Kindergarten*. We interviewed him and videotaped a class he taught. During the production, we videotaped visiting lecturer William Sloane Coffin, chaplain of Yale University and a former CIA agent-turned-antiwar-activist.

Kitchell conducted the interviews, and he asked thought-provoking questions that would help weave the story about the "calling" that students had discovered that would fulfill their lives' purposes. In an interview with the dean of students, Kitchell asked the dean to describe God, and the dean would use only the phrase "what some people refer to as God." The school president helped clarify these students' quests during her interview. The president, an accomplished cellist, created the music track for the video. We filmed alumni giving sermons at their own congregations and others performing community service. The video served as a public relations document, a recruiting tool, and a visual aid to assist with fund-raising efforts.

Progressive Way

The United Way is one of the largest charities in the United States. However, some critics have stated that too much of the money they raise goes to administrative costs rather than to the organizations they fund. So a competitor, Progressive Way, incorporated itself to attract donors who want more efficient use of their dollars. Similar to the program of the United Way, Progressive Way arranges with employees of companies to make donations through payroll deductions.

In the past, United Way was allowed to speak directly to employee groups. Now many companies require United Way and also Progressive Way to make their pitch via video. Our company made a 4-minute video for Progressive Way that they sent to participating companies to show to employees.

The video used a documentary approach that included brief interviews with the organizations that receive funding. The interviewees described the programs they were able to develop with the funds. Each interview could be no longer than 30 seconds, and as the director, I needed to coach the interviewees, in advance, to present their statements in succinct sound bites. In addition to the interview, the crew shot B-roll and collected existing photos and video clips of each group.

Voice-over narration with B-roll introduced each organization, and that motif was used for the conclusion. To keep the budget low, we used photos, newspaper headlines, shots of posters, video clips, and whatever material was available. The result was that Progressive Way was able to solicit employee donations on a level playing field with their Goliath competitor United Way.

Project SEED

A credit roll at the head of a corporate video? Well, it's not my style, but it was a requirement of this local nonprofit that had managed to get support from a great number of the largest corporations in the San Francisco Bay area. Despite my protests, the video starts with the organization's distinguished list of donors. Our contact specialist, who was their fund-raiser, explained to me that the audience consisted of people who want to develop contacts with these local power-brokers. It was an attention-getting opening that addressed the intended audience.

Project SEED teaches college-level math skills to inner-city fifth and sixth graders. The organization hires university instructors and scientists to be their classroom instructors. These teachers engage the students using a Socratic method of teaching. This technique involves asking the students questions and engaging their participation in solving problems.

One of the most powerful segments of this video was interviews with former students. Among those alumni interviewed were a successful lawyer, a social services administrator, and an actor. Our crew filmed two classes, each with two cameras and each in front of an audience of donors. One of these demos was held at a downtown hotel. That shoot included hiring a gaffer and a grip, who set up lights in the ceiling the night before the filming. Each camera's footage was recorded onto an individual VTR, and the sequence was compiled together in post. In order to complete this production within the organization's limited budget, we donated much of our time. I now have a letter in my file from Project SEED stating that our modest $10 K production yielded them over $100 K in donations. That became my calling card for future nonprofit clients.

Universities

Universities are major producers of educational videos, and the video manager at a university usually is part of a larger instructional media center. The media centers provide classroom support in the form of AV equipment, closed-circuit television (CCTV), and the infrastructures for live streaming of classroom presentations.

Some universities have spearheaded research into video streaming as well as software and hardware development. Frequently this technology gets transferred to major corporations, or former students themselves form a corporation.

For example, many years ago, some Stanford University students ran Ethernet cables between campus buildings. They called it the Stanford University Network (SUN), and later they created Sun Microsystems. The router that they used became one of the first products of Cisco Systems. At the MIT Media Lab, students developed MPEG-4 Structured Audio. MPEG-4 now is a popular compression codec for AV data for the web.

In conjunction with curricula in broadcasting, many universities operate their own broadcast TV channels. These are usually public television stations, and many produce programming for their communities. The video manager at a university may be involved in consulting with the station or serving on its board of directors. Students have an opportunity for hands-on training, internships, and possibly employment with these stations.

iTunes and YouTube at the University of California

The UC Berkeley Haas School of Business is one of the most prestigious business schools in the country, providing MBA grads for Fortune 100 corporations. Wouldn't YouTube or iTunes be more of a distraction to business communications rather than a vehicle for it? Hardly so, says Dana Lund, the business school's manager of media services. The school's custom YouTube channel frees up valuable in-house server space and enables those who might not be able to attend a special presentation to view it on demand. This audience includes the working professionals who enroll in the evening MBA program.

Some programs are streamed live, such as the Berkeley Entrepreneur Forums that my company films. Live streaming not only accommodates an overflow crowd, but it enables the university to reach out to the larger community. My company also makes a video-on-demand (VOD) version that gets posted to YouTube. Faculty members from the Haas School of Business travel to Europe and Asia to provide business start-up consultation. Some of the businesspeople in these areas have already viewed select videos online by the time the faculty visit. The videos provide not only valuable education, but they help make the visits more cordial and productive.

In addition to the Berkeley Entrepreneur Forums, the YouTube channel includes presentations by visiting lecturers, corporate presidents, and Nobel laureates. The university also maintains its own server, the Video Room, with classroom content that may be recorded from any of the several camera-equipped classrooms. One of the classrooms has four cameras and 40 microphones. Two cameras capture images from the stage, and the other two get shots of student interactions. The classroom can accommodate 80 students, with microphones in desks between each two students. An automatic mixer handles the audio. The technician operates the four cameras using a joystick control from the booth in the rear. He or she can also mix in images, such as PowerPoint from the instructor's computer.

The Haas School uses Real Media as their streaming platform. According to Dana Lund, they chose Real because it is easy to stream with, it outputs in H.264 (for YouTube), and it may be edited with Adobe Premiere. Real has its own editor with a 10-frame accuracy, and Lund says they frequently use that editor when all they need to do is slap a title on the head and tail of a video. Lund added that they like Real because it plays in a standalone window; they do not need to embed the video into a page, as is the case with Flash. Lund said that the school uses real-time webcasting in place of videoconferences because they can avoid the ISDN costs.

The Haas School of Business is part of the larger UC Berkeley system. While Haas Media Services has its own budget and runs independently from the campus-wide Office of Educational Technology Services, ETS provides high-end video production services and maintains the university's "Berkeley Webcast" video server, also known as "webcast.berkeley," as well as the entire YouTube channel.

ETS manages the Berkeley Multimedia Research Center (BRMC), which was an outgrowth of the Berkeley Internet Broadcasting System. With a National Science Foundation grant in 1995, the center produced and distributed its first webcast seminar. The site now includes over 100 courses available via Real Media streaming, YouTube distribution, streaming audio, and downloadable iTunes podcasts. Over a dozen of the classrooms on campus are equipped with a system to automatically record lectures and post them to the website. Among the video-on-demand choices is a lecture by President Bill Clinton recorded in February 2010.

Hospitals and Medical Centers

Color television had its first practical demonstration not by a television network but at the 1949 convention of the American Medical Association. As reported in *Life Magazine* (June 6, 1949), CBS designed a remote-controlled color camera for use in the operating room, and they transmitted the signal to 20 specially built receivers at the convention in Atlanta. This color television system was developed not for entertainment but as a new method of visual education for the medical profession. Since the FCC had not yet approved the CBS system (it was different from the soon-to-be-adopted NBC system), it could not be received on standard black and white sets. Later, CBS modified its system for broadcasting.

This tradition of video for medical education continued through the years, and television became integrated in the teaching programs at hospitals and medical centers. Pharmaceutical companies and medical device manufacturers sponsored the production and distribution of scores of films of surgical procedures. Hospitals that already had TV sets in patient rooms could use those receivers to provide education to patients.

The health care industry also uses video for marketing pharmaceuticals and medical equipment. While these companies are for-profits, their customers are the nonprofit health care providers. Video producers working in this industry (both on-staff and freelance) sometimes switch between working with the for-profit manufacturers and the nonprofit providers. While the corporate cultures are different, production techniques and audiences are frequently the same.

Government

Government entities are structured and operate much like corporations. Shareholders elect a board of directors, and constituents elect their city councils, legislatures, and the president. The employees in government fulfill the directives of the board of directors in much the same way as employees do in a corporation. In a similar manner as nonprofits, governments provide a service to their communities.

One important distinction between nonprofit organizations and government is that government doesn't have to constantly ask for donations. Taxes continuously support governments. And that is why government contracting is a lucrative business. Budgets for government-funded videos usually are generous. The downside is that the proposal process can be onerous.

In Chapter 2, we discuss ways you can get on bid lists and apply for government contracts. If you are a video manager working in the public service sector, you may have a generous budget and the opportunity to purchase new equipment. However, as many government entities downsize, you may be stuck with obsolete equipment and perhaps a minimal staff.

Government video projects range from live streaming of city council meetings to producing recruiting films for the military. Fire departments, police departments, and transit agencies all need training films. The House of Representatives has three mobile recording "studios" that are designed to be operated by a single technician/director. The system includes remote-controlled cameras inside a hearing room and a "crash cart" in the hallway operated by the director. They also have their own cable television channel, C-SPAN.

Many city governments use cable television channels to broadcast city council meetings, and some municipalities have contracted with the cable companies to provide local access channels. The cable companies offer production equipment and even full studios to woo the cities into signing exclusive cable TV contracts in their communities. Local cable channels are frequent employers of video producers, and the programming sometimes extends to covering local events and producing documentaries about community nonprofits.

Nonprofits come in many shapes and colors. Whether it is in government, universities, health care institutions, religious groups, or community organizations, the nonprofit sector is huge. While fund-raising can be a large part of the job at a nonprofit, this sector can include documentary production, development of instructional videos, staff training, and even involvement in cutting-edge research in video technology. The size and largess of some nonprofit corporations can offer bountiful opportunities for the video producer who wants to make a difference in the world.

YouTube Program for Nonprofits

Program Benefits

- Premium branding capabilities and increased uploading capacity
- The option to drive fund-raising through a Google Checkout "Donate" button
- Listing on the nonprofit channels and the nonprofit videos pages
- Ability to add a call-to-action overlay on your videos to drive campaigns
- Posting a video opportunity on the YouTube Video Volunteers platform to find a skilled YouTube user to create a video for your cause

Program Requirements

Organizations applying for the nonprofit program must meet the following criteria:

- Organizations must be U.S.-based nonprofits with IRS 501(c)(3) tax status.
- Organizations cannot be religious or political in nature.
- Organizations cannot focus primarily on lobbying for political or policy change.
- Commercial organizations, credit counseling services, donation middleman services, fee-based organizations, universities, and nonprofit portals are not eligible for the program.

From http://www.youtube.com/nonprofits.

50 Largest U.S. Charities

1. Mayo Foundation
2. YMCAs in the United States
3. United Way
4. Cleveland Clinic Foundation
5. Catholic Charities USA
6. American National Red Cross
7. Salvation Army
8. Goodwill Industries International
9. New York-Presbyterian Hospital
10. The Arc of the United States
11. Mount Sinai
12. Memorial Sloan-Kettering Cancer Center
13. Cedars-Sinai Medical Center
14. Henry Ford Health System
15. Boys & Girls Clubs of America
16. Children's Hospital of Philadelphia

(*Continued*)

50 Largest U.S. Charities (Continued)

17. Feed the Children
18. Shriners Hospitals for Children
19. American Cancer Society
20. Habitat for Humanity International
21. Children's Hospital
22. Planned Parenthood Federation of America
23. Nature Conservancy
24. Gifts in Kind International
25. Easter Seals
26. Beth Israel Deaconess Medical Center
27. World Vision
28. AmeriCares
29. YWCA of the USA
30. Girl Scouts of the USA
31. Boy Scouts of America National Council
32. Volunteers of America
33. Food for the Poor
34. CARE USA
35. American Heart Association
36. Catholic Relief Services
37. America's Second Harvest
38. St. Jude Children's Research Hospital
39. United Cerebral Palsy Association
40. Dana-Farber Cancer Institute
41. Public Broadcasting Service
42. Smithsonian Institution
43. Children's Hospital Los Angeles
44. Children's Memorial Hospital
45. City of Hope
46. Campus Crusade for Christ International
47. Children's National Medical Center
48. Children's Hospital
49. Metropolitan Museum of Art
50. Museum of Fine Arts, Houston

VIDEO DISTRIBUTION: LIVE STREAMING, VIDEO ON DEMAND, AND VIDEOCONFERENCING

Introduction

The speed of corporate communications requires that video information be delivered to employees almost instantly, if not transmitted live. Storage and access of audio and video files must be addressed, and the system should accommodate video on demand (VOD). The existing enterprise computer network is the ideal platform for live streaming, but the corporate video manager and IT team need to plan for this integration.

The corporate IT department may already have adequate bandwidth, as well as a management system for access control and usage-based reporting. It may also feature an enterprise webcast tool. However, many organizations have not allocated adequate bandwidth for high-quality video streaming or two-way videoconferencing. Live streaming in some organizations limits the quantity of viewers, and some systems may not have the security and reporting features that help ensure that employees are viewing.

As your company grows, you will need a system that provides enterprise-grade interactivity in a robust system. Users expect broadcast-quality video with high resolution and smooth frame rates. The audio should be clear, and, ideally, it should be in perfect sync with the video. Both video and audio should have minimal latency.

Jeffrey Marino of consulting firm Booz, Allen and Hamilton said that his team intentionally encodes their media at lower data rates than they would prefer "in order to give the viewer a more seamless experience." He said they want to avoid interruptions as the player buffers, which would happen with higher-bandwidth files. Their network is based on a gigabit backbone with 100 MB to the desktop for most users. Marino added that at his company, e-mail and telephone data are prioritized over streaming media, and streaming media is "at the bottom of the stack." He said they use Flash video instead of QuickTime and Windows because he found that Flash videos tend to work better on congested networks.

As companies grow and as the video library expands, the traditional corporate network infrastructure may not support high-quality video for a large employee pool. Employees need easy access to video on demand (VOD), and management needs security and accountability. Video streaming solutions may not support high resolution (720 × 480) or full-motion frame rate (30 frames per second). Webcams and popular video conferencing systems usually operate at lower bandwidths and low frame rates. Employees and customers expect television quality, but the low resolution or jerky motion of a low frame rate could cause them to become distracted by the technology and not focused on the content.

Employee training, product demonstrations, executive communications, company newscasts, and multinode videoconferencing are part of an enterprise-wide video solution. The lines between video streaming and videoconferencing sometimes become blurred as videoconferencing systems become more vigorous and lifelike. We will look at some videoconferencing systems that make you feel like your colleagues across the continent are sitting across the table from you. But first let's look at live video streaming solutions that can get your company started in an enterprise-wide video delivery platform.

Live Streaming

Corporations sometimes stream their videos to customers as well as employees. Therefore, if you are considering a streaming system for transmitting video to computers outside of the IT network, choose a system that detects local bandwidth and CPU conditions and seamlessly switches the video quality to the highest level accepted. That way, consumers with a fast connection may experience HD-quality streaming, and the corporation does not need to reduce the video quality to the lowest common denominator within the audience base.

Kontiki is a SaaS (software as a service) provider that streams through progressive download, and the company says they can

Figure 19.1 The capacity audience helped the client decide on live streaming. Notice camera-one in the background.

provide video programming within the enterprise without over-loading the network.

A system using distributed HTTP-based web servers performs the media download as a series of very small progressive down-loads, rather than a large single progressive download. Known as adaptive streaming, this technique uses generic HTTP caches or proxies, and it doesn't require specialized servers at each node. Start-up and seeking can be initiated at a lower bit rate, and then the files move at the high bit rate. The system should have no buffering or stuttering. Adaptive bit rate streaming adjusts the properties of the stream based on network conditions to maxi-mize the quality of the stream. When streaming occurs, the net-work server and the client's computer establish a connection. Connection speeds can fluctuate when using DSL connections or a LAN (local area network). Sometimes the video playback can stutter, become jerky, or stop altogether. This occurs because the client's computer memory runs out and the computer needs to wait to get more video. This is called buffering; the incoming stream exceeds the current available bandwidth.

Adaptive bit rate streaming systems detect the available bandwidth, and then the server adjusts the transmission to deliver a stream at the most appropriate bit rate. The server sends several streams simultaneously, and it switches to a lower bit rate stream when needed. During video playback, should the client computer's bandwidth increase, a good adaptive bit rate streaming system will change to a faster stream. However, it rarely will return to the highest bit rate.

In come cases, to avoid buffering, a system will employ "stream thinning" to intentionally decrease the image quality. Usually the only quality difference is the frame rate; rather than sending 30 frames per second (fps), it may slow the stream to 15 or even 10 frames per second. In some cases, if bandwidth decreases drastically, the system will send audio without video.

Computer media players improve with each new release. Windows Media Player (http://www.microsoft.com/windows/windowsmedia/default.mspx), Apple QuickTime (http://www.apple.com/quicktime), RealPlayer (www.real.com), and VLC (www.videolan.org) all incorporate enhancement technologies to filter such artifacts as ghosting, ringing, and enlarged pixels. When the user's computer receives video at a low bit rate, the resolution can decrease, causing the larger pixels. The pixels can become so large they become visible as blocks. Processing filters built into the players smooth the edges of the blocks and help remove the image artifacts.

H.264, VP8, Flash, HTML5, and WebM

H.264, also known as MPEG-4, is a popular compression codec for sending audio and video over the Internet. It is considered a "family of standards" that includes H.264/AVC (advanced video codec). A specific decoder decodes at least one but not necessarily all profiles. It provides high quality with lower bit rate than MPEG-2—about half the bit rate. The codec is popular because it is flexible enough to work in both low- and high-resolution video, DVD storage, and packet networks.

VP8 is an open-source codec developed by On2 Technologies, which is, as of this writing, owned by Google. VP8 is a royalty-free web video format. Google also provides WebM as the container format. WebM files have a .webm extension and play in HTML5-compatible browsers updated to support WebM. According to the WebM Project, "WebM defines the file container structure, video, and audio formats. WebM files consist of video streams compressed with the VP8 video codec and audio streams compressed with the open-source Vorbis audio codec."

Adobe Flash is a popular method of streaming video over the Internet. Flash video files have a .flv extension, and they may be placed in an embedded player on a web page. Flash files may also have the .swf extension (shock wave flash) that needs a standalone player. The Flash player is a browser plug-in. Flash videos are not directly playable from an e-mail or a document, but they need a link to the web page where they reside.

The downside of Flash, as of this writing, is that Flash videos don't play on Apple mobile devices such as the iPhone and the iPad. Many corporate video producers have created a YouTube page for their companies so their videos will display on a smart phone. YouTube will distribute Flash videos, but they convert Flash into a JavaScript so it is playable on iPhones and iPads.

One of the criticisms of Flash video is the issue of security. Adobe products have become a popular target for attackers. Symantec's "Internet Security Threat Report" states that "a remote code execution in Adobe Reader and Flash Player was the second most attacked vulnerability in 2009." Symantec also suggests that when a user visits an untrusted site, he or she should disable the Flash Player. McAfee reports similar high levels of attacks on Adobe applications.

Unlike a standard media player, the Flash Player animates on top of a video rendering, possibly making it more resource intensive than dedicated video player software. For smart phones, this translates into reduced battery life, among other things. Windows seems to display Flash easier than Mac OS or Linux platforms. According to StreamingLearningCenter's Jan Ozer (www.streaminglearningcenter.com), the Flash Player 10.1 "is extremely efficient on platforms where it can access hardware acceleration for video playback." Smart phones using the Android platform support Flash, as does Nokia.

The alternative to Flash is HTML5, which supports embedding video on an HTML page. Its creators hope that HTML5 will overshadow Flash as the standard for playing videos on the Internet. With the popularity of Apple's iPad, many Internet sites have been quick to adopt HTML5 as an option for playing videos, and it is something you should consider as a corporate video producer.

Media players, such as Windows Media Player, QuickTime, and RealPlayer, play back video using dedicated software on the user's computer. This is different from Flash and HTML5, which play video from a website. Windows Media Player is bundled into Windows computers, and the QuickTime Player comes with Macs. Both are available for either platform. These media players have onscreen buttons for playback controls, and some players let you adjust the playback speed and the display size. Some computers come with third-party players, and several players are available for free downloads, such as RealPlayer and VLC Player.

Streaming Appliances

For the department that would rather purchase a turnkey streaming system, there are "appliances" on the market that include a CPU, a capture board, and software. They come configured as either a rack-mounted unit or as a tabletop touch-screen unit. Consider purchasing a dual-channel system that supports both Flash and Windows Silverlight. Microsoft Silverlight operates similar to Adobe Flash to integrate video, graphics, and interactivity. It supports Windows Media Video (WMV), Windows Media Audio (WMA), and MP3 in browsers without requiring Windows Media Player (WMP).

By the time you read this, streaming appliances may also support HTML5. The appliance should have an intuitive web-based interface. Some include a front panel LCD readout or even a small video display. Look for a unit with three Ethernet ports. The first is the primary video feed that connects to the content delivery network (CDN). The second port is for backup. The third port provides remote management so you can monitor your stream from your office computer. You should be able to create multiple, simultaneous streams at different resolutions. Other features to look for include scaling, cropping, deinterlacing, inverse telecine, filtering, noise reduction, and closed-caption rendering.

According to Mike Nann of Digital Rapids, a supplier of streaming appliances, live streaming to multiple users is similar to sending your video signal to a video distribution amplifier (DA). "As an analogy, let's say you have a video camera with only SDI output, and you want to send the live video from it to ten different TVs that only have composite inputs. You'll take the SDI output of the camera, use a device to convert it to composite, and then route that composite signal to a distribution amplifier. The DA takes that one composite signal and makes ten out of it; the ten outputs of the DA then go to the individual TVs.

"For live streaming, the encoder basically plays the role of the SDI-to-composite converter unit, and the streaming server plays the role of the distribution amplifier—taking a single source stream in and creating ten output streams for ten viewers. (The ten is just an example number.)

"Instead of video cables, though, the connections are all virtual on a network, and the data rate of each connection (stream) plays a role. With a physical distribution amplifier, if you have one source cable coming in

Figure 19.2 Digital Rapids TouchStream video and audio streaming appliances combine live streaming with an intuitive touch-screen interface in a fully self-contained, portable unit for professional streaming applications.

and X number of viewers, you need X cables coming out. With streaming, if you have a 750 Kbps stream coming into the streaming server, and you have X number of viewers, you have a total of 750 Kbps coming out—and you need enough speed on your Internet connection to handle it. Ten viewers of that stream = 7,500 Kbps = 7.5 Mbps."

If no Internet connection is available, you can consider a system that uses cellular technology to stream video. Ustream offers the Livepack—what they call "a satellite truck in a backpack: a complete portable video broadcast encoding and streaming solution in a backpack." Ustream's Livepack is a customized computer that operates over several mobile phone carrier networks. The pack has six data modems that are load-balanced over three networks (AT&T, Verizon, and Sprint). The company says it is "capable of transmitting live video of up to 1 Mbps for up to six hours when fully loaded." Ustream says their Livepack is perfect for any situation where there is no feasible Internet connection, such as sporting events, on-the-street interviews, live music concerts, red carpet events, or mobile productions.

You can set up your own streaming computer with a capture board with real-time video processing and software. Choose a capture board that accepts both standard-definition and high-definition inputs. It should have independent settings for sizing, scaling, and bit rate speeds. Other features to look for are loss of video detection, color space conversion, automatic telecine detection and processing, and automatic optimization for changing motion content. Grass Valley EDIUS and the BlueFish Epoch are HD boards with these specifications.

When purchasing streaming software, look for such features as the ability to adjust compression settings and hardware pre-processing options. An important feature is batch encoding so you can capture any input format to an uncompressed media file in real time and automatically transcode it to multiple formats. Another feature enables independent video and audio encodes to be multiplexed into selected container formats. You want to be able to create multiple, parallel multiplexed outputs from the same encodes, eliminating redundant encoding when creating multiple deliverables from the same source.

Videoconferencing and Collaboration Technology

The corporate video producer or manager may be involved with managing or even purchasing a videoconference system. Companies that have multiple locations with employees spread

Figure 19.3 Cisco Systems' TelePresence videoconferencing system uses high-definition cameras and monitors plus an 18 Mbps Internet connection to give users the feeling they are in the same room with their colleagues on the screen.

across the country or around the world use videoconferencing as an alternative to employees to traveling to meetings.

TelePresence systems are high-end videoconferencing systems that incorporate large screen displays—and sometimes multiple displays—that give a realistic view of the parties on the other end. The Cisco Systems TelePresence system incorporates large HD monitors and loudspeakers positioned near the images of individuals speaking to create the illusion of a live conference. Cisco designs the systems to look alike, even to the details of the table design and wall colors. This contributes to the realistic feel of a live conference.

We visited the TelePresence room at one of the 50 Kaiser Permanente sites equipped with Cisco TelePresence systems. The room has three 60-inch monitors and a wraparound conference table that appears to continue into the image on the monitors. The colleagues on the monitors are framed and positioned so their images are their actual size. Six people can sit at the conference table as three cameras capture their images. Voice-activated mikes ensure that the sound is clear, and a cove light behind the monitors creates an even and unobtrusive illumination. Additional participants can sit behind the six front seats. Video is transmitted in high-definition and displayed in HD at 1080p.

According to Larry Kless, videoconferencing production manager at Kaiser Permanente Northern California, "People love this because you're right there. You look like you're looking at them." Kless explained that Kaiser Permanente leases the systems, and some of the basic systems have only a single monitor. The Tele-Presence systems allow the users of WebEx to join the conversation, and anyone can plug in a laptop computer to display PowerPoint, Excel spreadsheets, and other imagery. Those images are displayed from a projector that illuminates a white screen below the main monitors.

Kaiser Permanente also has a multicam videoconference room in the Northern California regional offices with three robotic cameras, each with TelePrompters and an overhead camera to display printed graphics. There is a scan converter for images from a laptop computer or from a desktop computer in the adjacent control room. Inside the control room, Kless can operate the cameras and mix audio. Most live productions only require two staff members to operate all the audio and video equipment. The system includes four Tandberg 6000 Integrators, which provide video codecs, tape playback, and archive capabilities.

Kaiser Permanente, with 35 medical centers, 431 medical offices, and over 160,000 employees, operates an extensive enterprise WAN, or enterprise wide area network. Kaiser Permanente first adopted videoconferencing in the late 1980s with the rollout of their first private microwave network. The company is now migrating to an IP-based network, which will take several years. KP adopted Cisco's WebEx as a desktop web conferencing platform and TelePresence technology to combat the rising cost of travel. The adoption rate of WebEx has been remarkable. In March 2010, the company conducted 35,000 WebEx conferences comprising 8 million meeting minutes. WebEx users can also connect webcams and share documents; this extends the video-conference room capabilities to the desktop.

Figure 19.4 In a control room that we created on location, the shader uses the camera control units (CCUs) as well as waveform monitor and vectorscope to adjust the color and brightness of the cameras.

Content Distribution Networks

The video manager who needs to select a video distribution system is faced with a challenge: conserve the company's financial resources and bandwidth, while providing all employees with a realistic video experience. If the corporation has been using a single server to send data to employees' terminals, they

Figure 19.5 The live streaming team brings an encoding working station, a backup system, and other signal processing and monitoring gear.

may want to consider using a content delivery network (CDN). A CDN lets you distribute to a larger number of viewers and can be useful when your upload speed is limited. It also eliminates the need to invest in your own distribution server.

A CDN may be able to multicast your video, since it has the bandwidth and control of the network architecture that a videographer rarely has. However, as the enterprise grows, a standard CDN may be limited. Some providers of software as a service (SaaS) offer what they call an enterprise video platform, or EVP. This scalable technology works with the corporation's existing network and uses the provider's hardware in a cloud computing environment.

The video team uploads their videos, and the service provider does the encoding and storage. Look for a provider that can target and push video to select groups and users. You'll want to make sure the system syndicates to the intranet and provides secure access via integration with the corporate directory. In addition, the system should provide metadata management, as well as reports on the use by employees and network utilization.

The system should provide full-motion, full-resolution video; be scalable to accept new employees and groups; and be relatively easy to use by employees. Furthermore, the system should leverage your existing videoconferencing equipment to deliver the conference sessions to each employee's desktop.

The employees should be able to receive the highest-quality video and audio stream based on their bandwidth. Make sure that VOD (video on demand) does not interfere with other business traffic on the network. A good system should minimize WAN usage and provide network efficiency similar to multicasting. Feedback to the central IT department and end-to-end security are a must.

Additionally, the audio support should include remote control audio transfer. The software should transfer audio across the network and play it to the speakers attached to the local computer. Music playback software usually works with sound control hardware to send audio to the locally attached speakers. Network audio support should include a remote-control software package that supports audio transfer to remote computers.

Your network audio and video distribution system should also support cobrowsing. That ensures that everyone who is part of a live interactive webinar with video sees the desired scenes. When the session leader selects a different video scene or chapter, all participants should see that same clip. The cobrowsing system should have a video player that supports embedded multimedia. That way, the session leader can synchronize playback for all users. The cobrowsing tool should allow all users to operate the Play, Stop, and Pause buttons.

Another consideration is file transfer so all the users on a network can transfer audio and video files between local and remote computers. This should be built into the program's user interface. In addition to AV files, users should also be able to transfer PowerPoint, Keynote, and PDF files. A remote mouse pointer and markup tools will let the presenter focus on particular elements within the images.

Web conferencing using webcams may not provide the resolution or frame rate that more sophisticated systems such as Cisco's TelePresence offers. However, there are some low-cost technologies worth considering. Microsoft Office Live Meeting can create a 360-degree view by stitching together several USB-based video cameras. The system will automatically determine which person in a room is speaking and then switch to that camera only. Users first see the 360-degree view, and then they see an enlarged view of the individual speaking.

Figure 19.6 In our makeshift control room (in a storeroom), we directed the camera operators. Notice the monitor with Multiview software that displays several cameras at once.

Satellite Distribution

Some corporations have built their own virtual private networks (VPNs) that handle videoconferencing, telephone service, e-mail service, and Internet file transfer as well as video. In

Figure 19.7 In our control room, the client monitors (with laptop) feedback from online participants and selects questions from them that will be asked of the presenter during question and answer sessions.

some cases the system includes terrestrial transmission via fiber together with satellite communication. They may have their own satellite antennas at their buildings and some contract with outside video service providers to transmit individual meetings, conferences, and events. While IP (Internet protocol) video distribution continues to improve, when you want to be certain of live, broadcast-quality transmissions, satellite distribution may be the best bet.

When an organization contracts with a service provider, that contractor arranges for time on a particular satellite. They provide a truck with a satellite antenna, or they send the signal via microwave to a satellite transmission facility in the area. Sometimes a teleport is used as a bridge to transmit or modify the signal. In this case, the signal is downlinked (taken into the teleport), where the signal is adjusted, if needed, to the format required at the receiving end. This is important when the company has divisions in other countries and needs to change the television standard to that of the receiving country. Then the signal is uplinked to the satellite where it is distributed.

The "earth station" may be permanently mounted on the roof of the building. When the earth station is on a truck, it is called a transportable earth station, or TES. Some of the satellite trucks include video production and editing equipment. Rather than take the chance that your equipment is not compatible with theirs, it is sometimes more convenient to use their gear, and sometimes even their personnel. Once you have established a rapport with a particular TES provider, you may want to save your corporation some money by providing your own cameras and crew.

The satellite technician will need to have a line-of-sight to the satellite or microwave tower. You may need to obtain a special permit from your city to allow the truck to park on a sidewalk or an alley. Some trucks have their own generators, but if you can supply power, you can avoid them running their engines.

Satellite trucks operate in two different bands: C-Band and Ku Band. Ku Band trucks use a smaller antenna and are easier to set up. They need only be mounted on a van or even a good-sized SUV, rather than a large truck. Television stations use them, since they are relatively quick to set up.

Although they are larger and require a wired telephone line, the C-Band systems are popular because they work in the rain. Ku Band has a less robust signal and is known to be susceptible to "rain fade." Some C-Band systems now can bypass the wired phone line and work with a cellular phone. In either case, you need to make sure the satellite service provider is licensed by the FCC to operate.

The Enterprise Content Delivery System

The video manager may be asked to join a team to design or improve the corporation's content delivery network, or he or she may wish to propose additions to the current system. We have listed some attributes for a modern enterprise-wide video distribution system. Certainly each organization has its own culture, resources, and needs, and the video manager can use that information to help propose the delivery network for the enterprise.

Consider using the network for all distribution of AV materials. Rather than replicate DVDs or CDs, if the network has available bandwidth, audio and video files are easily distributed via the portal. Employee training and sales collateral can be delivered on demand through a content delivery system. For example, employees can learn how to utilize a new software application by viewing a short instructional video. Sales staff in the field can show a filmed customer testimonial to their prospects, or the system can provide them with ready access to new product information and store display materials. The company CEO can speak to all the employees live over the network, or a division director can speak with select staffers in that division.

Teams or individual employees may subscribe to a specific channel to be notified of updates to materials in their areas. Employees on the go could have access to the network via their smart phones. A good content delivery system will automatically convert audio and video files into the format needed for users to view video clips on their mobile devices and tablet displays. Employees could subscribe to appropriate news feeds, with the approval of management, and they would have access to the latest videos and blog messages in their fields.

Video has become an integral communications tool in the enterprise. The corporate IT network is a natural delivery system for video communications, and the video manager can join the IT team to help design and develop a robust and flexible video content delivery network.

APPENDIX

Sample 1

Fringe assumptions:

Payroll Tax	23%	Length:	30 min.
Overtime	10%	Format:	Video (DVCam)
		Prep:	4 weeks
		Shoot:	9 days
		Post:	6 weeks (Off/On-Line Nonlinear to DigiBeta)
		Unions:	None

SUMMARY BUDGET

02-00 Script	4,680	
03-00 Producers Unit	25,600	
04-00 Direction	12,300	
05-00 Cast	554	
TOTAL ABOVE-THE-LINE		**43,134**
10-00 Production Staff	12,792	
15-00 Set Operations	211	
21-00 Electrical	4,853	
22-00 Camera	9,851	
23-00 Sound	3,965	
24-00 Transportation	495	
25-00 Location Expenses	936	
27-00 Stock—Production	736	
TOTAL PRODUCTION		**33,838**
30-00 Editorial	13,717	
33-00 Music	2,000	
34-00 Post Production Sound	4,475	
35-00 Titles & Graphics	2,400	
TOTAL POST-PRODUCTION		**22,592**

(Continued)

SUMMARY BUDGET (Continued)

37-00 Insurance	5,700		
38-00 General & Administrative	4,350		
TOTAL OTHER		**10,050**	
Total Above-The-Line		**43,134**	
Total Below-The-Line		**66,480**	
Total Above and Below-the-Line		**109,614**	
Contingency @ 10 %		**10,961**	
GRAND TOTAL		**$120,575**	

ABOVE-THE-LINE

		Amount	Units	x	Rate	Sub-Total	Total	
02-00 Script								
02-01 Writer Salaries (non-union)		1	Flat	1	3,500	3,500	3,500	
02-03 Title Registration		1	Allow	1	375	375	375	
	Payroll				3,500	805	805	
					Total for 02-00			**4,680**
03-00 Producers Unit								
03-02 Producer		1	Flat	1	20,000	20,000	20,000	
03-06 Consultants		1	Allow	1	1,000	1,000	1,000	
	Payroll				20,000	4,600	4,600	
					Total for 03-00			**25,600**
04-00 Direction								
04-01 Director (non-union)		1	Flat	1	10,000	10,000	10,000	
	Payroll				10,000	2,300	2,300	
					Total for 04-00			**12,300**
05-00 Cast								
05-08 Narrator (non-union)		1	Day	1	450	450	450	
	Payroll				450	104	104	
					Total for 05-00			**554**

BELOW-THE-LINE

10-00 Production Staff

10-01 Unit Production Manager	6	Weeks	1	800	4,800	4,800

Prep: 4 weeks
Shoot: 1 week
Wrap: 1 week

10-08 Production Assistant	10	Weeks	1	550	5,500	5,500	
Prep: 4 weeks							
Shoot: 1 week							
Wrap: 5 weeks							
Runner	1	Days	1	100	100	100	
Payroll				10,400	2,392	2,392	
Total for 10-00							**12,792**

15-00 Set Operations

15-01 First Grip							
Shoot	1	Days	14	25	350		
15-05 Craft Service (PA)							
Purchases	7	Days	1	30	30	30	
Rentals	1	Allow	1	100	100	100	
Payroll				350	81	81	
Total for 15-00							**211**

21-00 Electrical

21-01 Gaffer							
Prep	1	Day	10	25	250		
Shoot (10 hrs.)	7	Days	14	25	2,450		
Overtime				2,700	270	2,970	
21-06 Equip. Rental							
Light/Grip Pckg	7	Days	1	100	700	700	
Extra Package	1	Day	1	500	500	500	
Payroll				2,970	683	683	
Total for 21-00							**4,853**

22-00 Camera

22-01 Director of Photography/Op.							
Scout	1	Day	12	$32.14	386		
Shoot (10 hrs.)	9	Days	14	$32.14	4,050		
Overtime				4,435	444	4,879	
22-07 Camera Pckg Rentals (Video)	7	Days	1	550	3,850	3,850	
Payroll				4,879	1,122	1,122	
Total for 22-00							**9,851**

23-00 Sound

23-01 Mixer	Shoot (10 hrs.)	7	Days	1	350	2,450	
	Overtime				2,450	245	2,695
23-03 Expendables (Batteries, etc)		1	Allow	1	150	150	150
23-06 Radio Mics		5	Days	2	50	500	500
Payroll					2,695	620	620
Total for 23-00							**3,965**

(Continued)

BELOW-THE-LINE (Continued)

24-00 Transportation

24-03 Production Van	9	Days	1	55	495	495	
			Total for 24-00				**495**

25-00 Location Expenses

25-06 Catering Service

Crew Meals (6 crew + 4 guests)	6	Lunch	12	13	936	936	
			Total for 25-00				**936**

27-00 Stock — Production

28-03 Videotape Stock — Production	46	Tapes	1	16	736	736	
(Allow 6/day × 7days)			**Total for 27-00**				**736**

30-00 Editorial

30-08 Editor		5	Weeks	1	1,500	7,500	7,500	
30-09 Off/On-Line Edit System		5	Weeks	1	750	3,750	3,750	
30-12 Videotape Dubs/Stock & Transfers								
	VHS Off-Line Dubs	50	Tapes	1	20	1,000		
	Off-Line Misc. dubs	1	Allow	1	50	50		
30-13 DVD Screening Copies		20	DVD	1	35	700	700	
30-14 Video Masters/Safeties/Textless						0	0	
	DigiBeta Master	1	Tape	1	21	21	21	
	DigiBeta Protection	1	Tape	1	21	21	21	
	Payroll				7,500	1,725	1,725	
			Total for 30-00					**13,717**

33-00 Music

33-01 Composer	1	Allow	1	2,000	2,000	2,000	
(All-In Package includes: Arrangers,					0	0	
Copyists, Musicians, Instruments,							
Studio, Engineers, Stock, etc)							
			Total for 33-00				**2,000**

34-00 Post Production Sound

34-01 Spotting for Music/Sound Efx	3	Hours	1	150	450	450	
34-05 Narration Record	1	Hour	1	175	175	175	
34-14 Laydown	1	Hour	1	175	175	175	
34-15 Pre-Lay	6	Hours	1	150	900	900	
34-16 Mix	10	Hours	1	200	2,000	2,000	
34-17 Layback	1	Hour	1	375	375	375	
34-18 Stock/Dubs/Transfers (Video)	1	Allow	1	400	400	400	
			Total for 34-00				**4,475**

35-00 Titles & Graphics

35-01 Graphic Design & Workstation	1	Allow	1	2,000	2,000	2,000
35-02 Stocks and Dubs	1	Allow	1	400	400	400
				Total for 35-00		**2,400**

37-00 Insurance

37-01 Producers Entertainment Pckg	1	Allow	1	2,000	2,000	2,000
Negative					0	0
Faulty Stock					0	0
Equipment					0	0
Props/Sets					0	0
Extra Expense					0	0
3rd Party Property Damage					0	0
Office Contents					0	0
37-02 General Liability (Included)					0	0
37-03 Hired Auto					0	0
37-04 Cast Insurance					0	0
37-05 Workers Compensation	1	Allow	1	1,200	1,200	1,200
37-06 Errors & Omissions	1	Allow	1	2,500	2,500	2,500
				Total for 37-00		**5,700**

38-00 General & Administrative Expenses

38-02 Legal	1	Allow	1	1,500	1,500	1,500
38-03 Accounting fees	1	Allow	1	500	500	500
38-05 Telephone/FAX	1	Allow	1	500	500	500
38-06 Copying	1	Allow	1	125	125	125
38-07 Postage & Freight	1	Allow	1	200	200	200
38-08 Office Space Rental				0	0	0
38-09 Ofice Furniture				0	0	0
38-10 Office Equipment & Supplies	1	Allow	1	200	200	200
38-11 Computer Rental	1	Allow	1	0	0	0
38-13 Transcription (5 hrs × 3)	15	Hours	1	25	375	375
38-14 Messenger/Overnight	1	Allow	1	125	125	125
38-15 Parking	1	Allow	1	100	100	100
38-16 Storage	1	Allow	1	150	150	150
38-17 Still Photographer	1	Allow	1	250	250	250
Equip./Supplies/Film/Processing	1	Allow	1	125	125	125
38-18 Publicity	1	Allow	1	0	0	0
38-20 Hospitality	1	Allow	1	200	200	200
38-21 Production Fee	1	Allow	1	0	0	0
				Total for 38-00		**4,350**

Contingency @ 10%	10,961	10,961
GRAND TOTAL		**$120,575**

(Continued)

BELOW-THE-LINE (Continued)

Total Above-The-Line	**43,134**
Total Below-The-Line	**66,480**
Total Above and Below-the-Line	**109,614**

Check budget 120,575 120,575
totals

Budgets provided by Michael Wiese Productions. Excerpted from Film and Video Budgets, 5th Edition by Deke Simon www.mwp.com

Sample 2

Fringe assumptions:

Payroll Tax	23%	Shoot Days:	2
WGA	14%	Location:	Local
DGA	13%	Unions:	AFTRA
SAG	14%	Production:	Super 16 mm film
AFTRA	12%		DVCam
Agency Fees	10%	Off-Line:	Non-linear — 5 days
		On-Line	Non-linear — 12 hrs.

SUMMARY BUDGET

02-00 Script	2,460	
03-00 Producers Unit	7,700	
04-00 Direction	0	
05-00 Cast	1,416	
TOTAL ABOVE-THE-LINE		**11,576**
10-00 Production Staff	1,661	
13-00 Production Design	2,844	
14-00 Set Construction	2,000	
15-00 Set Operations	4,302	
16-00 Special Effects	750	
19-00 Wardrobe	2,032	
20-00 Make-Up and Hairdressing	461	
21-00 Electrical	3,652	
22-00 Camera	9,249	
23-00 Sound	619	
24-00 Transportation	660	
25-00 Location Expenses	2,700	
27-00 Film & Lab	3,476	
TOTAL PRODUCTION		**34,405**

30-00 Editorial				7,060		
33-00 Music				2,000		
34-00 Post Production Sound				3,075		
35-00 Titles & Graphics				2,500		
36-00 Stock Footage				2,700		
	TOTAL POST-PRODUCTION					**17,335**
37-00 Insurance				0		
38-00 General & Administrative				0		
	TOTAL OTHER					**0**
Total Above-The-Line						**11,576**
Total Below-The-Line						**51,740**
Total Above and Below-the-Line						**63,316**
Contingency @ 10 %						**6,332**
	GRAND TOTAL					**$69,648**

ABOVE-THE-LINE

		Amount	Units	x	Rate	Sub-Total	Total	
02-00 Script								
02-01 Writer's Salaries		5	Days	1	400	2,000	2,000	
	Payroll				2,000	460	460	
					Total for 02-00			**2,460**
03-00 Producers Unit								
03-02 Producer		14	Days	1	500	7,000	7,000	
	Payroll				7,000	700	700	
					Total for 03-00			**7,700**
04-00 Direction								
04-01 Director						0	0	
					Total for 04-00			**0**
05-00 Cast								
05-01 Lead Actors								
	Basketball star					0	0	
	Scientist	1	Day	1	380	380	380	
	Narrator (2x scale)	1	Hour	1	622	622	622	
	Agency fee @ 10%	1	Allow	1	622	62	62	
	Payroll				1,002	230	230	
	AFTRA				1,002	121	121	
					Total for 05-00			**1,416**

BELOW-THE-LINE

10-00 Production Staff
10-08 Production Assistants

Set PA	8	Days	1	150	1,200	1,200	
PA/Script	1	Day	1	150	150	150	
Payroll				1,350	311	311	
				Total for 10-00			**1,661**

13-00 Production Design
13-02 Art Director

Prep	3	Days	1	325	975		
Shoot	2	Days	1	325	650	1,625	

13-03 Assistant

Prep	3	Days	1	125	375		
Shoot	2	Days	1	125	250		
Wrap	0.5	Day	1	125	63	688	
Payroll				2,313	532	532	
				Total for 13-00			**2,844**

14-00 Set Construction

14-06 Purchases (Bld. materials)	1	Allow	1	1,000	1,000	1,000	
14-07 Rentals (Greens/drapery etc.)	1	Allow	1	1,000	1,000	1,000	
				Total for 14-00			**2,000**

15-00 Set Operations
15-01 First Grip

Prod. shot Shoot	1	Day	12	25	300		
Talent Shoot	1	Day	12	25	300	600	

15-02 Second Grip (Best Boy)

Prod. shot Shoot	1	Day	12	22	264		
Talent Shoot	1	Day	12	22	264	528	

15-04 Dolly Grip

Prod. shot Shoot	1	Day	12	22	264		
Talent Shoot	1	Day	12	22	264	528	

15-05 Craft Service

Prep	1	Day	6	13	78		
Shoot	2	Days	12	13	312	390	
Purchases	2	Days	1	100	200	200	

15-06 Grip Rentals

Package	2	Days	1	250	500	500	
Dolly	2	Days	1	250	500	500	
Cartage	1	Allow	1	75	75	75	

	Smoke cracker	1	Day	1	200	200	200	
15-07 Grip Expendables		1	Allow	1	200	200	200	
15-08 Box Rentals						0	0	
Key Grip		2	Days	1	30	60	60	
Craft Service		2	Days	1	25	50	50	
	Payroll				2,046	471	471	
				Total for 15-00				**4,302**

16-00 Special Effects

16-05 Special Effects-Squishy Shoe		1	Allow	1	750	750	750	
				Total for 16-00				**750**

19-00 Wardrobe

19-01 Stylist

	Prep (shoes/ wrdrobe)	2	Days	1	350	700		
	Shoot	2	Days	1	350	700	1,400	
19-04 Expendables		1	Allow	1	50	50	50	
19-05 Purchases		1	Allow	1	100	100	100	
19-10 Box Rentals		2	Days	1	30	60	160	
	Payroll				1,400	322	322	
				Total for 19-00				**2,032**

20-00 Make-Up and Hairdressing

20-01 Key Make-Up Artist		1	Day	1	350	350	350	
20-07 Box Rentals		1	Day	1	30	30	30	
	Payroll				350	81	81	
				Total for 20-00				**461**

21-00 Electrical

21-01 Gaffer

	Prod. shot Shoot	1	Day	12	25	300		
	Talent Shoot	1	Day	12	25	300	600	
21-02 Best Boy								
	Prod. shot Shoot	1	Day	12	22	264		
	Talent Shoot/ Wrap	1	Day	14	22	308	572	
21-05 Purchases		1	Allow	1	350	350	350	
21-06 Equipment Rentals		2	Days	1	900	1,800	1,800	
21-10 Box Rentals								
	Gaffer	2	Days	1	30	60	60	
	Payroll				1,172	270	270	
				Total for 21-00				**3,652**

(Continued)

BELOW-THE-LINE (Continued)

22-00 Camera

22-01 Director/DP/Op

Prod. Shot:	Prep	1	Day	1	1,000	1,000		
	Shoot	1	Day	1	2,000	2,000		
	Invoice fee @ 10%	1	Allow	1	300	300	3,300	
Talent Shoot:	DP/Op							
	Prep	1	Day	1	450	450		
	Shoot	1	Day	1	750	750	1,200	
22-03 1st Asst. Camera								
	Prep	1	Day	6	30	180		
	Shoot	1	Day	12	30	360	540	
22-06 Expendables		1	Allow	1	250	250	250	
22-07 Camera Package Rental								
Prod. Shot:	Arri 16SR2 (MOS)	1	Day	1	200	200		
	Prime lense set	1	Day	1	250	250		
	Cam. accessories	1	Day	1	450	450	900	
Talent shoot:	DXC-D30 Pckge.	1	Day	1	650	650	650	
22-12 Teleprompter/Operator		1	Day	1	450	450	450	
22-13 Video Assist/Operator		1	Day	1	800	800	800	
	Payroll				5,040	1,159	1,159	
	Total for 22-00							**9,249**

23-00 Sound

23-01 Mixer

	Talent Shoot:	1	Day	12	25	300	300	
23-03 Expendables (Batteries, etc)		1	Allow	1	100	100	100	
23-04 Sound Pckg (Incl. w/cam pckg)						0	0	
23-06 Radio Mikes		1	Allow	1	150	150	150	
	Payroll				300	69	69	
	Total for 23-00							**619**

24-00 Transportation

24-03 Equipment Rental

Production Van		4	Days	1	65	260	260	
Set Dressing		4	Days	1	75	300	300	
24-04 Gas & Oil		1	Allow	1	100	100	100	
	Total for 24-00							**660**

25-00 Location Expenses

25-09 Catering Service							
Crew Meals (2 days)		25	Meals	2	12	600	600
Tent/Tables/Chairs		1	Allow	1	100	100	100
25-17 Location Site Rental							
	Gym	2	Days	1	1,000	2,000	2,000
				Total for 25-00			**2,700**

27-00 Film & Lab—Production

27-01 Raw Stock (Film-Production)		3200	Feet	1	$0.46	1,472	
Sales Tax		1	Allow	1	1,472	121	1,593
27-02 Lab-Negative Prep & Proc.		3200	Feet	1	$0.12	368	368
27-03 Videotape Stock—Production							
	DVCam	3	Cass.	1	17	51	51
27-08 Telecine (sc. to sc.-circled takes @ 5:1)							
		4	Hours	1	350	1,400	1,400
27-09 D2 Tape Stock (1 hr.)		1	Allow	1	64	64	64
				Total for 27-00			**3,476**

30-00 Editorial

30-08 Off-Line Editor		5	Days	1	450	2,250	2,250
30-09 Off-Line Editing System							
	Non-linear	5	Days	1	150	750	750
30-10 On-Line System & Editor		12	Hours	1	300	3,600	3,600
	D2 Record/ D2 + BSP playback						
30-12 Videotape Dubs/Stock & Transfers							
Prod. shot:	D2 to BetaSP	1	Allow	1	70	70	70
	Misc.	1	Allow	1	100	100	100
30-13 Screening Copies (DVD)		10	disks	1	12	120	120
30-14 Video Masters/Safeties/Textless							
	D2 Edit Master-10:00	1	Cass.	1	85	85	85
	D2 Safety (textless)	1	Cass.	1	85	85	85
				Total for 30-00			**7,060**

33-00 Music

33-01 Composer		1	Allow	1	2,000	2,000	2,000
(All-In Package includes: Arrangers, Copyists, Musicians, Instruments, Studio, Engineers, Stock, etc)						0	0
				Total for 33-00			**2,000**

(Continued)

BELOW-THE-LINE (Continued)

34-00 Post Production Sound

34-01 Spotting for Music/Sound Efx	3	Hours	1	150	450	450
34-05 Narration Record	0.5	Hour	1	200	100	100
34-14 Laydown	0.5	Hour	1	250	125	125
34-15 Pre-Lay	6	Hours	1	150	900	900
34-16 Mix	5	Hours	1	250	1,250	1,250
34-17 Layback	0.5	Hour	1	200	100	100
34-18 Stock/Dubs/Transfers (Video)	1	Allow	1	150	150	150

Total for 34-00   **3,075**

35-00 Titles & Graphics

35-01 Graphic Designer & Workstation	Package	1	Allow	1	2,500	2,500	2,500

Total for 35-00   **2,500**

36-00 Stock Footage

36-01 Film and Tape Clips Licensing	60	Seconds	1	45	2,700	2,700

Total for 36-00   **2,700**

37-00 Insurance

37-01 Producers Entertainment Package	0	0
Negative	0	0
Faulty Stock	0	0
Equipment	0	0
Props/Sets	0	0
Extra Expense	0	0
3rd Party Property Damage	0	0
Office Contents	0	0
37-02 General Liability	0	0
37-03 Hired Auto	0	0
37-04 Cast Insurance	0	0
37-05 Workers Compensation	0	0
37-06 Errors & Omissions	0	0

Total for 37-00   **0**

38-00 General & Administrative Expenses

	0	
38-02 Legal	0	0
38-03 Accounting fees	0	0
38-05 Telephone/FAX	0	0
38-06 Copying	0	0
38-07 Postage & Freight	0	0
38-08 Office Space Rental	0	0
38-09 Ofice Furniture	0	0
38-10 Office Equipment & Supplies	0	0
38-11 Computer Rental	0	0

38-12 Software		0	0
38-14 Messenger/Overnight		0	0
38-15 Parking		0	0
	Total for 38-00		**0**
Contingency @ 10%		6,332	6,332
	GRAND TOTAL		**$69,648**
Total Above-The-Line			11,576
Total Below-The-Line			51,740
Total Above and Below-the-Line			63,316
	Check	*69,648*	*69,648*
	budget		
	totals		

Budgets provided by Michael Wiese Productions. Excerpted from Film and Video Budgets, 5th Edition by Deke Simon www.mwp.com

Sample 3

SAMPLE BUDGET			
4 hours	Production Planning	110	440
1 day	Video Production	900	900
10 ea	Digital Videotapes	10	100
10 ea	Window Dubs	25	250
50 hrs	Post Production	115	5750
1 ea	Narrator and Studio	600	600
10 hrs	Graphics Production	115	1150
15 hrs	DVD Authoring	115	1725
5 hrs	Magic Bullet Digital Filter	115	575
3000 ea	DVD Copies	0.85	2550
1 ea	Packaging & Printing	1873	1873
(package design will be oursourced at additional fee per client artwork)			
Total			**15913**

PRODUCTION STILLS

Photo Credits: Richard Cash

A green screen background may be made of muslin cloth, or it could be seamless photo paper, as shown here. Seamless comes in either a six-foot or a nine-foot roll, and are 36 feet long. One advantage of using seamless, rather than cloth, is that cloth can wrinkle. If the paper develops a wrinkle, tear it off and advance the roll to a clean area.

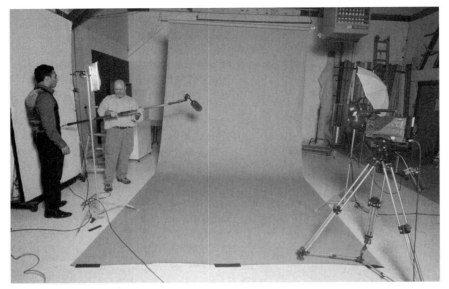

The author shows a production assistant how to hold a microphone boom pole, sometimes called a "fishpole." The pole enables the microphone to be positioned just above camera range. In this case, an actor, who is not in this particular scene, doubles as a production assistant. Union crew regulations usually prohibit this practice, but if yours is a nonunion shoot, an actor may be willing to help in this capacity.

A green screen set up in a studio, or a blue screen, enables the producer to place the talent in virtually any setting. In postproduction, you substitute stock footage or photography for the green background. The talent needs to know not to wear green clothing; that area would become replaced by the virtual background. Sometimes in a close-up, even green eyes can be a problem; that's one reason why blue screens are less popular.

Industrial locations provide a realistic setting for video shoots. While a host in a tie in front of a forklift may appear incongruous, it captures the attention of the viewer. It also shows that executives in the company spend time at the plant. Through subtle imagery, the video producer can convey an aspect of the company culture.

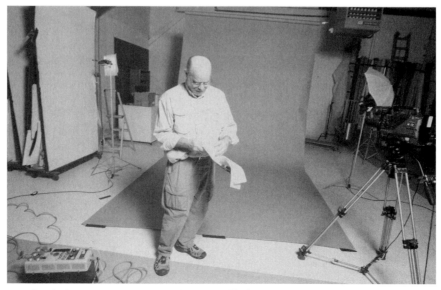

Author reviews script during green screen setup in the studio. With a green screen or a blue screen (also called "chroma key") the video editor may use any photo or moving picture in place of the green background. You may use a simple background such as a photo of an office or something more elaborate such as employees operating machinery in a factory.

The author, on right, directs a video shoot in the studio. Notice that he used a faux background that looks like a brick wall, to give the scene an industrial look. The interviewer sits as close to the camera lens as possible, so the subject's face is seen fully. The fuzzy thing above the talent is a windscreen for the microphone. Even when used inside, a windscreen avoids any noise that could occur when a very sensitive mike is moved quickly.

When filming in a studio or in any interior location, consider using a reflector to bounce some light to fill in shadows. In this case, the production assistant aims a pop-open reflector at the subject. Notice that he uses the silver side of the reflector. The white side is generally used outside to reflect sunlight without it being too harsh.

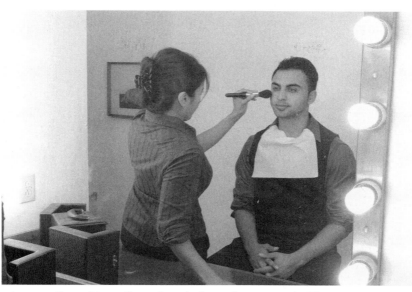

The makeup artist uses disposable appliers when placing makeup on each different subject. The subject should shield his or her clothing with a paper protector or paper towel. You can build your own makeup room or booth with lighting strips available at a home supply store. Make sure the bulbs are color balanced for the color of the lighting you plan to use during the shoot. For example, if you are filming outside, use daylight-balanced compact fluorescent bulbs.

The author reviews the script before a conference room shoot. Sometimes tight quarters require the camera to be positioned very close to a wall. Computer screens may need to be brightened or dimmed, depending on the video lighting used. To avoid light reflections off the screens, adjust lights or add flags.

The author and a production assistant arrange items in the bookcase behind the talent. Backgrounds are important; when poorly selected, they can distract the viewer's attention from the main subject. Sometimes a background can be arranged out of focus, and with proper lighting and composition, it can add an artistic touch to the scene.

A reaction shot, used as a cutaway shot, can add drama to a scene. In this case, a worker has just fallen, after using a chair rather than a ladder to try to retrieve a box. A coworker, hearing the fall, walks in and appears startled. The viewer can identify with the startled coworker, and this creates an added level of involvement for the audience of your video.

GLOSSARY

180-degree rule: Keeping camera angles on one side of an imaginary line running through the set. Crossing the line can cause confusing discontinuity.

4:4:2 (and 4:4:4): Chroma sampling rates. 4:4:4 means that the color and luminance components of the picture are sampled at the same rate, as is performed in cinematic postproduction. With 4:2:2, the two chroma components are sampled at half the rate of the luminance components; this reduces bandwidth by one-third with little or no visible difference.

After Effects: An Adobe software application for motion graphics and compositing.

Alpha compositing: The process of combining an image with a background to create the appearance of partial transparency. An alpha channel is used extensively when combining computer-rendered image elements with live footage.

AFTRA: American Federation of Television and Radio Artists.

Analog: Standard audio/video recording. When copied, signal loss results. Digital eliminates the signal loss.

Archival copy: A copy recorded on a high-quality disc that is designed to preserve the recording. It is a good idea to make a second copy and store it at a different location.

Aspect ratio: The ratio of length to height of a picture. Standard definition video is 4:3, while most high-definition video is 16:9.

AVC: Advanced video coding. A digital video compression format sometimes referred to as MPEG-4.

AVCHD: Advanced video coding high definition. A format for recording and playback of HD video onto removable flash media and hard drives. It uses the MPEG-4, H.264 video compression codec.

AVI: Audio video interleaved. An audio/video film format used during digital video editing frequently displayed as ".avi."

Betacam SP: Broadcast-quality, analog video standard. This format is popular with television stations, but it is slowly being phased out. Betamax is an old home video format. Betacam XS is a digital broadcast Betacam format.

Blue screen: A chroma-keying technique where the subject is shot in front of a blue background and that background is replaced during postproduction.

Blu-ray: A high-definition disc format similar in size and operation to a DVD but capable of holding eight times the data. Sony and Panasonic support Blu-Ray, while Microsoft and Toshiba support HD DVD.

BNC connector: A broadcast standard video connector used with coax cable. A single BNC connector is used for analog video. Multiple BNC connectors carry SDI or serial digital interface video.

Bokeh: A background so out of focus that it appears to be soft and cloudlike. Very narrow depth of field to draw attention to the main subject. It is obtained when using a digital still camera for video or when using a neutral density filter.

Broadcast quality: Video and audio quality standards developed by the National Association of Broadcasters. Frequently used to describe a broadcast camera.

Broadcast-quality camera: A high-resolution video camera with three chips for each of the primary colors of light: red, blue, and green. Furthermore, a broadcast-quality camera allows for internal adjustments to achieve the best contrast and color rendition possible.

B-roll: During a video production, in addition to video shot with actors or participants speaking on camera, the camera operator shoots other shots of interiors and exteriors to help illustrate the story.

Camcorder: A combination video camera and recorder. Camcorders may record on videotape, DVDs, hard drives, or flash cards.

CD-DA: Compact disc digital audio. The standard digital music CD format that is playable on all CD players.

CDN: Content distribution network. A service that distributes online videos as live streaming or video on demand.

Chapter: A segment on a DVD that is used during navigation. Authored DVDs have their glossarys created at specific points to divide the video for easy navigation and interactivity.

Character generator: Software that is part of video editing used to create titles. The titles may be over video or by themselves.

Chip: A small circuit board for processing data. Camcorders have one or three optical chips.

Chroma-key: A compositing technique where the subject is shot in front of a green or blue background. In postproduction, the background is replaced with a different image.

Chroma subsampling: Applying more compression to the chrominance portion of the signal than to the luminance. Humans process luminance with more precision than chrominance. There is no perceptible loss by compressing chrominance at a higher level than the luminance portion of the signal.

Chrominance: The color level or color saturation.

Closed-captioning: Transcript of the words that are spoken on a film or video, usually displayed as text at the bottom of the screen.

Cloud computing: Internet-based shared computing. Video and other IT resources may be shared. Cloud computing customers do not own the infrastructure but rather pay for it on a per-use basis, similar to paying for traditional utility services, such as electricity.

Coaster: A sarcastic name for a disc that will not play. It could be used as a coaster for drinks.

Coax or coaxial cable: A video cable that consists of an inner conductor, an insulating layer, and a conducting shield consisting usually of braided metal. Coax is thicker than shielded audio cables because of the higher frequencies of video. RG59 is a common size for coax cable.

Cobrowsing: Navigation of Internet pages by two or more users. Some cobrowsing tools offer synchronized playback of video with start, pause, and stop functionality.

Codec: Encoder-decoder. Used in digital video and audio, files are encoded for such applications as Internet video and then decoded when displayed from a website.

Component video: Separating primary colors and picture information of a video signal into three cables, usually colored red, green, and blue. This allows for a sharper display of video.

Composite video: Combining video signal and color into a single cable, usually the yellow RCA-type connector on a monitor, camcorder, or DVD player.

Compositing: Combining several images together, sometimes using layering, to create a single scene. Chroma-key and green screen are examples of compositing.

Composition: Refers to composing shots to conform to aesthetic principals such as the rule of thirds, using leading lines, and avoiding distracting backgrounds.

Compression: A method of squeezing data into a smaller size for storing on a computer, on a disc, and for sending via the Internet.

Crossing the line: Also known as the 180-degree rule. Keeping camera angles on one side of an imaginary line running through the set. Crossing the line can cause confusing discontinuity.

Cutaway: A reaction shot or a shot that is away from the main action. Cutaway shots are sometimes used to cover up a jump-cut.

Cut-in: A close-up shot that shows detail of the subject. In multicamera filming or during editing of single-camera footage, the director will ask for a cut-in to show the detail.

DivX: A trade name for a digital video compression format based on the MPEG-4 standard that compresses video into a small file.

Data DVD/CD: Unlike a video DVD or audio CD that plays on a standard machine, a data DVD or CD is designed to store AV files in a computer format. Data discs such as these are used for further editing or for Internet uploading.

DGA: Directors Guild of America.

Digital compositing: The process of digitally assembling multiple images to make a final image. Adobe After Effects, Apple Shake, and Autodesk Smoke are digital compositing applications.

Digital file conversion: Transferring one type of audio/video file to another for the purpose of uploading it to the Internet or making a CD or DVD.

Digital recording: Audio and video are converted to bits of data. This results in no signal loss when digital copies are made. DVDs are digital, while VHS tape is analog.

Digital video editing: Using a computer to perform video editing, the scenes are assembled in the order required. Like word processing, the scenes may be rearranged.

Display: Another word for monitor, whether it is a computer monitor or video monitor.

Dissolve: A smooth blend from one image to the other. As the first image fades away, the second image overlaps and fades in.

Dolly: Wheeled cart to hold the camera and allow for smooth movements. Sometimes refers to the movement itself.

Downloadable video: Video that may be downloaded from a website and stored on the user's computer. Downloadable video takes longer to start playing than streaming video, but streaming video may not be stored.

DSLR: Digital single-lens reflex camera, some of which record HD video.

Duplication: Making copies of DVDs, CDs, or videotapes. The process usually includes verification to confirm that the signals had been properly recorded on the discs or tapes. Frequently, labels and boxes are included with duplication.

DVCAM: A popular digital videotape format. It is used in broadcast-quality camcorders and in digital video editing.

DVD: Digital versatile disc. Can be used to store video and other kinds of data.

DVD authoring: The process of creating a custom DVD by dividing a video into glossarys. Chapters are listed in a menu and allow for easy navigation and interactivity.

DVD video: A DVD disc that has standard video and audio recorded on it. Will play in a standard DVD player or a computer.

DVI: Connector for HD video display on a monitor. It is similar and compatible with HDMI, but it carries no audio.

Edit decision list (EDL): A list of time code numbers of the start and stop times of scenes. An EDL greatly shortens billable editing time. The list may be written by hand or generated by a computer. The video editor enters these numbers into the computer during the editing process.

Editing: Combining video shots together in an organized method. Includes addition of voice-over narration, music, titles, graphics, and special effects. See also *Postproduction*.

Editor: The professional technician who performs video editing, postproduction, photo montages, and digital file conversion.

Enterprise WAN: Enterprise wide area network. The network links corporate offices from different locations.

File-based editing: Instead of videotape, editing is done using file-based media such as a hard drive, optical disc, or solid-state storage.

FireWire: A digital cable and connector that handles audio, video, and other information between computers, camcorders, and other digital devices. Also known as IEEE 1359.

Fishpole: A boom for holding a shotgun microphone. The boom may be extended and is usually held by a sound technician.

Flash: A computer program from Adobe that allows photos, graphics, and video to be displayed on home and office computers. The file extension is .swf.

Flickr: Flickr provides both private and public image storage. A user uploading an image can set privacy controls that determine who can view the image. A photo can be flagged as either public or private.

Flypack: Rack-mounted video production equipment encased in a shipping case that is approved for airline shipping.

Frame-accurate: A term to describe the highest precision in video editing. A frame is 1/30 of a second, and it is the smallest measurement of time in a video or audio recording.

French flag: A shade that mounts above the lens to help keep light out of the lens. It looks like a single barn door.

Google video: Sometimes known as YouTube videos, but Google's search engine will display videos from any website.

GOP: A group of successive pictures within a coded video stream. Each coded video stream consists of successive GOPs. From the pictures contained in it, the visible frames are generated. The GOP is composed of I-frames, which are the least compressible but don't require other video frames to decode; P-frames, which use data from previous frames to decompress and are more compressible than I-frames; and B-frames, which can use both previous and forward frames for data reference to get the highest amount of data compression.

Green screen: A chroma-keying technique where the subject is shot in front of a green background and that background is replaced during postproduction.

H.264 encoding: MPEG-4 AVC (advanced video coding) compression designed to record at lower bit rates than MPEG-2.

HDD: Hard drive disk. The hard drive in a computer or used as an external hard drive for a computer or video camera.

HDMI: High-definition media interface. The HD connector on a monitor or recording device that carries audio and video. It supports uncompressed video and up to eight channels of audio.

HDTV: High-definition television. Sharper than standard definition, it displays up to 1,050 lines of resolution.

HDV: A type of high-definition video that is popular with camcorders.

High definition: Video with resolutions greater than standard definition. High definition usually starts at 720 lines, and 1,080 p refers to 1,080 lines with progressive scanning.

HTML5: A tag of Hypertext Markup Language that adds support for embedding video in an HTML page. This is an alternative to Adobe Flash.

Hue: The tint of color.

IATSE: International Alliance of Theatrical and Stage Employees, sometimes referred to as the "I.A."

IEEE 1359: A digital cable and connector that handles audio, video, and other information between computers, camcorders, and other digital devices. Also known as FireWire.

IFP: Interruptible feedback. Intercom used for remote broadcasting. Usually includes earpieces that the host and guest wear to hear both each other and the director.

iMAG: Image magnification. Frequently used at conferences and conventions, a camera video output is connected to a data projector to project a live image onto a projection screen.

Interlaced scanning: To economize bandwidth for CRT monitors, lines of video are recorded as separate fields of odd lines followed by scans of the even lines. Sometimes still frames in interlace scanning produce a flicker. Progressive scanning produces sharper images but requires greater bandwidth.

Instructional DVD: Unlike a training video, an instructional DVD is marketed to the general public or to a special interest group. Instructional DVDs include how-to videos.

Interframe: Compression using interframe prediction. This kind of prediction tries to take advantage of the redundancy between neighboring frames to achieve high compression rates with minimal loss.

Intraframe: A compression system used for videoconferencing and some video editing platforms. It is part of the GOP (group of pictures) with interframes. Compression is done only to the individual frame and not to the adjoining frames.

Intranet: The organization's internal website, but may be a more extensive part of the organization's information technology infrastructure.

I/O: Input/output. Refers to connectors and cables going between the computer and AV devices. In computing, I/O also refers to the communication between an information processing system and the user.

IPTV: Internet protocol television.

ISDN: Integrated Services Digital Network. A set of communications standards for simultaneous digital transmission of voice, video, data, and other network services over the traditional circuits of the public switched telephone network.

IT: Informational technology. The department in an organization that manages computer-based information systems, particularly software applications and computer hardware.

JPEG: Joint photographic experts group. JPEG is the most popular compression technique for still photos.

Jump cut: An error that may occur during editing where the subject appears to jump from one shot to the next. This is common when the recording was stopped or paused and then resumed.

LCD: Liquid crystal diode. This is popular for flat-screen displays.

Lossless data compression: A compression technique that allows the original data to be reconstructed when uncompressed. This is in contrast to lossy data compression, where only an approximation of the original data is available.

Lossy data compression: Compression used to minimize bit rate for editing and processing. Video can sometimes be compressed 100:1 without noticeable quality loss. Audio can be compressed 10:1 before noticing loss.

LTO: Linear Tape Open is a magnetic tape storage system that uses open standards. Popular for backups in larger computer systems, each tape cartridge can store up to 1.5 TB of uncompressed data.

Menu: The opening screen of an authored DVD that shows the glossarys. Frequently the glossarys are shown as thumbnails.

Metadata: Hidden within an audio or video file is information about the file such as the camera settings, date recorded, and other data.

Mini-DV: A popular digital video format used in consumer and prosumer camcorders.

Motion effects: During editing and postproduction, still images can be made to move or look like the camera is zooming, panning, or tilting movements.

Mov: The file format used by QuickTime for compressing audio and video for computer and Internet displays.

MP3: The most popular method of compressing audio for recording on a solid-state player, a disc, or the Internet.

MPEG: Moving Picture Experts Group. Standards for compressing video for recording on discs, hard drives, and the Internet.

MPEG-1: The standard for video CDs and audio MP3 compression.

MPEG-2: The standard for video DVD compression, high-definition compression for camcorders.

MPEG-4: A digital video compression format sometimes referred to as advanced video coding, or AVC. MPEG-4 is frequently used for compressing video for solid-state devices such as mobile phones and iPods.

NAS: Network Attached Storage. System of multiple hard drives, such as a RAID, that may be accessed by all terminals on a network.

Noddies: Shots where the host nods in reaction to what the guest has said. These may be shot after the guest has left.

Noise: Tiny dots that sometimes appear in low-quality video. The hiss that sometimes is heard in low-quality audio.

NTSC: National Television Standards Commission. The video system used in the United States and Japan.

On-disc printing: Rather than use paper labels, discs with an inkjet printable surface allow label art to be printed directly on the disc.

OTS: Over the shoulder. Camera is placed behind the interviewer and is focused on the interviewee. Sometimes the back of the shoulder and side of the head of the interviewer are visible in the frame.

PAL: Phase Alternate Line. The video system used in Europe and other countries. PAL videotapes and discs need to be converted to NTSC for viewing in the United States.

Pan: When the camera operator moves the camera left to right or right to left during filming. Generally a good pan goes in a single direction and is done slowly and smoothly. This effect may be applied to a still image during postproduction.

PA system: Public address system of microphones, amplifiers, and speakers, usually installed in an auditorium or meeting room. Can also be a portable PA system that may be brought to a room.

Pay per view: Streaming or downloadable videos that require payment to view.

Photomontage: A video DVD of photos combined with music. This is usually produced at a video editing workstation by a professional video editor. Images frequently have dissolves for smooth transitions, and movements such as zooms, pans, and tilts may be applied.

Podcast: Streaming video or audio that is regularly scheduled in a similar way as a radio or television broadcast.

Progressive scanning: A method for displaying, storing, or transmitting moving images in which all the lines of each frame are drawn in sequence. This is in contrast to the interlacing used in traditional television systems, where first the odd lines and then the even lines of each frame (each image now called a field) are drawn alternately.

Prompter: The generic term for the popular brand TelePrompTer. Prompters display the script for the talent to read. The text is displayed onto a clear glass panel that may be placed in front of the camera lens.

ProRes 422: An intraframe-only codec that is part of Apple Final Cut Studio. Designed for lossy compression of HD, it is designed to be simpler to decode than distribution-oriented formats such as H.264. It is comparable to Avid's DNxHD codec, which has the same purpose and uses similar bit rates.

Prosumer: A cross between consumer and professional equipment. Frequently used to distinguish a three-chip camcorder from a consumer, single-chip camcorder.

Proxy editing: Creating a low bit rate copy of your HD source footage that uses less computer resources. After editing at that low resolution, the editor switches to HD and renders the finished video in full quality.

Pull focus: Changing focus to sharpen objects at different distances from the camera to draw attention of the viewer.

QuickTime: A computer program from Apple that allows audio/video to be displayed on home and office computers. The file extension is .mov.

RAID: Redundant array of independent disks. A hard drive system comprised of two or more drives that have the same data. If one drive fails, the other takes over.

RealPlayer: A computer program from Real Networks that allows audio/video to be displayed on home and office computers. The file extension is .rv, .rm, or .rmvb.

Red One: Brand name of a camera that can record at resolutions up to 4,096 horizontal by 2,304 vertical pixels, directly to flash or hard disk storage. It features a single Super 35–sized CMOS sensor and a cinematography industry standard PL lens mount.

Resolution: The capacity of a recording system to show distinct thin lines of a picture. Higher resolution results in the viewer being able to see a greater number of distinct lines in a given area.

RGB: Red, green, and blue. An additive color model that cameras use for individual image capture chips and displays use for processing color. Dividing the color spectrum into RGB enables each primary color to be separately processed.

Rule of thirds: Mentally dividing the frame into thirds horizontally and vertically to position key elements on those axes.

SaaS: Software as a service over the Internet. Rather than purchase the software, the user is licensed to use the software through a subscription or based on the usage, similar to a traditional utility service such as electricity.

Safe title area: On a video monitor, the center 80 percent of the picture within which text should be limited. Some playback monitors cut off the edges of the text, so a safe title area is used when creating text during postproduction.

Safety training video: A video or DVD that shows exact procedures for security or safety training. Rather than read a manual, employees learn from the video, which is the next best thing to a live class.

SAG: Screen Actors Guild.

Sales motivation video: Training video used to teach selling techniques and to stimulate viewers to improve their sales.

SAN: Storage area network. A system to attach external storage devices to servers so the devices appear as attached locally to the operating system.

SDI: Serial digital interface. A broadcast video interface that consists of BNC connectors that send video divided into its components. HD-SDI is a high-definition version of the interface that provides a nominal data rate of 1.485 Gbit/s. Dual-link HD-SDI consists of a pair of SDI connectors that provide a nominal data rate of 2.970 Gbit/s. 3G-SDI consists of a single 2.970 Gbit/s serial link.

SEG: Screen Extras Guild.

SEO: Search engine optimization. The optimization of a website so search engines find it fast.

Standard definition: Standard video that is currently used on DVDs and VHS tapes. It is limited to approximately 480 lines of resolution. High definition goes up to 1,080 lines.

Streaming video: Video that may be viewed from a website but not stored on the user's computer. Streaming videos usually start playing faster than downloadable videos.

Tape to DVD/CD/HDD/flash drive transfers: Tape is dead, or they may wear out soon. Hard drives, flash drives, and discs are designed for archival storage and are easier to search through than tapes.

TBC: Time base corrector. Used during copying or transferring from videotape to correct distortions caused by tape. Also used for color and brightness correction.

Telecine: The process of converting motion picture film to video.

Telepresence: A high-end videoconferencing system that simulates a live conference. Large monitors and loudspeakers positioned near the images of individuals speaking create the illusion of a live conference.

Thumbnail: A small photo or frame of video that identifies the contents.

Tie-in: Connecting to an existing sound system, such as those found in auditoriums or meeting rooms. A tie-in allows the videographer to get high-quality sound from the microphones in that room.

Tilt: When the camera moves the camera up or down during filming. This effect may be applied to a still image during postproduction.

Time code: A method of identifying shots on a tape, disc, or hard drive. The recording is measured in hours, minutes, seconds, and frames, based on a time code signal embedded in the recording.

Titles: Text on the video screen; sometimes referred as character generator.

Training video: A video, DVD, or online video used to train employees on the procedures and policies of the organization.

Triaxial cable (triax): Similar to coax, but with the addition of an extra layer of insulation and a second conducting sheath. It provides greater bandwidth and rejects interference better than coax.

Tweet: A post on Twitter with no more than 140 characters. Retweeting refers to forwarding a tweet to others.

VCR: Videocassette recorder. The older type of home videorecording device.

Vectorscope: A hardware monitor or software plug-in that enables the technical director to ensure that the colors coming from cameras are accurate.

VHS: Video home system. The format of videotape and VCR that has been popular with consumers but is gradually being phased out.

Videoconference: Two-way audio and video is displayed at two or more locations for several people to speak to one another from different sites.

Video editing workstation: An ensemble of digital video editing computers, monitors, postproduction VCRs, DVD recorders, and other equipment used for video postproduction and production of photomontages.

Video on demand (VOD): Streaming videos that users view from a website whenever they want, as opposed to a webcast, where the video streams at only certain times.

Video production: The process of planning, videotaping, editing, and other procedures to come up with a finished video or DVD.

Viral video: Online videos that users send to one another via e-mails with a link to the video. Sometimes written comments accompany the video.

WAN: Wide area network.

Waveform monitor: A hardware device or software plug-in that allows the camera technician to accurately adjust the brightness and contrast with either lighting or the camera's internal white and black levels.

Webcast video: Video that may be viewed online at a scheduled time.

WGA: Writers Guild of America.

Widget: Small applications that allow users to turn personal content into dynamic web apps that can be shared on just about any website.

Window dub: A copy of a master video, usually on DVD, where the time code numbers are displayed in a window on the monitor.

Windows Media Player: A computer program from Microsoft that allows for audio/video to be displayed on home and office computers. The file extension is .wmv.

Wireless microphone: A microphone that does not need a cord. Usually it consists of a clip-on microphone attached to a small belt pack transmitter. At the camera is the receiver portion of the system.

Xsan: An enterprise shared disk file system that encourages collaborative postproduction. It allows several computers to read and write to the same storage volume at the same time.

YCbCr: A way of encoding RGB color. Y is the luminance or the black and white element of the signal. Cb is the "color difference," which is represented as the color blue minus the luminance (B − Y). C5 is the red minus the luminance (R − Y). In analog video it is referred to as "YUV."

YouTube video: Videos, usually under 10 minutes in length, that can be uploaded and displayed on YouTube at no charge.

Zoom: When the camera lens enlarges the image so the viewer sees a closer view. Also used in postproduction to give the effect of zooming in on a still image.

BIBLIOGRAPHY

Scriptwriting

Cartwright, S. (1996). *Pre-production planning for video, film, and multimedia.* Focal Press.

Matrazzo, D. (1986). *Corporate scriptwriting.* Communicom Publishing Company.

Scriptwriting Software

Final Draft (www.finaldraft.com).

Movie Magic (www.screenplay.com).

Scriptware (www.scriptware.com).

Budgeting

Simon, D. (2006). *Film and video budgets.* Michael Wiese Productions.

Easy Budget Movie Budgeting Software (www.easy-budget.com).

Michael Weise Productions. Download sample budgets at: (http://shop.mwp.com/pages/film-making-resources).

Movie Magic Budgeting (www.entertainmentpartners.com).

TV/Film Budgeting Templates (www.boilerplate.net).

Producing

Carlsberg, S. (1991). *Corporate video survival.* Knowledge Industry Publications.

DiZazzo, R. (2000). *Corporate media production.* Focal Press.

Gayleski, D. M. (1983). *Corporate and instructional video.* Prentice Hall.

Richardson, A. R. (1992). *Corporate and organizational video.* McGraw Hill.

Directing

Kennedy, T. (1989). *Directing video.* Knowledge Industry Publications.

McCoy, M. (2000). *Sound and look professional on television and the internet.* Bonus Books, Inc.

Production Coordination

Garvey, H. (1988). *Before you shoot.* Shire Press.

McQuillan, L. (1983). *Video production handbook.* Howard W. Sams & Co. Publishers.

Patz, D. S. (2002). *Film production management 101.* Michael Wiese Productions.

Shooting and Editing

Browne, S. E. (2007). *High definition postproduction.* Focal Press.

Freeman, M. (2007). *The photographer's eye: Composition and design for better digital photos.* Focal Press.

Utz, P. (1987). *Today's video.* McFarland & Company.

Wheeler, P. (2009). *High definition cinematography.* Focal Press.

Winston, B., & Keydel, J. (1986). *Working with video.* Watson-Guptill Publications.

Training

Cartwright, S. R. (1986). *Training with video.* Knowledge Industry Publications.

Independent Video Production

Dawson, R. (2010). *Refocus.* Peachpit Press.

Jacobs, B. (1986). *How to be an independent video producer.* Knowledge Industry Publications.

Kamoroff, B. B. (2009). *Small time operator: How to start your own business, keep your books, pay your taxes, and stay out of trouble!* Bell Springs Publishing.

Phillips, M., & Rasberry, S. (1996). *Honest business.* Shambhala Pocket Editions.

Phillips, M. (2002). *The seven laws of money.* Clear Glass Publications.

Yankee, S. (2010). Doc's Marketing Mojo. www.docsmarketingmojo.com.

Legal Considerations

Miller, P. (2003). *Media law for producers.* Focal Press.

INDEX